Jesus in the Talmud

Babylonian Talmud, Ms. Munich Cod. hebr. 95, fol. 342r (tractate Sanhedrin, fol. 43a–b), with erasures by the censor. By courtesy of the Bayerische Staatsbibliothek, Munich.

Jesus in the Talmud

Peter Schäfer

Princeton University Press
Princeton and Oxford

Published by Princeton University Press, 41 William Street, Princeton, New Jersey 08540

In the United Kingdom: Princeton University Press, 3 Market Place, Woodstock, Oxfordshire OX20 1SY

Schäfer, Peter, 1943–
    Jesus in the Talmud / Peter Schäfer.
        p.   cm.
    Includes bibliographical references and index.
    ISBN-13: 978-0-691-12926-6 (alk. paper)
    ISBN-10: 0-691-12926-6 (alk. paper)
    1. Jesus Christ—Jewish interpretations.   2. Talmud—Criticism, interpretation, etc.
3. Rabbinical literature—History and criticism.   4. Bible. N.T.—Controversial literature—
History and criticism.   I. Title.
    BM620.S27 2007
    296.1'206—dc22   2006050392

British Library Cataloging-in-Publication Data is available

This book has been composed in Electra

pup.princeton.edu

10 9 8 7 6 5 4 3 2 1

———————————————

For Martin Hengel

mentor, colleague, friend

Contents

Acknowledgments

This study has two roots. The first goes back to the late 1970s, when I read Johann Maier's book *Jesus von Nazareth in der talmudischen Überlieferung*, which appeared in 1978. I was stunned by the erudition and meticulous scholarship of my colleague at that time at Cologne University, which nevertheless left me deeply dissatisfied. Having worked my way through the book's sophisticated arguments and painstakingly prepared charts, I was left wondering: what an expenditure of time and energy, just to prove that there is no Jesus in the Talmud and that the Talmud is an unreliable historical source for Jesus and early Christianity. I had the feeling that somehow the wrong questions were asked, or rather that the chimera of a rationalistic and positivistic historicity was evoked, almost as if to evade the real questions. True, and to be fair, our notion of Judaism and Christianity—and of their mutual relationship—has changed considerably over the last thirty years, but still the sources cry out for a more nuanced approach that takes into consideration the difference between pure factuality and a longer and complex process of *Wirkungsgeschichte* (reception history).

I always wanted to get back to the subject, but it took until the spring term of 2004 at Princeton University that I finally had a chance to realize this desire. When my friend Israel Yuval of the Hebrew University, who spent that term at Princeton as a visiting professor in the Department of Religion, suggested that we address in a joint seminar the topic of "How Much Christianity in Talmud and Midrash?"—the larger and much discussed question of rabbinic responses to Christianity—I enthusiastically agreed and proposed to include the Jesus passages in the Talmud. This memorable seminar belongs among the most exciting and rewarding teaching experiences in my life, not only because of a uniquely congenial group of students (undergraduate and graduate) as well as of colleagues (our Princeton colleagues Martha Himmelfarb and John Gager honored us with their presence), but also and above all because of the time Israel and I spent together preparing the seminar. At first we wanted to meet briefly to discuss the structure and strategy of the seminar sessions, but soon our meetings became longer and longer, until we spent hours reading the texts together—brainstorming together and driving each other to ever bolder interpretations and conclusions. Much of what will appear on the following pages, in particular with regard to the exegeses of the talmudic sources, has its root in these preparations and the subsequent seminar sessions. It would be a fruitless exercise to seek to divide up the birthright of certain ideas and suggestions, but I do not hesitate to acknowledge gladly and gratefully that this book in its present form could not have been written without the experience of this joint enterprise. The students', the colleagues', and above all Israel Yuval's creativity and ingenuity contributed greatly to many of the ideas developed in this book.

Research on the Babylonian Talmud has considerably advanced recently. Venturing into a field that is not my primary research area, I had the good fortune that Richard Kalmin of the Jewish Theological Seminary of America in New York was kind enough to read a draft of the manuscript. I owe him thanks for his many helpful suggestions, further clarifications of complicated talmudic texts, and corrections of several mistakes or misreadings. With regard to the New Testament—a field of which I can claim even less competence—Martin Hengel, my longtime mentor, senior colleague, and friend, generously commented on the manuscript and showered upon me an embarrassingly rich cornucopia of advice, improvement, further insights, bibliographical details, and, not least, corrections. (I wish I had taken advantage of his erudition at an earlier stage of writing the manuscript: it would have been considerably improved.) It is with admiration for his work and with heartfelt gratitude for his continuous support since I became his assistant at the University of Tübingen that I dedicate this small volume to him. My Princeton colleagues Martha Himmelfarb and Elaine Pagels read parts of the manuscript and made many helpful suggestions. The two anonymous readers for the Press took the trouble of reading an early draft of the manuscript and giving me much useful advice. I am deeply grateful to all of them. As always, I must take the responsibility for any remaining shortcomings. Finally, I would like to thank Brigitta van Rheinberg, the executive history editor at Princeton University Press, for her constructive enthusiasm; Baru Saul, my secretary/assistant, for correcting my English and proofreading the manuscript; and Molan Goldstein, the copyeditor, for a marvelous job.

Abbreviations

AMS	*Acta Martyrum et Sanctorum*
Ant.	Josephus, *Antiquitates*
Apol.	Justin, *Apology*
art.	article
AZ	tractate Avodah Zarah
b	Talmud Bavli (Babylonian Talmud)
b.	ben ("son of")
BamR	Midrash Bamidbar Rabba (on Numbers)
BB	tractate Bava Batra
Bekh	tractate Bekhorot
Bell.	Josephus, *Bellum*
Ber	tractate Berakhot
BerR	Midrash Bereshit Rabba (on Genesis)
Bes	tractate Betza
BM	tractate Bava Metzia
Col.	Letter to the Colossians
cols.	columns
Cor.	Letter to the Corinthians
Dan.	Book of Daniel
Deut.	Deuteronomy
Eccl.	Ecclesiastes (Qohelet)
EJ	*Encyclopaedia Judaica*
Eph.	Letter to the Ephesians
Er	tractate Eruvin
Esth.	Esther
Ex.	Exodus
Ez.	Ezekiel
fol.	folio
Gen.	Genesis
Git	tractate Gittin
Hag	tractate Hagiga

Hebr.	Letter to the Hebrews
HTR	*Harvard Theological Review*
HUCA	*Hebrew Union College Annual*
Hul	tractate Hullin
Isa.	Isaiah
Jer.	Jeremiah
JJS	Journal of Jewish Studies
Josh.	Joshua
JPS	Jewish Publication Society
JQR	*Jewish Quarterly Review*
JRS	*Journal of Roman Studies*
JSJ	*Journal for the Study of Judaism*
JSQ	*Jewish Studies Quarterly*
JTS	Jewish Theological Seminary
Lam.	Lamentations
Lev.	Leviticus
Lit.	literally
Lk.	Gospel of Luke
m	Mishna
Makh	tractate Makhshirin
Men	tractate Menahot
MGWJ	*Monatsschrift für die Geschichte und Wissenschaft des Judentums*
Mic.	Micah
Mk.	Gospel of Mark
Ms.	Manuscript
Mss.	Manuscripts
Mt.	Gospel of Matthew
n.	note
nos.	numbers
N.S.	New Series
Num.	Numbers
OTP	*Old Testament Pseudepigrapha*
PesR	Midrash Pesiqta Rabbati
PGM	Papyri Graecae Magicae
Prov.	Proverbs

Ps.	Psalms
Qid	tractate Qiddushin
QohR	Midrash Qohelet Rabba
R.	Rabbi
RAC	*Reallexikon für Antike und Christentum*
Rev.	Revelation
Rom.	Letter to the Romans
Sam.	Samuel
Sanh	tractate Sanhedrin
Shab	tractate Shabbat
Sot	tractate Sota
s.v.	sub voce
t	Tosefta
TRE	*Theologische Realenzyklopädie*
v.	verse
vol.	volume
y	Talmud Yerushalmi (Jerusalem Talmud)
Yev	tractate Yevamot
Zech.	Zechariah

Jesus in the Talmud

Introduction

This book is about the perception of Jesus of Nazareth, the founder of Christianity, in the Talmud, the foundation document of rabbinic Judaism in Late Antiquity. What do these two—Jesus and the Talmud— have in common? The obvious answer is: not much. There is, on the one hand, the collection of writings called the New Testament, undisputedly our major source for Jesus' life, teaching, and death, most of it written in the second half of the first century C.E.[1] And there is "the" Talmud, on the other, the most influential literary product of rabbinic Judaism, developed over several centuries in its two versions in Palestine and in Babylonia (the first, the Palestinian or Jerusalem Talmud, was edited in fifth-century Palestine, and the second, the Babylonian Talmud, reached its final form in the early seventh century in Babylonia). Both documents, the New Testament and the Talmud, could not be more different in form and content: the one, written in Greek, is concerned about the mission of this Jesus of Nazareth, who, regarded as the Messiah and the Son of God, was rejected in this claim by most of his fellow Jews, put to death by the Roman governor Pontius Pilate, and resurrected on the third day after his crucifixion and taken up into heaven; the other, written mostly in Aramaic, is a huge collection of mainly legal discussions that deal with the intricacies of a daily life conducted according to the rabbinic interpretations of Jewish law.

Moreover, and here things become much more complicated, with the juxtaposition of "Jesus" and the "Talmud" bordering on an oxymoron, both stand in a highly charged and antagonistic relationship with each other. The Jewish sect triggered by Jesus in Palestine would eventually evolve into a religion of its own, a religion to boot that would claim to have superseded its mother religion and position itself as the new covenant against the old and outdated covenant of the people of Israel by birth. And at precisely the time when Christianity rose from modest beginnings to its first triumphs, the Talmud (or rather the two Talmudim) would become the defining document of those who refused to accept the new covenant, who so obstinately insisted on the fact that nothing had changed and that the old covenant was still valid.

Yet strangely enough, the figure of Jesus does appear in the Talmud, as does his mother Mary—not in a coherent narrative, but scattered throughout the rabbinic literature in general and the Talmud in particular[2] and often dealt with in passing, in conjunction with another subject pursued as the major theme. In fact, Jesus is mentioned in the Talmud so sparingly that in relation to the huge quantity of literary production culminating in the Talmud, the Jesus passages can be compared to the proverbial drop in the *yam ha-talmud* ("the ocean of the Talmud"). The earliest coherent narrative about Jesus' life from a Jewish viewpoint that we possess is the (in)famous polemical tract *Toledot Yeshu* ("History of Jesus"), which, however, took shape in Western Europe in the early Middle Ages, well beyond the period of our concern here (although, to be sure, some earlier versions may go back to Late Antiquity).[3]

So why bother? If the rabbis of rabbinic Judaism did not care much about Jesus, why should we care about the few details that they do transmit, apart from simply stating the fact that they did not care much? This is one possible approach, and, as we will see, the one that has been taken in the most recent research on our subject. But I do not think that it is an appropriate response to the problem posed by the admittedly meager evidence. First, the question of Jesus in the Talmud is, of course, part of the much larger question of whether and how the nascent Christian movement is reflected in the literary output of rabbinic Judaism. And here we are standing on much firmer ground: Jesus may not be directly mentioned, but Christianity, the movement that he set in motion, may well be discussed. Second, the starkly antagonistic paradigm of "Judaism" versus "Christianity," forever frozen, as it were, in splendid isolation from each other, has come under closer scrutiny over the past two decades. The overly simplistic black-and-white model of the one sister religion ("Christianity") emerging out of the other and almost simultaneously breaking off from it and choosing its own and independent path, and of the other ("Judaism"), remarkably unimpressed by this epoch-making event, steering its own course until being overcome by the historic momentum of the stronger "religion," no longer holds; the reality as it transpires from more detailed and unbiased research is much more complex and perplexing.[4] Hence, no matter what the accumulation of quantitative evidence, we need to take very seriously any trace of a discourse between Judaism and Christianity, let alone of a reaction to Christianity's founder.

As a matter of fact, some scholars have taken it exceptionally seriously. The history of research on how the Jews of Late Antiquity discussed Christianity in general and Jesus in particular is impressively rich and deserves a study of its own.[5] It takes as its starting point the scattered rabbinic evidence about Jesus and Christianity in talmudic sources as well as the tract *Toledot Yeshu*, which was widely disseminated in the Middle Ages and the early modern period and became the major source for Jewish knowledge about Jesus. One of the first landmarks of a Christian examination of these Jewish sources, made increasingly accessible through Jewish converts, was the polemical treatise *Pugio fidei* ("The Dagger of Faith") composed by the Spanish Dominican friar Raymond Martini (d. 1285), which uses many extracts from talmudic and later rabbinic sources. It influenced most of the subsequent polemical, anti-Jewish pamphlets, particularly after the lost manuscript was rediscovered by the humanist scholar Justus Scaliger (d. 1609) and republished in 1651 (Paris) and 1678 (Leipzig). In 1681 the Christian Hebraist and polyhistorian Johann Christoph Wagenseil, a professor at the University of Altdorf in Germany,[6] published his collection of Jewish anti-Christian polemics *Tela ignea Satanae. Hoc est: arcani et horribiles Judaeorum adversus Christum Deum et Christianam religionem libri* ("Flaming Arrows of Satan; that is, the secret and horrible books of the Jews against Christ, God, and the Christian religion"), also drawing on the talmudic literature and the *Toledot Yeshu*.[7] The first book solely devoted to Jesus in the talmudic literature was the

1699 dissertation, submitted at the University of Altdorf by the Protestant Orientalist Rudolf Martin Meelführer, *Jesus in Talmude* ("Jesus in the Talmud").[8] Unlike Wagenseil, who was highly influential and widely read, his student Meelführer was almost immediately forgotten; both, however, were surpassed in their influence by Johann Andreas Eisenmenger's German work in two volumes, *Entdecktes Judenthum* ("Judaism Unmasked"), which would become—until well into the modern period—a major source for anti-Semitic attacks against the Jews.[9]

Whereas in the early modern period the "Jesus in the Talmud" paradigm served almost solely as an inexhaustible source for anti-Jewish sentiments, the subject gained more serious and critical recognition in the nineteenth and twentieth centuries. Among the extensive relevant literature a few authors deserve special attention:[10] Samuel Krauss presented the first scholarly analysis of the *Toledot Yeshu*, based on an edition and comprehensive analysis of the variant versions of the text (1902), which even today remains the authoritative treatment of the subject.[11] A year later, in 1903, Travers Herford published his *Christianity in Talmud and Midrash*,[12] which would become the standard book about Christianity and Jesus in rabbinic sources, particularly in the English-speaking world. Herford's approach can be called maximalistic in every regard: not only are the many passages that mention the *minim* ("heretics" in the broadest sense of the term) dealing almost without exception with Christians, but he also concludes that almost all the passages in the rabbinic literature that have been remotely connected with Jesus and his life indeed refer to Jesus. The fact that he is rather restrained with regard to the value of the rabbinic sources as evidence for the attempt to reconstruct the *historical* Jesus[13] does not detract from his generally maximalistic and quite naive approach.

The first attempt to examine the relevant rabbinic passages about Jesus and Christianity critically and to provide a text critical edition and translation was made in 1910 by the Christian German scholar Hermann L. Strack (the same Strack who gained enormous reputation through his famous *Introduction to the Talmud and Midrash*)[14] in his 1910 monograph *Jesus, die Häretiker und die Christen nach den ältesten jüdischen Angaben.*[15] Strack set a sober tone, not only with regard to the historical value of the rabbinic evidence but also with regard to the number of the relevant passages, that was to become a major trend particularly in German-language research.[16] The first major scholarly book on Jesus in Hebrew, published in 1922 by the Hebrew University professor Joseph Klausner,[17] follows in its assessment of the Jesus passages a similar critical tendency: the evidence is scanty and does not contribute much to our knowledge of the historical Jesus; much of it is legendary and reflects the Jewish attempt to counter Christian claims and reproaches. The same is true for Morris Goldstein's *Jesus in the Jewish Tradition* of 1950[18] and a long (and rather convoluted) essay by Jacob Lauerbach, published in 1951.[19]

The climax of the latest development in the scholarly literature concerned with Jesus in the Talmud is Johann Maier's book of 1978, *Jesus von Nazareth in der talmudischen Überlieferung.*[20] This is, in many respects, an amazing and disturbing book. It presents the most comprehensive, painstakingly erudite treatment of the subject so far. Maier has sifted through all the secondary literature, even if only remotely relevant, and showers the reader with excruciating details about who wrote what, and when. More important, all the rabbinic sources that have ever been brought into connection with Jesus are analyzed in every possible regard, with Maier taking great pains not just to discuss bits and pieces ripped out of context but to examine them always within the larger literary structure in which they are preserved. This is definitely a huge step forward in comparison with the rather atomistic efforts of his predecessors. But it is achieved at a high price. The reader who has followed Maier through all his endless and winding analyses, peppered with sophisticated charts, is left with the quite unsatisfying question: what is the purpose of all of this? For what Maier ultimately presents is an excess in scholarly acumen that leads nowhere or, to put a slightly more positive spin on it, that leads to the frustrating conclusion of "much ado about nothing." His book is the epitome of a minimalist exercise, just the opposite of Herford. According to Maier, there is hardly any passage left in the rabbinic literature that can be justifiably used as evidence of the Jesus of the New Testament. The rabbis did not care about Jesus, they did not know anything reliable about him, and what they might have alluded to is legendary at best and rubbish at worst—not worthy of any serious scholarly attention, at least after Maier has finally and successfully deconstructed the "evidence."

To be sure, he does not say so in these words; in fact, it is rather difficult to determine what he really thinks about the results of his exercise.

Clearly, he wants to position himself between or, more precisely, beyond the two alternatives of the anti-Jewish Christian and the apologetic Jewish approach. Whereas the former—charged with emotion—uses as its yardstick the theological truth of New Testament Christology, and finds everything that deviates from this "truth" appalling, the latter—painfully embarrassed by what their forefathers might have thought up—opts for a more restrained attitude and calls for moderation and distinction. Maier, naturally, dismisses the Christian anti-Jewish bias and finds the Jewish approach more appealing because he regards it altogether as more "critical" and "skeptical" and as capable—in what he regards as the epitome of modern critical scholarship—of distinguishing between the historical Jesus and the Jesus of the Christian faith. But he disapproves of its apologetic tendency to tone down the anti-Christian polemic in the Jewish sources, and he even lets himself be carried away in this context by the highly charged question: why shouldn't the Jews have allowed themselves to polemicize, since, after all, the holy Church Fathers and the Christian theologians did precisely this, over and over again, and with considerable political and social consequences?[21] Indeed, why shouldn't they have? Maier's question should have become the starting point of a much deeper inquiry into the subject. But unfortunately, these and very few similar remarks are the only "emotional outbursts" that Maier grants himself. In general he remains the "objective" and "rational" scholar, who has overcome, with his literary deconstruction of the sources, Christian anti-Judaism and Jewish apologetics alike.

Is this, then, the last word? Is there no other option beyond Christian anti-Judaism, Jewish apologetics, and Maier's almost "scientific" explaining away of the evidence? I strongly believe there is, and I intend to demonstrate that in the chapters of this book. Before we enter the detailed discussion of the relevant sources, I will set forth some of the principal considerations that will guide me through this discussion.

Since this book is not aimed just at specialists, let me first clarify what I mean by discussing Jesus in the Talmud. By "Talmud" in the broadest sense of the term I mean the entire corpus of rabbinic literature, that is, the literature left to us by the rabbis, the self-appointed heroes of the Judaism of the classical period between the first and the seventh century C.E.[22] This literature includes the Mishna and the Tosefta (the early twin collections of legal decisions, edited around 200 C.E. and in the third century respectively), the midrashim (the rabbinic commentaries on the Hebrew Bible in their manifold form), and—in the more narrowly defined and technical sense of the word—the Talmud in its two manifestations, the Jerusalem or Palestinian Talmud (edited in the rabbinic academies of Palestine in the fifth century) and the Babylonian Talmud (edited in the rabbinic academies of Babylonia in the seventh century C.E.). The later polemical tract *Toledot Yeshu* is not part of this investigation, although I do hope to turn to it in a follow-up project and, in addition to preparing a modern edition and translation, to clarify further its relationship with the talmudic evidence.[23]

I follow the traditional distinction between the earlier tannaitic sources (i.e., sources that are ascribed to the rabbis of the first and second centuries) and the later amoraic sources (i.e., sources that are ascribed to rabbis of the third through the sixth centuries) of the relevant talmudic literature. In addition, I put great emphasis on whether a certain tradition appears in Palestinian and Babylonian sources or solely in Babylonian sources, that is, in the Babylonian Talmud alone. Indeed, in calling the book Jesus in *the Talmud* I emphasize the highly significant role played by the Babylonian Talmud and Babylonian Jewry.

The source material that I have chosen for analysis focuses on Jesus and his family. In other words, I am not claiming to deal with the much broader subject of how Christianity as such is reflected in the literature of rabbinic Judaism. One could argue that a book about "Jesus" in the Talmud cannot adequately be written without taking this broader context of "Christianity" into full consideration. To a certain extent I agree with such an approach (and sometimes I will venture into more comprehensive categories); yet I nevertheless take the risk of limiting myself to this more narrowly defined question because I believe that Jesus, along with his family, was indeed perceived in our sources as a subject of its own.

Unlike Maier and many of his predecessors, I start with the deliberately naive assumption that the relevant sources do refer to the figure of Jesus unless proven otherwise. Hence, I put the heavier burden of proof on those who want to decline the validity of the Jesus passages. More precisely, I do not see any reason why the tannaitic Jesus ben Pantera/Pandera ("Jesus son of Pantera/Pandera") and Ben Stada ("son of Stada") passages should not refer to Jesus, and I will justify this claim in the book. Here I substantially disagree with Maier who vehemently denies the possibility that there are authentic tannaitic Jesus passages and even declares the amoraic passages as all belonging to the post-talmudic rather than to the talmudic period.[24]

However, we need to make here an important qualification. The fact that I accept most of the relevant sources as referring to Jesus (and his family, particularly his mother), does not, by any means, assume the historicity of these sources. As I see it, Maier's most fateful mistake is the way he poses the problem of the historicity of his texts. He takes it for granted that in having purged the bulk of rabbinic literature from Jesus and in allowing for "authentic" Jesus passages to appear only in the very late talmudic and preferably the post-talmudic sources, he has solved the historicity problem once and forever: the few authentic passages, he maintains, are all very late and hence do not contribute anything to the historical Jesus. For what he is concerned about, almost obsessed with, is the historical Jesus. This is why he is so fond of the distinction, in (mostly) Jewish authors, between the historical Jesus and the Jesus of the faith (following, of course, the differentiation being made in critical New Testament scholarship). The historical Jesus does not appear in our rabbinic sources; they do not provide any reliable evidence of him, let alone historical "facts" that deviate from the New Testament and therefore must be taken seriously. According to Maier, that's the end of the story: since the rabbinic literature is meaningless in our quest for the historical Jesus, it is altogether worthless for serious scholarly attention with regard to our subject matter.

I agree that much of our Jesus material is relatively late; in fact, I will argue that the most explicit Jesus passages (those passages that deal with him as a person) appear only in the Babylonian Talmud and can be dated, at the earliest, to the late third–early fourth century C.E. Yet I strongly disagree with Maier that this is the end of the story. On the contrary, I will claim that it is only here that our real inquiry begins. I propose that these (mainly) Babylonian stories about Jesus and his family are deliberate and highly sophisticated counternarratives to the stories about Jesus' life and death in the Gospels—narratives that presuppose a detailed knowledge of the New Testament, in particular of the Gospel of John, presumably through the Diatessaron and/or the Peshitta, the New Testament of the

Syrian Church.[25] More precisely, I will argue—following indeed some of the older research—that they are polemical counternarratives that parody the New Testament stories, most notably the story of Jesus' birth and death. They ridicule Jesus' birth from a virgin, as maintained by the Gospels of Matthew and Luke, and they contest fervently the claim that Jesus is the Messiah and the Son of God. Most remarkably, they counter the New Testament Passion story with its message of the Jews' guilt and shame as Christ killers. Instead, they reverse it completely: yes, they maintain, we accept responsibility for it, but there is no reason to feel ashamed because we rightfully executed a blasphemer and idolater. Jesus deserved death, and he got what he deserved. Accordingly, they subvert the Christian idea of Jesus' resurrection by having him punished forever in hell and by making clear that this fate awaits his followers as well, who believe in this impostor. There is no resurrection, they insist, not for him and not for his followers; in other words, there is no justification whatsoever for this Christian sect that impudently claims to be the new covenant and that is on its way to establish itself as a new religion (not least as a "Church" with political power).

This, I will posit, is the historical message of the (late) talmudic evidence of Jesus. A proud and self-confident message that runs counter to all that we know from Christian and later Jewish sources. I will demonstrate that this message was possible only under the specific historical circumstances in Sasanian Babylonia, with a Jewish community that lived in relative freedom, at least with regard to Christians—quite different from conditions in Roman and Byzantine Palestine, with Christianity becoming an ever more visible and aggressive political power. This is not to say that the Palestinian sources are devoid of any knowledge of Christianity and Jesus. On the contrary, they are vividly and painfully aware of the spread of Christianity. They are not simply denying or ignoring it (in a kind of Freudian mechanism of denial and repression), as has often been suggested; rather they are acknowledging Christianity and engaged in a remarkably intense exchange with it. But still, Jesus as a person, his life, and his fate are much less prominent in the Palestinian sources. So my claim is that it is not so much the distinction between earlier and later sources that matters but the distinction between Palestinian and Babylonian sources, between the two major centers of Jewish life in antiquity. As we shall see, the different political and religious conditions under which the Jews lived created very different attitudes toward Christianity and its founder.

Finally, what kind of Jewish society was it that dealt in this particular way with the question of Jesus and Christianity—daringly self-confident in Babylonia, and so much more restrained in Palestine? The answer is simple but probably not very satisfying for a social historian: it was no doubt an elitist society of the rabbinic academies. The creators and addressees of this discourse were the rabbis and their students, not the ordinary Jew who did not have access to the rabbinic deliberations—although the possibility cannot be ruled out that the academic discourse also penetrated into sermons delivered in synagogues and therefore did reach the "ordinary man," but there is no evidence of this. Moreover, it needs to be reemphasized that the Jesus passages in the Talmud are the proverbial drop of water in the ocean, neither quantitatively significant nor presented in a coherent manner nor, in many cases, a subject of their own. Yet they are much more than just figments of imagination, scattered fragments of lost memory. Adequately analyzed and read in conjunction with one another, they are powerful evidence of bold discourse with the Christian society, of interaction between Jews and Christians, which was remarkably different in Palestine and Babylonia.

The chapters of this book follow the story of Jesus as it emerges from the talmudic sources as we combine them and put them in sequence. This is to say, I have set up the headings under which I present the evidence in order to present the material in a meaningful structure, not just as literary fragments. Although I do not wish to impose on the reader the notion of a coherent Jesus narrative in the Talmud, I do want to point out major thematic topics with regard to Jesus with which the rabbis were concerned. The first chapter ("Jesus' Family") deals with the first cornerstone of the New Testament Jesus narrative, his birth from the Virgin Mary. I will show that the rabbis drafted here, in just a few words, a powerful counternarrative that was meant to shake the foundations of the Christian message: for, according to them, Jesus was not born from a virgin, as his followers claimed, but out of wedlock, the son of a whore and her lover; therefore, he could not be the Messiah of Davidic descent, let alone the Son of God.

The two following chapters focus on a subject of particular importance to the rabbis: their relationship with their students. A bad student was one of the worst disasters that could happen to the rabbinic elite, not only for the poor student but also for his rabbi who was responsible for him. In counting Jesus among the students who turned out badly, the rabbis passed upon him their harshest judgment. Moreover, I will show that in Jesus' case, the reproach with which they confronted him clearly had sexual undertones and emphasized the suspicion of his dubious origin (chapter 2). The same is true for the story about Jesus, the frivolous disciple. Not only did he entertain lewd sexual thoughts, but, when rebuked by his rabbi, he became apostate and established a new cult. The message, therefore, is that the new Christian sect/religion stemmed from a failed and insubordinate rabbinical student (chapter 3).

The next chapter ("The Torah Teacher") does not deal with Jesus directly but with a famous late first–early second century C.E. rabbi (Eliezer b. Hyrkanos), whom the Roman authorities accused of heresy. The precise kind of heresy is not specified, but I will argue that it is indeed the Christian heresy that is at stake and that R. Eliezer was accused of being closely associated with a student of Jesus. Moreover, I will demonstrate that again sexual transgressions are involved because the Christian cult was characterized as enticing its members into secret licentious and orgiastic rites. R. Eliezer became the rabbinic doppelgänger of Jesus, indulging in sexual excesses and exercising magical power. The rabbis needed to punish him with the full thrust of the means at their disposal (excommunication) for threatening the core of their rabbinic authority.

Similar mechanisms are at work in the stories that deal with the magical healing power connected with the name of Jesus (chapter 5). In one story a rabbi is bitten by a snake and wants to be healed by the name of Jesus, spoken over his wound by one of Jesus' followers. His fellow rabbis do not allow the Christian heretic to perform his healing, and the poor rabbi dies. In another story the grandson of a famous rabbi, choking on something that he has swallowed, survives when a Christian heretic manages to whisper the name of Jesus upon him. Rather than being relieved, however, his grandfather curses the heretic and wishes that his grandson had died instead of being healed through the name of Jesus. In both cases it is not the magical power as such that poses a problem (for, on the contrary, the efficiency of the magical power is taken for granted, even if exercised by a heretic and in the name of Jesus); rather, what is at stake is again the wrong magical power: the magical power that competes with the authority of the rabbis and that invokes another authority—Jesus and the Christian community.

With the sixth chapter ("Jesus' Execution") we return to the fate of Jesus himself. Here, a quite elaborate story—again only in the Babylonian Talmud—details the halakhic procedure of Jesus' trial and execution: Jesus was not crucified but, according to Jewish law, stoned to death and then, as the ultimate postmortem punishment reserved for the worst criminals, hanged on a tree. This took place on the eve of Passover, which happened to be Sabbath eve (Friday). The reason for his execution was because he was convicted of sorcery and of enticing Israel into idolatry. As required by the Jewish law, a herald made the announcement of his death sentence—in order to allow for witnesses in his favor, in case there were some—but nobody came to his defense. Finally, he was regarded as being close to the Roman government, but this did not help him either. My comparison of this rabbinic narrative with the Gospels shows some remarkable congruencies and differences: most conspicuous among the former is the day before Passover as the day of Jesus' trial and execution (which concurs with the Gospel of John) and among the latter is the rabbinic insistence on the fact that Jesus was indeed sentenced and executed according to Jewish and not to Roman law. I interpret this as a deliberate "misreading" of the New Testament, (re)claiming Jesus, as it were, for the Jewish people, and proudly acknowledging that he was rightly and legally executed because he was a Jewish heretic.

The story about Jesus' five disciples (chapter 7) continues such charges. In contrast to the futile exercises of most scholars to find here some dark reminiscences of Jesus' historical disciples, I read the story as a highly sophisticated battle with biblical verses, a battle between the rabbis and their Christian opponents, challenging the Christian claim that he is the Messiah and Son of God, that he was resurrected after his horrible death, and that this death is the culmination of the new covenant. Hence, as we shall see, this story, instead of adding just another bizarre facet to the fantastic rabbinic stories about Jesus, is nothing short of an elaborate theological discourse that foreshadows the disputations between Jews and Christians in the Middle Ages.

The most bizarre of all the Jesus stories is the one that tells how Jesus shares his place in the Netherworld with Titus and Balaam, the notorious archenemies of the Jewish people. Whereas Titus is punished for the destruction of the Temple by being burned to ashes, reassembled, and burned over and over again, and whereas Balaam is castigated by sitting in hot semen, Jesus' fate consists of sitting forever in boiling excrement. This obscene story has occupied scholars for a long time, without any satisfactory solution. I will speculate that it is again the deliberate, and quite graphic, answer to a New Testament claim, this time Jesus' promise that eating his flesh and drinking his blood guarantees eternal life to his followers. Understood this way, the story conveys an ironic message: not only did Jesus *not* rise from the dead, he is punished in hell forever; accordingly, his followers—the blossoming Church, which maintains to be the new Israel—are nothing but a bunch of fools, misled by a cunning deceiver.

The concluding chapter ("Jesus in the Talmud") attempts to connect the various and multifarious aspects of the Jesus narrative in the rabbinic literature and to place them into historical perspective. Only when the fruitless search for fragments of information about the historical Jesus, hidden in the "ocean of the Talmud," has been given up and when the right questions are asked, regardless of apologetic, polemic, or other considerations, can we discover the "historical truth" behind our sources: that they are literary answers to a literary text, the New Testament, given under very concrete historical circumstances. I will address the major topics that appear almost as leitmotifs in the texts—sex, magic, idolatry, blasphemy, resurrection, and the Eucharist—and place them in their contemporary, literary as well as historical, context.

Finally, since one of the most striking results of my inquiry is the difference in attitude of the Palestinian and the Babylonian sources, I will pose the question of why we find the most significant, radical, and daring statements about Jesus' life and destiny in the Babylonian Talmud rather than in the Palestinian sources. In pursuing this question I will try to outline the historical reality of the Jews and the Christians living in the Sasanian

Empire in Late Antiquity, in contrast to that of the Jews living in Palestine under Roman rule and subsequently under Christian rule. Then I will summarize the New Testament evidence as it emerges from our rabbinical texts and will again ask the concrete question of why the Gospel of John takes such a prominent place among references to the New Testament. In an appendix, I will address the problem of the manuscript tradition of the Babylonian Talmud and the phenomenon of censorship.

A brief technical note: the translations of the Hebrew Bible and of the rabbinical sources are my own (I checked, however, the Jewish Publication Society translation of the Tanakh, the *New Oxford Annotated Bible*, and the Soncino translation of the Talmud and of Midrash Rabba); for the New Testament I used the *New Oxford Annotated Bible*, third edition with the Apocryphal/Deuterocanonical Books, New Revised Standard Version, edited by Michael D. Coogan, Oxford: Oxford University Press, 2001. All translations of other sources are documented in the notes.

For the Jerusalem and the Babylonian Talmud (in Hebrew *ha-Talmud ha-Yerushalmi* and *ha-Talmud ha-Bavli* respectively) I use both the English terms and the Hebrew abbreviations Yerushalmi and Bavli.

1. Jesus' Family

The rabbinic literature is almost completely silent about Jesus' lineage and his family background. The rabbis do not seem to know—or else do not care to mention—what the New Testament tells us: that he was the son of a certain Mary and her husband (or rather betrothed) Joseph, a carpenter of the city of Nazareth, and that he was born in Bethlehem, the city of David, and hence of Davidic origin. It is only in the Babylonian Talmud, and there in two almost identical passages, that we do get some strange information that may be regarded as a faint and distorted echo of the Gospels' stories about Jesus' family background and his parents.[1] Since neither source mentions, however, the name "Jesus" but instead resorts to the enigmatic names "Ben Stada" and "Ben Pandera/Pantera" respectively, their relationship to Jesus is hotly disputed. I will analyze the Bavli text in detail and demonstrate that it indeed refers to the Jesus of the New Testament and is not just a remote and corrupt echo of the New Testament story; rather, it presents—with few words and in the typically discursive style of the Bavli—a highly ambitious and devastating counternarrative to the infant story of the New Testament.

The version of our story in Shab 104b is embedded in an exposition of the mishnaic law, which regards the writing of two or more letters as work and hence forbidden on the Sabbath (m Shab 12:4). The Mishna discusses all kind of materials that might be used for writing, and of objects upon which one might write, and states that the prohibition of writing includes also the use of one's own body as a writing object. From this the logical question arises: But what about tattoos?[2] Are they, too, to be regarded as writing and hence forbidden on Sabbath?[3] According to R. Eliezer, the answer is yes (they are forbidden on Sabbath), whereas R. Yehoshua allows it (in the Tosefta parallel it is the Sages).

The Tosefta and both the Jerusalem and the Babylonian Talmud elaborate further upon this Mishna. According to the Tosefta, R. Eliezer responds to the Sages: "But did not Ben Satra *learn* only in such a way?"[4] — in other words, did he not use the tattoos on his body as an aid to facilitate his learning (hence, weren't they clearly letters and therefore forbidden to be "written" on Sabbath)? This is bad enough, but the two Talmudim come up with an even worse explanation of why tattooing one's body on Sabbath is forbidden, when they have Eliezer ask: "But did not Ben Stada bring forth witchcraft from Egypt by means of scratches/tattoos (*biseritah*) upon his flesh?"[5] In all three versions the Sages dismiss R. Eliezer's objection with the counterargument that Ben Satra/Stada[6] was a fool and that they would not let one fool's behavior influence the implementation of Sabbath laws.

It is within this context that the Talmud (Shab 104b)[7] proceeds with a clarification of the enigmatic "fool's" family background. The text is only preserved in the uncensored manuscripts and printed editions of the Bavli; I quote according to Ms. Munich 95 (written 1342 in Paris), with some variations in the footnotes:

(Was he) the son of Stada[8] (and not on the contrary) the son of Pandera?

Said Rav Hisda: the husband (*baʿal*) was Stada, (and) the cohabiter/lover (*boʿel*) was Pandera.

(But was not) the husband (*baʿal*) Pappos ben Yehuda and rather his mother Stada?[9]

His mother was [Miriam],[10] (the woman who) let (her) women's [hair][11] grow long (*megadla [seʿar] neshayya*).[12]

This[13] is as they say about her[14] in Pumbeditha: This one turned away from (was unfaithful to) her husband (*saṭat da mi-baʿalah*).

This is a typical discourse of the Bavli, which tries to clarify the contradiction between two traditions: according to one received tradition, the fool/magician is called "son of Stada" and according to another one he is called "son of Pandera."[15] What, then, is his correct name?[16] In other words, the Talmud is concerned about the problem that the same person is called by two different names and not about the question of who this person is (the answer to this latter question is obviously presupposed: everybody seems to know it). Two different answers are provided.

First, Rav Hisda (a Babylonian amora of the third generation and an important teacher at the academy of Sura; d. 309 C.E.) suggests that the person in question had, as it were, two "fathers" because his mother had a husband and a lover,[17] and that he was called "son of Stada," when referring to the husband and "son of Pandera," when referring to the lover. Against this, an anonymous author comes up with a different solution: No, he argues, his mother's husband was not some "Stada" but rather Pappos b. Yehuda, a Palestinian scholar (not portrayed as a sage and without the title "Rabbi") of the first half of the second century C.E., and in fact it was his mother who was called "Stada."[18] If this is so, the last step of the mini-discourse in the Bavli continues, we need to explain this strange name "Stada" for his mother. The answer: His mother's true name was Miriam, and "Stada" is an epithet which derives from the Hebrew/Aramaic root *saṭah/seṭe'* ("to deviate from the right path, to go astray, to be unfaithful"). In other words, his mother Miriam was also called "Stada" because she was a *soṭah*, a woman suspected, or rather convicted, of adultery. This anonymous explanation is located in Pumbeditha, Sura's rival academy in Babylonia.

Hence, it becomes clear that both explanations begin with the assumption that our hero's mother had both a husband and a lover, and that they only disagree about the name of the husband (Stada versus Pappos b. Yehuda). The name Pandera for the lover is made explicit only by Rav Hisda but seems to be accepted in the Pumbeditha explanation as well, because it presupposes the mother's adultery and does not suggest another name for the lover. That Pappos b. Yehuda is identified as the husband originates from another story in the Bavli, transmitted in the name of R. Meir, that Pappos b. Yehuda, when he went out, used to lock his wife in their house—obviously because he had reason to doubt her fidelity (b Git 90a). This behavior on the part of Pappos b. Yehuda is quite drastically compared to that of a man who, if a fly falls into his cup, puts the cup aside and does not drink from it any more—meaning that Pappos b. Yehuda not only locks away his wife so that she cannot go astray but that he also refrains from intercourse with her because she has become doubtful.

The dubious reputation of our hero's mother is further emphasized by the statement that she grew her hair to a great length. Whatever the original meaning of the odd phrase,[19] the context in Shabbat 104b/Sanhedrin 67a clearly suggests that Miriam's long and apparently unfastened hair was indicative of her indecent behavior. Another passage in the Talmud (Er 100b) describes the epitome of a "bad woman" as follows: "She grows long hair like Lilith (*megaddelt śaʿar ke-Lilit*),[20] she sits when making water like a beast, and she serves as a bolster for her husband." Similarly, the story in Gittin continues with a "bad man who sees his wife go out with her hair unfastened[21] and spin cloth in the street with her armpits uncovered and bathe with (other) people"—such a man, it concludes, should immediately divorce his wife instead of continuing to live with her and having intercourse with her. A woman who appears bareheaded and with long hair in public, this seems to be presupposed here, is prone to all kinds of licentious behavior and deserves to be divorced.[22]

If the Bavli takes it for granted that our hero's mother was an adulteress, then the logical conclusion follows that he was a *mamzer*, a bastard or illegitimate child. In order to be put in this *mamzer* category it did not matter whether his biological father was indeed his mother's lover and not her legal husband—the very fact that she had a lover made his legal status dubious. Hence the uncertainty that he is sometimes called Ben Stada and sometimes Ben Pandera. But nevertheless, the Talmud seems to be convinced that his true father was Pandera,[23] his mother's lover, and that he was a bastard in the full sense of the word.

Searching for evidence outside the rabbinic corpus, scholars have long pointed to a remarkable parallel in the pagan philosopher Celsus' polemical treatise *Alethēs Logos*, written in the second half of the second century C.E.[24] and preserved only in quotations in the Church Father Origen's reply *Contra Celsum* (written ca. 231–233 C.E.). There, Celsus presents a Jew[25] as having a conversation with Jesus himself and accusing him of having "fabricated the story of his birth from a virgin." In reality, the Jew argues, he [Jesus] came from a Jewish village and from a poor country woman who earned her living by spinning. He [the Jew] says that she was driven out by her husband, who was a carpenter by trade, as she was convicted of adultery. Then he says that after she had been driven out by her husband and while she was wandering about in a disgraceful way she secretly gave birth to Jesus. And he says that because he [Jesus] was poor he hired himself out as a workman in Egypt, and there tried his hand at certain magical powers on which the Egyptians pride themselves; he returned full of conceit, because of these powers, and on account of them gave himself the title of God.[26]

In another quotation Celsus repeats these allegations put into the mouth of a Jew and even communicates the name of Jesus' father:

Let us return, however, to the words put into the mouth of the Jew, where the mother of Jesus is described as having been turned out by the carpenter who was betrothed to her, as she had been convicted of adultery and had a child by a certain soldier named Panthera (*Panthēra*).[27]

This story has much in common with the short discourse in the Talmud: the hero is the son of an adulteress, he returned from Egypt with magical powers and, most important, the name of his mother's lover (his father) was Panthera. The only difference between the versions in the Talmud and in Celsus is the fact that Celsus makes it explicit that the child, born from the poor Jewish adulteress and the soldier Panthera, was the very Jesus whom the Christians regard as the founder of their faith, whereas the Talmud keeps silent about the proper name of the child.[28] But this does not pose a real problem because the Talmud, as we have seen, is not concerned about the identity of the child but about the strange phenomenon of two different names used for his father. Moreover, several rabbinic sources do mention Jesus as the son of Pandera,[29] and it can be safely assumed, therefore, that the Talmud presupposes the knowledge of this identity. The punch line of this attribution, of course, is the fact that Jesus, through his father Panthera/Pandera, becomes not only a bastard but even the son of a non-Jew.[30]

These congruencies make it highly probable that both the Talmud and Celsus draw on common sources (most likely originally Jewish sources) that relate that Jesus of Nazareth was a bastard because his mother was an adulteress (Miriam)[31] and his father was her lover (Pandera/Panthera). Some scholars, most radically among them Johann Maier, want to conclude from the fact that the name Panthera is relatively common in Latin inscriptions[32] and that the spelling of its equivalent in the Hebrew sources varies considerably, that there must have been some different Jesus with the patronymic Panthera/Pandera/Pantiri (or similar forms) who cannot and should not be traced back to the one and only Jesus of Nazareth.[33] Although such a possibility cannot be excluded, it does not seem very likely. The different versions of the name Panthera are still similar enough to be attributed to the same person, and such an attribution certainly does not require that all of the various forms of the name be *philologically* traced back to one *ur*-form (Panthera).[34] Moreover, and more important, the name is not common at all in Hebrew or Aramaic, and this fact alone makes the connection with Celsus' Panthera obvious.

Celsus' Jew in the late second century C.E. and the Babylonian Talmud in a presumably early fourth-century tradition refer to the same counternarrative of Jesus' family background, which evidently is an inversion of and polemic against the New Testament narrative of Jesus' birth. Several motifs are characteristic:

1. Jesus "returns" from Egypt as a magician. In the New Testament, Jesus' parents Mary and Joseph flee to Egypt with the newborn infant because King Herod threatens to kill the child (Mt. 2:13ff.). Herod had heard about Jesus from the magicians who came from the East to pay tribute to Jesus as the newborn King of the Jews (Mt. 2:2). Egypt was regarded in antiquity as the classical land of magic,[35] and Jesus is portrayed in the New Testament[36] as well as in rabbinic sources[37] as someone with supernatural powers (healing, commanding the demons, etc.). That Jesus is labeled a magician in a derogatory sense is, therefore, an inversion of the New Testament, which connects him (positively) with magicians, with Egypt, and with healing powers.

2. Celsus portrays Jesus' parents as poor: his father was a carpenter and his mother a poor countrywoman who earned her living by spinning. The

New Testament does not say anything about Mary's family background, but it mentions explicitly that Joseph, her betrothed, was a carpenter (Mt. 13:55).[38] The Talmud remains silent about his parents' means—unless one wants to see in the strange epithet *megadla neshayya* given to his mother an allusion not to her long hair but to her profession as a manual worker (the Aramaic word *megadla* can mean "plaiting" but also "weaving").

3. The most pungent counterargument against the evangelists' narrative is, of course, the assertion of Jesus' illegitimate birth from an adulterous mother and some insignificant lover. It parries the claim of Jesus' noble Davidic lineage to which the New Testament attaches such great value: Matthew starts with his genealogy (Mt. 1) which leads back directly to David and calls him, as well as his "father" Joseph, "son of David" (Mt. 1:1, 20; Lk. 1:27, 2:4); he is born in Bethlehem, the city of David (Mt. 2:5f.; Lk. 2:4), and hence is the Davidic Messiah (Mt. 2:4; Lk. 2:11). No, the Jewish counternarrative argues, this is all nonsense; he is anything but of noble origins. His father was by no means a descendant of David but the otherwise unknown Panthera/Pandera (just a Roman soldier, according to Celsus, in other words a non-Jew and a member of the hated Roman Empire that so visibly and horribly oppressed the Jews).

Much worse, in turning Jesus into a bastard, the counternarrative takes up the contradictions within the New Testament story about Jesus' origins and ridicules the claim that he was born from a virgin (parthenogenesis). The New Testament itself is remarkably vague about this claim. Matthew, having established Jesus' genealogy from Abraham down to Joseph, concludes with Jacob who "fathered Joseph, the husband[39] of Mary, who gave birth to Jesus, who is called Messiah" (Mt. 1:16). This is clear enough: Jesus is the son of the couple Joseph and Mary, and the Davidic lineage comes from his father Joseph, not from his mother. Only under this premise, that Joseph was his real father, does the emphasis put on his genealogy make sense.[40] Yet after this dramatic beginning Matthew suddenly reveals that Mary was not married to Joseph but just betrothed and that she expected a child before they were legally married (1:18). This discovery troubled Joseph,[41] who was a just man, and he decided to dismiss her (1:19)—but in a dream it was revealed to him that her child was "from the

Holy Spirit" (1:20). When he woke up from his dream, Joseph took Mary
as his legal wife and accepted her son (1:24f.).[42]

The Jewish counternarrative points to the inconsistencies within
Matthew's birth story. It does not spend time on the legal intricacies of be-
trothal and marriage but maintains that Joseph and Mary were indeed
married, not just betrothed. The bizarre idea of having the Holy Spirit in-
tervene to make him the father of Mary's child is nothing but a cover-up of
the truth, it maintains, namely that Mary, Joseph's legal wife, had a secret
lover and that her child was just a bastard like any other bastard. Joseph's
suspicion, whether he was Mary's husband or her betrothed, was absolutely
warranted: Mary had indeed been unfaithful to him. He should have dismissed her immediately as was customary according to Jewish law.

This powerful counternarrative shakes the foundations of the Christian
message. It is not just a malicious distortion of the birth story (any such
moralizing categories are completely out of place here); rather, it posits
that the whole idea of Jesus' Davidic descent, his claim to be the Messiah,
and ultimately his claim to be the son of God, are based on fraud. His
mother, his alleged father (insofar as he helped covering up the truth), his
real father, and not least Jesus himself (the would-be magician) are all impostors that deceived the Jewish people and deserve to be unmasked, exposed to ridicule, and thereby neutralized. Most striking, this counter–New
Testament in a nutshell has been preserved in rabbinic sources only in
the Babylonian Talmud,[43] and there almost in passing.

I conclude this chapter with yet another story from the Babylonian Talmud (again, only in the Bavli) that can be read as a parody of Jesus' birth
from a virgin. It is part of a long disputation between "the" notorious Roman emperor and R. Yehoshua b. Hananya,[44] in the course of which
R. Yehoshua travels to Athens to meet the Greek Sages. R. Yehoshua and
the Athenians engage in a long discussion that aims at finding out who is
cleverer, the Greek Sages or the rabbi. Asked to tell them some fiction stories (*milei di-bedi'ei*), he comes up with the following tale:

There was this mule which gave birth, and [round its neck] was
hanging a document upon which was written, "there is a claim
against my father's house of one hundred thousand Zuz." They [the

Athenian Sages] asked him: "Can a mule give birth"? He [R. Yeho-shua] answered them: "This is one of these fiction stories".

[Again, the Athenian Sages asked:] "When salt becomes unsavory, wherewith is it salted"? He replied: "With the afterbirth of a mule."—"And is there an afterbirth of a mule"?—"And can salt become unsavory"?[45]

These brief stories center around the well-known fact that mules, the off-spring of a cross between a male donkey and a female horse, almost al-ways are sterile. Both play with a double element of surprise: in the first case the allegation that a mule not only can give birth to a cub, but that a particular cub was even born with a debt document bound around its neck; and in the second case that salt not only can become unsavory, but that it can regain its flavor with the afterbirth of a mule. This, of course, has nothing to do with Jesus. But why the strange idea of a sterile mule giving birth, coupled with the not-less-strange idea of unsavory salt, that is, presumably salt that lost its taste? One could argue that what we have here are remnants of some kind of an early "scientific" discourse about the sterility of mules, and this is probably the easiest answer. But still, the connection of the miraculous offspring of a sterile mule with the salt re-gaining its taste by the afterbirth of a mule is suspicious. With regard to the unsavory—most likely insipid—salt one immediately thinks of Jesus' famous dictum in the Sermon on the Mount:

You are the salt of the earth; but if the salt has lost its taste, how can its saltiness be restored? It is no longer good for anything, but is thrown out and trampled underfoot.[46]

Jesus addresses here his disciples as the salt of the earth, more precisely as the new salt of the earth because there is some other salt that has lost its saltiness and hence it taste. This other salt, with no taste anymore, can easily be understood as the people of the old covenant which is "no longer good for anything," "thrown out," and "trampled under foot." If we take this saying of Jesus as the foil against which our Bavli story was con-strued, the brief tale turns into a pungent parody of the New Testament claim of Jesus' followers as the new salt of the earth: these Christians, it argues, maintain that the salt of the old covenant has become insipid, and hence useless, and that its taste was restored by the people of the new covenant—through the afterbirth of a mule! But we all know that there is no such thing as the afterbirth of a mule because the mule does not give birth, as much as we know that salt does not lose its taste.

On this background, the miraculous offspring of the mule in the first story (and the afterbirth in the second one) gets an even more significant meaning. It can well be understood as a parody of Jesus' miraculous birth from a virgin: an offspring from a virgin is as likely as an offspring from a mule.[47] The Christians' claim of Jesus' birth from a virgin and without a father belongs to the category of fiction stories, fairy tales just for fun. Moreover, this is the punch line of the second story: Jesus' followers, who claim to be the new salt of the earth, are nothing but the afterbirth of that imagined offspring of the mule, a fiction of a fiction. Read this way, our two little Bavli stories become indeed much more than an amusing exchange between the rabbis and the Greek Sages; rather, they offer another biting ridicule of one of the cornerstones of Christian theology.

2. The Son/Disciple Who Turned out Badly

The next stage in Jesus' "career," of which we find an echo in the Talmud, is his appearance as a quite grown-up son or disciple. To be sure, the Talmud does not convey any information about Jesus' growing up in his family or his youth, let alone about his education and his teachers; it just mentions him, again in passing, as an example of a son or a disciple who turns out badly—the nightmare of any decent parent. Interestingly enough, the New Testament, too, does not tell us much about Jesus' childhood: Matthew moves directly from his return from Egypt with his parents after Herod's death to his baptism as an adult in the Jordan by John the Baptist, his temptation in the desert, and then to his first public appearance in Galilee; Mark starts with his baptism, temptation, and first public appearance; and John opens his narrative with John the Baptist's testimony about Jesus' mission and his first disciples. It is only Luke who relates the story about the twelve-year-old Jesus who, instead of joining his parents on their trip back from Jerusalem to Nazareth, prefers to stay calmly in the Temple among the teachers in order to listen to them and to ask them questions (Lk. 2:46).

The talmudic story about the wicked son/disciple is preserved in two different contexts. The first, in Bavli Sanhedrin 103a, presents itself as an exegesis of Psalm 91:10:[1]

Rav Hisda said in the name of R. Yirmeya bar Abba: What is meant by the verse: No evil (*ra'ah*) will befall you, no plague (*nega'*) will approach your tent (Ps. 91:10)?

No evil (*ra'ah*) will befall you (ibid.): that the evil inclination (*yetzer ha-ra'*) shall have no power over you!

No plague (*nega'*) will approach your tent (ibid.): that you will not find your wife a [doubtful][2] Niddah[3] when you return from a journey.

Another interpretation: No evil (*ra'ah*) will befall you (ibid.): that bad dreams and bad thoughts will not frighten you.

No plague (*nega'*) will approach your tent (ibid.): that you will not have a son or a disciple who publicly spoils his food/dish (*maqdiah tavshilo*) like Jesus the Nazarene (*Yeshu ha-Notzri*).[4]

This is a symmetrically structured exposition, transmitted by the same Rav Hisda (the Babylonian amora from the academy of Sura) who played an important role in the discussion about Miriam's husband and lover; R. Yirmeya b. Abba, the authority he quotes, is a Babylonian amora of the second generation (mid-third century C.E.). Rav Hisda's first interpretation of the Psalm verse suggests that "evil" refers to the "evil inclination" (most likely not just any evil inclination but specifically some sexual temptation) and "plague" to the dreaded situation in which a husband returns home, presumably after a long journey, only to find his wife in a state in which it is doubtful whether she may be menstruating (and hence impure and unfit for intercourse) or not. This condition, Rav Hisda assumes, is even crueler for the poor husband than if his wife is definitely menstruating because he might be tempted to dismiss the doubt and have intercourse with her, although, in fact, she is menstruating and therefore forbidden.

The second interpretation[5] applies the "evil" in the Psalm verse to bad dreams/thoughts and the "plague" to a son or disciple who publicly spoils his food. What kind of "bad dreams/thoughts" our author has in mind is not spelled out, but the clearly sexual coloring of the first interpretation— "evil inclination" (often connected with sexual misconduct) and Niddah— suggests that he is not just referring to nightmares but more concretely to sexual dreams. It is highly likely, therefore, that the difficult and unusual phrase "who publicly spoils his food" has also a sexual connotation. The literary meaning of the phrase is "to cause burning to a dish," that is, to make a dish inedible by oversalting[6] or overspicing it.[7] This literal meaning can hardly be the misdeed of which the son/disciple is accused. Rather, the symmetrical structure of Rav Hisda's exegesis actually requires that "burning the dish" has something to do with the son's/disciple's sexual relationship to his wife, in other words that some kind of sexual misconduct is at stake here:

a. evil: evil (sexual) inclination/plague: doubtful menstrual status of the wife

b. evil: bad (sexual) dreams and thoughts/plague: he does something to his wife(?)

In order to elucidate the meaning of our strange phrase further, let us look at some parallels. A similar phrase is used in a discussion between the houses of Hillel and Shammai regarding the question of the proper reason for a man to divorce his wife: according to the house of Shammai a man should divorce his wife only when he has found her guilty of some unseemly conduct, whereas according to the house of Hillel a man may have sufficient grounds for divorce "if she has spoilt his food" (*hiqdiha tavshilo*: m Git 9:10). It does not seem very likely that the wife's spoiling her husband's food simply refers to preparing some oversalted or overspiced dishes. The controversy between Hillel and Shammai rests on a different understanding of the biblical proof text for their legal reasoning: "If a man takes a wife and has intercourse with her, and it happens that she fails to please him because he finds some unseemly thing in her—he writes her a bill of divorcement, hands it to her and sends her away from his house" (Deut. 24:1). What is translated here as "some unseemly thing" is in Hebrew ʿerwat davar (literally "nakedness of a thing, indecency, lewdness"). Whereas Shammai puts the emphasis on ʿerwah ("nakedness, indecency"), arguing that only a clear case of the wife's sexual misconduct deserves divorce, Hillel stresses the word *davar* ("thing"), arguing that any "thing" that may be related to "indecency" (even a minor offense or probably just the rumor of an indiscretion)[8] can be used by the husband as a reason for divorce. Hillel's "thing" in this context is clearly not just anything that the husband can present against his wife (like spoiling his dinner), but anything that has to do with fornication.

This sexual context becomes even clearer if we take into consideration that the Hebrew word for the spoiled "dish" (*tavshil*) acquires in the Bavli also the meaning of intercourse. Thus the Talmud relates of Rav Kahana (a Babylonian amora of the second generation and student of Rav, who went to Palestine):

> Rav Kahana once went in and hid under Rav's bed. He heard him chatting (with his wife) and joking and doing what he required (having intercourse with her). He (Rav Kahana) said to him (Rav): "One would think that Abba's[9] mouth had never sipped the dish before (*śaref tavshila*)." He (Rav) said to him (R. Kahana): "Kahana, are you here? Get out because this is not what one is supposed to do!" He (Rav Kahana) replied: "It is a matter of Torah, and I require to learn!"[10]

Here the phrase "to sip/swallow the dish" undoubtedly refers to performing sexual intercourse. Accordingly, if a woman "spoils his [her husband's] dish," she does something that prohibits him from having intercourse with her—most likely some sexual misconduct that compromises her as well as his reputation. In the case of our son or disciple it is the man who spoils his dish, meaning that he does something that prohibits her from having intercourse with him—again presumably some sexual misconduct that compromises his as well as her reputation. The effect of this misconduct on the part of the son/disciple is intensified by the fact that he does so in public, making it impossible for her to ignore it.

Seen within this wider context the message of Rav Hisda's exegesis of the Psalm verse seems to be: the worst plague is a son or disciple who publicly leads a licentious life by which he compromises himself and his poor wife. It is hardly by coincidence that this interpretation comes from the same Rav Hisda who told us that Jesus' mother had a husband as well as a lover and that Jesus was the son of her lover. Now we learn: this Jesus isn't any better than his mother—it's in his blood. He is so spoiled that he has become the proverbial son or disciple who is unfaithful to his wife and a disgrace to his parents or his teachers.[11] This is quite an unexpected turn in Jesus' life that goes far beyond the New Testament narrative—unless one wants to follow the later identification of Mary Magdalene with the unknown "immoral woman" in Luke (7:36–50),[12] who wets Jesus' feet with her tears, wipes them with her hair, kisses them, and anoints them with myrrh (7:38). The Pharisees, who observe this scene, know her as a prostitute (7:39) and want to use this fact as proof that Jesus is no real prophet as he claims (because he did not seem to know what kind of woman she was), but Jesus, seeing through their bad intentions, publicly forgives the woman her sins and thus reveals that he did know of her bad reputation. The Talmud could again have inverted this New Testament story and insinuated that Jesus indeed knew her—but not in order to forgive her her sins and to unmask the Pharisees; rather, he knew her for what she really was (a prostitute) because he had an affair with her.

Another, and slightly different, possible background for the talmudic story could be the tradition preserved in some gnostic texts about Mary Magdalene. This is the tradition that has even made it into recent fiction,[13] namely that Jesus was indeed married—and to no less a person than Mary Magdalene. The gnostic library from Nag Hammadi contains a "Gospel of Mary Magdalene," presumably from the second century C.E., in which the jealous apostle Peter addresses her as someone whom Jesus loved more than the rest of women.[14] The "Gospel of Philip" (second half of the third century C.E.?) calls her his "companion"[15] and emphasizes that Jesus not only loved her more than all the disciples but that he "[used to] kiss her [often] on her [. . .]."[16] Unfortunately the last word is missing, but it is highly probable that the word "mouth" must be added.[17] Within the context of the gnostic writings it isn't very likely, however, that a plain conjugal relationship is at stake here. Rather, it seems that the "companion" (*koinonos*, a Greek loanword in the Coptic text) refers not to "spouse" in the technical sense of the word but to "sister" in the spiritual sense of the gnostic fellowship, just as the "kiss" does not refer to a sexual relationship but to a kiss of fellowship.[18] Yet one can easily see how this reading of the New Testament narrative could be turned— not only in modern fiction but already in the source used by the Talmud—into a tradition about Jesus being married to Mary Magdalene. Whether the wicked son/student Jesus was unfaithful to his spouse Mary Magdalene or had intercourse with her during her Niddah, or whether the Talmud wants to imply that the marriage with Mary Magdalene as such was suspicious (because she was a prostitute), or whether it wants to read its source creatively and to understand "sister" literally (insinuating some kind of incestuous relationship)—there is quite a variety of nasty implications to choose from. Whichever one wishes to adopt, the possibility that the Talmud might respond to a tradition that is preserved only in the gnostic[19] literature is in itself remarkable enough.

The second context (b Ber 17a–b) in which the Talmud presents the story of the wicked son/disciple is an exegesis of Psalm 144:14: "Our oxen are well loaded (*allufenu mesubbalim*). There is no breach (*peretz*) and no going forth (*yotzet*), and no outcry (*tzewahah*) in our streets." Like the first one, it is connected with Rav Hisda:

When the rabbis took leave from the school of Rav Hisda—others say, from the school of R. Shemuel bar Nahmani—they said to him (Rav Hisda):

Our oxen are well loaded (Ps. 144:14)—(this means): we are instructed, we are well loaded.[20]

Rav and Shemuel—others say, R. Yohanan and R. Eleazar—(give different explanations of this).

One says: We are instructed (ibid.)—(this means): we are instructed in Torah.

We are well loaded (ibid.)—(this means): we are well loaded with precepts.

The other says: We are instructed—(this means): we are instructed in Torah and precepts.

We are well loaded—(this means): we are well loaded with chastisements.[21]

There is no breach (ibid.)—(this means): may our company not be like that of David, from whom issued Ahitophel.

And no going forth (ibid.)—(this means): may our company not be like that of Saul, from whom issued Doeg the Edomite.

And no outcry (ibid.)—(this means): may our company not be like that of Elisha, from whom issued Gehazi.

In our streets (ibid.)—(this means): that we shall not have a son or a disciple who publicly spoils his food/dish (*maqdiah tavshilo*) like Jesus the Nazarene (*Yeshu ha-Notzri*).[22]

Here Jesus finds himself in the not particularly flattering company of Ahitophel, Doeg, and Gehazi. What is it that they did and why are they regarded as prime examples of bad company? First of all, the emphasis in the present context is on disciples and not on sons: the students leave the school of Rav Hisda, are well loaded with Torah and precepts, and dread a "breach," "going forth," and "outcry" in their "streets" (i.e., among them), meaning someone in their company who produces an unworthy student/follower. The examples are taken from no lesser "companions" than David, Saul, and Elisha. David "produced" Ahitophel, his unfaithful adviser, who advised David's son Absalom to rebel against his father by having intercourse with his concubines (2 Sam. 16:20–23) and to kill David (2 Sam. 17:2); when his counsel was rejected, he committed suicide (2 Sam. 17:23). Doeg the Edomite was the overseer over Saul's shepherds (1 Sam. 21:8) and loyal to King Saul: he informed Saul that the priests of Nob had supported David (1 Sam. 22:9f.) and killed the priests on Saul's request (1 Sam. 22:18f.). And finally Gehazi was the servant of the prophet Elisha whom Elisha cursed with leprosy because of his greed (2 Kings 5:20–27). Jesus clearly does not originally belong to this list because he breaks the pattern of the preceding examples ("may our company not be like that of X, from which issued Y"): his master is not mentioned because there was no appropriate candidate in the Bible; instead he is just introduced as a bad son or disciple with the same phrase as in b Sanhedrin. This makes it quite clear that the context in b Berakhot is secondary.

Such a conclusion based on the literary analysis of the story does not affect, however, the message of the version preserved in b Berakhot.[23] At first glance it simply reuses the Jesus dictum within the context of a list of "bad companions" all taken from the Hebrew Bible without adding substantial new information about Jesus. But this is only part of the evidence. Looking at it again and taking into consideration the original context of the "bad companions," it becomes clear that our version is in fact a very clever remodeling of a much earlier story. Our three "bad companions" are singled out, together with Balaam as the fourth and most prominent culprit, already in the famous passage in the Mishna of the four "commoners," who have no portion in the world to come.[24] The Mishna, after having stated categorically that "all Israel have a portion in the world to come" (Sanh 10:1),[25] nevertheless lists the exceptions of those who "have no portion in the world to come":

1. One who maintains that resurrection is not intimated [in the Torah];[26]
   that the Torah is not (revealed) from heaven;
   the Apikoros[27] (this part is transmitted anonymously).

2. One who reads "external books";[28]
   one who whispers over a wound (transmitted by R. Aqiva).
   One who pronounces the divine name according to its letters[29] (transmitted by Abba Shaul).

3. Three kings: Jeroboam, Ahab, Manasseh;
   Four commoners: Balaam, Doeg, Ahitophel, Gehazi (again transmitted anonymously).

From this Mishna it becomes clear that Doeg, Ahitophel, and Gehazi (and in addition Balaam) are listed together because they are the only four private individuals (in contrast to three kings) who are excluded from what is actually, as the Mishna maintains, reserved for all of Israel. The anonymous author of the Mishna does not give any justification for his harsh verdict; we need to turn to the Bible to find out what is so peculiarly dreadful about them that they are excluded from the world to come. We have seen already what was the rabbis' concern with Doeg, Ahitophel, and Gehazi. Balaam, the fourth culprit, is portrayed in the talmudic tradition as a pagan magician who nevertheless, when asked by the king of Moab to curse the Israelites, did just the opposite and uttered divine blessings (Num. 23; 24). There is nothing wrong with this, and hence the Talmud praises him as a genuine prophet among the nations.[30] On the other hand he is regarded as utterly wicked, because it was he who enticed Israel into the idolatry of Baal-Peor (Num. 25; 31:16).[31] That our text in b Berakhot leaves Balaam out is a tacit response to a problem apparent already in the Mishna: How is it that the Mishna counts Balaam among those who have no portion in the world to come when discussing the fate of Israel? Balaam after all was a pagan and not an Israelite![32]

Whatever the four culprits in the Mishna did—they are the only four commoners in history who are bound together in the horrible destiny of being categorically excluded from the world to come. Now the very fact that our talmudic text puts Jesus (instead of Balaam) in this company can only have the purpose of having him share the destiny of his companions, namely to have no portion in the world to come. This, however, is anything but an innocent statement. To be denied an afterlife is bad enough, but to deprive Jesus, of all persons, an afterlife reveals quite a wicked sense of humor. Did not his followers claim that he was resurrected (Rom. 8:34) and that the people of the new Israel would be saved only through him (Rom. 6:3–11)? By including Jesus among the very few of Israel who are categorically and on principle denied access to the world to come, the Talmud makes a very forceful and bold argument. It is difficult to imagine that such a statement is coincidental and not, on the contrary, a deliberate response to the New Testament's claim of Jesus' resurrection and his followers' participation in his destiny. Hence, what the talmudic passage wants to convey in reality is the message that not only Jesus is excluded from the world to come but that all of his followers in the Christian Church share this devastating verdict with him.

In transferring the dictum about Jesus publicly spoiling his food to the tradition of those who have no share in the world to come (and in replacing Balaam with Jesus) the Talmud considerably changes its meaning. The originally sexual connotation recedes into the background; instead, if we take the Balaam connection seriously, the accusation of idolatry becomes prominent—although, to be sure, the idolatry of Baal-Peor, into which Balaam enticed Israel, is clearly sexually oriented. Jesus-Balaam is now the paragon of an idolater, who spoiled his food by enticing all of Israel into idolatry. He did it "in our streets," that is, as the Talmud explains, publicly and unabashedly—just as Balaam did, his "master" and model.

3. The Frivolous Disciple

Jesus' role as a disciple and his relationship with his teacher is the subject of yet another colorful story preserved in the Bavli. This time Jesus has a teacher explicitly mentioned by name and is coupled only with Gehazi, one of the other ill-behaved disciples known from the Bible whom we encountered in the previous story. The fate of both Gehazi and Jesus is put under the rabbinic maxim: "Let the left hand push away but the right hand always draw near!"[1] Their teachers are now presented as prime examples of (bad) teachers who did not follow this maxim but pushed their students away with both their hands and did not help them to mend their wrongdoing: "Not as Elisha, who pushed Gehazi away with both hands, and not as Yehoshua b. Perahya, who pushed Jesus the Nazarene away with both hands."[2]

We know Elisha as Gehazi's master/teacher from the Bible—but what about the strange connection of Jesus with Yehoshua b. Perahya? The Talmud explains as follows:

What was the incident with Yehoshua b. Perahya? When King Yannai killed the rabbis,[3] R. Yehoshua b. Perahya[4] fled to Egyptian Alexandria. When there was peace, Shimon b. Shetah sent (the following message):

"From Jerusalem, the Holy City, to you, Alexandria in Egypt. O my sister, my husband dwells in your midst, and I remain desolate!"

He [Yehoshua b. Perahya] arose, went and found himself in a certain inn. They paid him great respect. He said: "How beautiful is this inn/innkeeper (*akhsanya*)!" He [one of his disciples/Jesus][5] said: "Rabbi, her eyes are narrow."[6] He [Yehoshua b. Perahya] replied: "(You) wicked (student), do you occupy yourself with such (a thought)?!" He sounded 400 Shofar blasts and excommunicated him.

He [the disciple] came before him [the rabbi] several times (and) said to him: "Receive me!", but he [Yehoshua b. Perahya] refused to take notice. One day, while he [Yehoshua b. Perahya] was reciting the Shema, he [the disciple] came (again) before him. (This time) he [Yehoshua b. Perahya] wanted to receive him (and) made a sign to him with his hand. But he [the disciple] thought that he [Yehoshua b. Perahya] was again repelling him. He [the disciple] went, set up a brick and worshipped it. He [Yehoshua b. Perahya] said to him [the student]: "Repent!", (but) he answered him: "Thus have I learned from you: Whoever sins and causes others to sin, is deprived of the power of doing penitence."

The master said: "Jesus the Nazarene[7] practiced magic and deceived and led Israel astray."

This story[8] is situated during the reign of the Hasmonean king (Alexander) Yannai, who ruled from 103 until 76 B.C.E. and who became entangled in a bloody conflict with the Pharisees. The Pharisees, who opposed his rule, instigated an open rebellion against the king that climaxed in a civil war. When the king finally succeeded in suppressing the rebellion, his opponents were either executed or forced to leave the country. These events are reported in detail by the Jewish historian Flavius Josephus,[9] and the rabbinic story is a faint echo thereof, anachronistically identifying the Pharisees with the much later rabbis. The hero of the rabbinic narrative, of which our story is a part, is Shimon b. Shetah.

Both Yehoshua b. Perahya and Shimon b. Shetah belong to the enigmatic "pairs" (*zugot*) that are affiliated with the famous "chain of tradition," connecting the leaders of rabbinic Judaism with the revelation of

the Torah to Moses on Mount Sinai.[10] After having established the chain
of tradition from Moses through the members of the "Great Assembly,"
the Mishna proceeds first with certain individuals (Shimon the Righteous, Antigonos from Sokho) and then with altogether five "pairs," all of
them shrouded in the mists of history, reaching safer historical ground
only with the last pair (Hillel and Shammai). Yehoshua b. Perahya belongs to the second "pair" (together with Nittai ha-Arbeli), whereas Shimon b. Shetah forms (together with Yehuda b. Tabbai) the third one.

Except for Shimon b. Shetah and Hillel/Shammai, little is known
about these early "pairs," who are presented as the "forefathers" of the rabbis. And why of all possible candidates Yehoshua b. Perahya is chosen as
the one who fled to Egypt (presumably together with his favorite student)
remains dubious.[11] A more plausible (although not necessarily historically
more reliable) setting is suggested by the parallel version of our story in
the Talmud Yerushalmi.[12] There, the heroes of the story are Yehuda b.
Tabbai and Shimon b. Shetah, the third "pair," and it is Yehuda b. Tabbai, who flees to Alexandria—not because of King Yannai's persecution of
the Pharisees/rabbis but for a much more mundane reason: he wanted to
escape his appointment as *naśi* (Patriarch) of the Jewish people. This is
but another anachronistic attempt of the rabbis to backdate a later (second century C.E.) rabbinic institution to a much earlier period, but at
least it explains why Shimon b. Shetah so desperately wanted him to return to Jerusalem.[13]

The framework plot of our narrative, in both the Bavli and in the
Yerushalmi versions, does not help much to understand and to locate historically the core of the story: the strange incident between a teacher
(Yehoshua b. Perahya/Yehuda b. Tabbai) and his favorite student (anony-
mous/Jesus). The incident occurs in an inn on their way back to
Jerusalem.[14] Satisfied with how they are received, the master praises the
inn, but his student, misunderstanding him as praising the (female)
innkeeper,[15] makes a disparaging remark about the less than beautiful appearance of the lady. The master is horrified by his student's frivolous
thoughts[16] and immediately excommunicates him. The poor student tries
to appease his master but initially in vain. When the master finally is
ready to forgive him, the student misunderstands his body language,[17]
leaves the master in despair and becomes an idolater. Now the master

begs him to repent, but the student is convinced that he has committed a capital sin, which forever excludes penitence and forgiveness.

This last part of the story (the excommunication of the student and the aborted repentance as well as the master's conclusion about Jesus' magic) is completely lacking in the Yerushalmi, where the story concludes with the remark that the master becomes angry and that the student leaves him or (in one manuscript)[18] dies.

It is obvious that the identification of the student with Jesus reflects a later stage in the development of the story: it is lacking in the Yerushalmi version and attested only in some manuscripts of the Bavli version. There can be no doubt, therefore, that Yehoshua b. Perahya, whatever historical reality stands behind this figure, has nothing to do with Jesus in the sense that the story preserves some historically reliable information about the founder of Christianity. But this is not what is at stake here. The fact that Jesus penetrated into the story at a later stage does not mean that the story does not contain any reliable information about *the Bavli's* perception of Jesus.[19] On the contrary, the manuscript evidence clearly shows a tendency during the editorial process of the Bavli to identify the unknown student of Yehoshua b. Perahya with Jesus, a tendency moreover that is peculiar to the Bavli and must have to do with the Bavli's understanding of Jesus and his personality.[20]

Two features in the story underline this assumption. The first is the kind of idolatry the heretical student adopts when he believes that he has been finally rejected by his teacher: he worships a brick, a custom that markedly points to the cultural context of Babylonia. Any attempt to find behind this brick worship some hidden allusions to Christian practices[21] is completely misguided and misses the point. Our Bavli editor did not know (and did not care) much about Christian worship and identified the idolatry of Jesus with what he regarded as idolatry in his Babylonian milieu—brick worship.[22]

The second distinctively Babylonian feature is the explicit reference to magic in the concluding statement by the master. We have seen already that Jesus was connected with Egyptian magic (reminiscent of the infancy story with the magicians coming from the East[!] and the subsequent flight of Jesus and his parents to Egypt in the Gospel of Matthew); now we are in the center of Babylonia, the most ancient motherland of magic, and Jesus' idolatry is identified as what many Babylonian Jews would have expected an idolater to do: to practice deviant or forbidden kinds of magic. However, the master's pious condemnation of magic cannot conceal the fact that magic was regarded as perfectly acceptable and was widespread, not least in Babylonia. The many magical bowls from Mesopotamia, which were written in all likelihood by Jewish practitioners of magic, attest to this.[23]

Most remarkable, among the names that appear on these Babylonian magic bowls are no less famous ones than our Yehoshua b. Perahya and, indeed, Jesus. Yehoshua b. Perahya issues a letter of divorce to female demons in order to stop their evil deeds—the prime example of a potent magician whose decree is sanctioned in heaven.[24] Clearly not by coincidence, he appears also in some fragments of the *Toledot Yeshu*, the infamous Jesus narrative.[25] Jesus has been discovered on a magic bowl published by Montgomery,[26] and recently Dan Levene has added another one from the Moussaieff collection.[27] The bowl (a curse) is written in Jewish Babylonian Aramaic and points to the cultural context of Sasanian Persia:[28]

> By the name of I-Am-that-I-Am (*ehyeh asher ehyeh*), the Lord of Hosts (*YHWH Tzevaot*), and by the name of Jesus (*'Ishu*), who conquered the height and the depth by his cross, and by the name of his exalted father, and by the name of the holy spirits forever and in eternity. Amen, amen, selah.[29]

This is a quite common adjuration that uses the most powerful names of God in the Hebrew Bible, the "I-Am-that-I-Am" from Exodus 3:14 (the name communicated to Moses by God), and the tetragrammaton YHWH (in the frequent combination "the Lord of Hosts"). What is unique, however, is the addition not only of Jesus (in the unusual spelling 'Ishu)[30] but also of the Father and the Holy Spirit,[31] that is, the invocation of the Christian Trinity after the God of the Hebrew Bible. Shaul Shaked has discussed the implications of this reference to Jesus and the Trinity in a bowl written in Jewish Aramaic and has convincingly concluded that our bowl was indeed written by a Jew.[32] Yet this does not necessarily mean that the bowl was written *for* a Jew; rather, he suggests, that the clients who ordered the bowl were Zoroastrians and that their opponent, against whom the curse should be directed, was a Christian.[33] Hence, the Jewish writer of the bowl used in the curse the most effective magic names he could think of for a Christian: the names of the God of the Old and New Testaments (from the Christian perspective). This does not imply, of course, that the Jewish writer believed in Jesus and the Trinity, but it certainly means that he knew of the name of Jesus and believed in its magical power.

It may well be the case, therefore, that the connection between Yehoshua b. Perahya and Jesus in the Bavli is made through "magic" as the common denominator of both figures:[34] Yehoshua b. Perahya, the arch-magician from Babylonia and Jesus, his master student. The fact that the editor of our Bavli sugya turns this into an anti-magic story only proves that the connection between the two heroes must be older than the story in its present form.

Finally, despite the critique of Jesus and his magic within the narrative itself, the context in which the Bavli editor puts the story is remarkable: he criticizes not Jesus, the magician, but rather his teacher Yehoshua b. Perahya, who pushes the poor student away with both his hands, that is, finally and irrevocably, instead of first punishing him (with one hand) and then forgiving him (with the other). This reading of the story by the editor is all the more ironical as, in fact, Yehoshua b. Perahya does want to receive Jesus (waving with one hand!), and it is Jesus who misunderstands this gesture as the ultimate rejection. Nevertheless, the teacher makes another effort to convince the student to repent (even after he has set up his brick worship), and it is again the student, not the teacher, who concludes that he is not eligible for repentance because of the magnitude of his sin.

Altogether, we observe a striking sequence of literary layers in the Bavli narrative: first, the story of an originally anonymous disciple, reprimanded for his frivolous behavior, who is later identified as Jesus. This story is extended by the abortive attempt on the part of the student to be forgiven by his teacher (which turns out to be a misunderstanding) and the student's brick worship as a result of this. A last attempt on the part of the teacher to save the student fails because of the student's insight that his sin forfeits repentance. In what clearly looks like an addendum, the "master" identifies this sin as magic and once again the student as Jesus. Finally, the Bavli editor puts the blame on the teacher (Yehoshua b. Perahya), who is ultimately responsible for the student's (Jesus') idolatry. In other words, according to the latest editorial layer in the Bavli, it is a distinguished rabbi (no less a figure than one of the famous "pairs"), who is responsible for the origin of Christianity.

4. The Torah Teacher

The Talmud does not relate anything about Jesus' life until his very end, his violent death. It does have, however, some vague notion of him as a Torah teacher, and this is quite in accordance with Jesus' portrayal in the New Testament (see in particular the so-called Sermon on the Mount in Matthew 5–7; according to Luke 19:47, Jesus was teaching every day in the Temple, and "the chief priests, the scribes, and the leaders of the people kept looking for a way to kill him").[1] One story in the Bavli presents Jesus as such a Torah teacher, in dialogue with the contemporary rabbis, and even preserves his halakhic exegesis. In the typical rabbinic fashion, his teaching is transmitted through the mouth of one of his faithful students. However, what is striking here is the fact that the story is not concerned with Jesus himself (and also very little with his student) but rather with a supposed *rabbinic* follower of Jesus and his teachings, in other words, that it attacks the Christian sect through the mirror of the rabbinic perception of Christianity. The story appears in Bavli Avodah Zarah 16b–17a, but this time we are in the possession of earlier Palestinian parallels.[2] I translate the Bavli version according to the Vilna edition and will refer to the variant readings in the Bavli manuscripts as well as in the parallels where necessary:

Our rabbis taught: When R. Eliezer was arrested because of heresy (*minut*), they brought him up to the tribune to be judged. The

[Roman] Governor (*hegemon*) said to him: "How can an old man like you occupy himself with such idle things?" He [R. Eliezer] answered: "I acknowledge the judge as reliable (*ne'eman*)!"[3] Since the Governor thought that he referred to him—though he really referred to his Father in Heaven—he said to him: "Because you have acknowledged me as reliable,[4] *dimissus*:[5] you are acquitted!"

When he [R. Eliezer] came home, his disciples arrived to comfort him, but he would accept no consolation. Said R. Aqiva to him: "Master, will you permit me to say one thing of what you have taught me?" He answered: "Say it!" He [Aqiva] said to him: "Master, perhaps you encountered (some kind of) heresy (*minut*) and you enjoyed it and because of that you were arrested?" He [R. Eliezer] answered him: "Aqiva, you have reminded me! Once I was walking in the upper market of Sepphoris when I came across[6] someone/one of the disciples of Jesus the Nazarene,[7] and Jacob of Kefar Sekhaniah[8] was his name.

He [Jacob] said to me:[9] It is written in your Torah: You shall not bring the hire of the harlot [or the pay of a dog into the house of the Lord, your God] (Deut. 23:19). May such money be used for making a latrine for the High Priest? To which I made no reply.

He [Jacob] said to me: Thus was I taught [by Jesus the Nazarene]:[10] For from the hire of a harlot was it gathered[11] and to the hire of a harlot shall it[12] return (Mic. 1:7)—it came from a place of filth, and let it return to a place of filth.

This word pleased me very much, and that is why I was arrested for heresy (*minut*). Because I transgressed what is written in the Torah: Keep your way far from her (Prov. 5:8)—this refers to heresy (*minut*); and do not come near to the door of her house (ibid.)—this refers to the ruling power (*rashut*)."

There are some who say: Keep your way far from her (Prov. 5:8)—this refers to heresy and the ruling power;[13] and do not come near to the door of her house (ibid.)—this refers to the harlot.[14]

And how far (is one to keep away)? Rav Hisda said: Four cubits.

This strange story, marked by its introductory formula as a Baraita and hence an early Palestinian tradition, leaves more questions open than it answers. First of all, it remains completely unclear why R. Eliezer was arrested and what the heresy was of which the Roman governor suspected him. R. Eliezer is the famous Eliezer b. Hyrkanos (late first–early second century C.E.), the favored disciple of Rabban Yohanan b. Zakkai and the paragon of rabbinic zeal and determination.[15] The Roman authorities, however, certainly did not arrest him for nothing, yet the only accusation we hear from the trial is that he was occupying himself with "such idle things."[16] The accused even does not bother to defend himself; he simply puts his fate into the hands of the heavenly judge. The earthly judge, believing that the accused refers to him, acquits the rabbi.

What can the "idle things" have been with which the rabbi was occupying himself and which provoked the wrath of the Roman authorities? Strangely enough, R. Eliezer does not know himself of what he was accused and he needs one of his students (Aqiva) to remind him. Even worse, the rabbi seems to accept the accusation because—instead of being happy about his obviously unexpected release—he needs to be comforted for what he did. A clue to the mysterious accusation may be found in an addition that is preserved only in the Tosefta Hullin version of our story. There, the governor says: "Since you have deemed me reliable for yourself, so thus I have said (= ruled): [. . .] *dimissus*: you are acquitted!" Unfortunately, what precisely the governor says before he reaches his conclusion of *dimissus* is difficult to understand. The Hebrew text reads: *efshar šhsybw hallalu to'im ba-devarim hallalu*, and the crucial word is *šhsybw*, which does not make much sense in the present context. Scholars have therefore suggested the conjecture *še-ha-sevot/sevot hallalu* (from *sevah/sevah*, "grey hair"), hence: "Is it possible that these grey hairs should err in such matters?"—whereupon the answer is: "Obviously not, therefore: *dimissus*: you are acquitted!"[17]

The problem with this conjecture is that it requires the addition of one letter that is not attested in the manuscripts (*šhsybwt = še-ha-sevot/sevot*) and, moreover, that it does not help us to understand the decision of the governor any better (just because the rabbi is old, he must be acquitted of what definitely was a grave accusation?).[18] Maier has suggested a quite plausible different solution. He proposes to read the problematic word as the verb *hesebu* and translates: "Is it possible that they (R. Eliezer and his friends) were lying down for a meal (reclining for dining in company)?

These [accusers] err with regard to these matters, therefore: *dimissus*: you are acquitted!"[19] Interpreted this way, the Roman governor acquits R. Eliezer of participating in a forbidden meal (symposium), either a Christian *agape* or some kind of orgiastic cult (*Bacchanalia*) or both because the Christian meal could easily be misunderstood as a mysterious and conspiratorial cult with orgiastic rites.[20] The heresy (*minut*) of which he was accused by some anonymous informers could therefore have been membership in a forbidden cult/Christianity, a serious accusation demanding the intervention of the Roman authorities.

If this was indeed the case, nothing in the supposedly heretical teaching that R. Eliezer hears from Jacob in the name of Jesus (ben Pandera) and enjoys so much supports such an accusation. Let us have a closer look at the version in Qohelet Rabba, which is more detailed and more coherent. There, Jacob—in the name of Jesus—argues as follows:[21]

[Jacob:] "It is written in your Torah: You shall not bring the hire of a harlot or the pay of a dog[22] into the house of the Lord, your God [in payment] for any vow [for both of these are abhorrent to the Lord, your God] (Deut. 23:19). What is to be done with them (the money)?"

I [R. Eliezer] told him: "They are prohibited [for every use]."

He [Jacob] said to me: "They are prohibited as an offering, but it is permissible to dispose of them."

I answered: "In that case, what is to be done with them?"

He said to me: "Let bath-houses and privies be made with them."

I answered: "You have well spoken because [this particular] Halakha[23] escaped my memory for the moment."

When he saw that I acknowledged his words, he said to me: "Thus said So-and-so (*ploni*): From filth they came and to filth shall they go out (= on filth they should be expended), as it is said: For from the hire of a harlot was it gathered, and to the hire of a harlot shall it return (Mic. 1:7)—Let them be spent on privies for the public!"

This [interpretation] pleased me, and on that account I was arrested for heresy (*minut*).

This is a well argued and perfectly acceptable Halakha: The Bible prohibits that money gained from prostitution[24] may be used to buy an offering in the Temple (in order to redeem a vow). The question that arises is whether this money is forbidden only for cultic purposes but can be used for some other purposes, or whether it is prohibited altogether. R. Eliezer, expressing the more stringent halakhic view, prohibits the prostitution money altogether, whereas Jesus/Jacob takes the more lenient approach and permits the money to be spent in the public interest: to build with it bathhouses and privies. Both bathhouses and privies are institutions that deal with the disposal of filth—and what better use could be made with money that owes its origins to filth (the Bavli almost ironically goes a step further: the money may even be used for building a privy for the High Priest, presumably on the site of the Temple)? R. Eliezer not only accepts Jacob/Jesus' halakhic ruling but enjoys in particular the biblical proof text Micah 1:7 and its application to the present case.

There is nothing peculiarly Christian about this halakhic discourse. That one rabbi expresses a more stringent and his opponent a more lenient view is commonplace, as is the result that the more lenient decision becomes the accepted one. So shall we dismiss R. Eliezer's own "discovery"—that he was convicted of heresy because he enjoyed this particular halakhic exposition—as completely unreliable? Two answers to this question are possible that do not exclude but mutually supplement each other. The first, and quite obvious, answer is that the question of whether or not the contents of the Halakha as such point to Christianity is irrelevant. The biblical command "Remove your way far from her, and do not come near to the door of her house" (Prov. 5:8) refers, according to R. Eliezer's own interpretation, to heresy and the ruling Roman power. He transgressed this verdict in getting involved with someone who was known as a student of Jesus and notorious for his heretical views. In other words, it is not important *what* has been said and taught but rather *who* did it. Even if the teachings of the heretic are concordant with the rabbis and hence halakhically correct—this does not matter: they are invalid and dangerous because they come from a heretic.

But still, even if any contact with a heretic is forbidden (the correctness of their halakhic deductions notwithstanding), this does not seem to be the full story. If we take a closer look at the biblical verse from Proverbs (5:8), we may discover a deeper meaning. This verse, with which R. Eliezer concludes his self-searching in all three versions of our story, originally refers to the "strange" or "loose woman," the prostitute, whose lips drip honey but whose end is death (5:3–5). The Tosefta version does not interpret the verse explicitly,[25] but both the Bavli and Qohelet Rabba relate one part of the verse to heresy and the other part to prostitution.[26] In other words, if we take the proof text literally, R. Eliezer admits[27] that his guilt consists of heresy that is connected to prostitution. This interpretation reinforces the reading of Tosefta Hullin where R. Eliezer was suspected of getting involved not just with prostitutes (bad enough for such a strict and pious rabbi) but of participating in sexual orgies.

The continuation of the "loose woman's" description in Proverbs is even more conspicuous. In chapter 7 she is explicitly called a prostitute who lies in wait for the young man to seduce him (Prov. 7:11–15):

> She is loud and wayward; her feet do not stay at home;
> now in the street, now in the squares, and at every corner she lies in
> wait.
> She seizes him and kisses him, and with impudent face she says to
> him:
> I had to offer sacrifices, and today I have paid my vows;
> so now I have come out to meet you, to seek you eagerly, and I have
> found you!

This colorful description of a prostitute is all the more remarkable in our context, as it establishes a quite unexpected connection between her seductive behavior and the Temple offering, the very connection Deuteronomy 23:19 prohibits and to which Jacob/Jesus' halakhic exegesis in our story refers. This can hardly be by coincidence. It seems therefore that the editor of our story wants to imply two things: first, R. Eliezer was indeed accused of being a member of a forbidden (orgiastic) sect; and second, in (allegedly) getting involved with a prostitute, who pays with her whore's wages for her Temple offering, he infringes Jesus' (and his own) Halakha according to which such money must not be used for purposes related to the Temple.

Scholars have tried hard to connect the historical R. Eliezer b. Hyrkanos with nascent Christianity at the end of the first and the beginning of the second century C.E.[28] They assume that Jacob, the disciple of Jesus, could have been either Jesus' brother James (Mk. 6:3; Mt. 13:55) or Jesus' disciple James, the son of Alphaeus (Mk. 3:18; Mt. 10:3; Lk. 6:15; Acts 1:13; 15:13) and that Eliezer's trial has to do with persecutions of the Christians in the early second century C.E.[29] This, however, presupposes quite a chronological stretch because the encounter with Jacob/James in Sepphoris must have taken place much earlier than the trial (if Jacob is James, the son of Alphaeus, the latter was stoned around 62 C.E.): not only must much time have passed between the heretical conspiracy in Sepphoris and the trial, but R. Eliezer must have lived to a very old age when he finally was put on trial (not to mention the fact that it took the Roman authorities unseemly long to prosecute his crime).

Such a historical reconstruction of R. Eliezer's heresy and inclination toward Christianity is not very likely and an easy victim for Maier's scholarly acumen.[30] It is highly improbable that our story reflects an encounter between the historical R. Eliezer and a historical disciple of Jesus in the city of Sepphoris in Galilee, let alone that the halakhic decision with regard to the hire of the harlot refers to an authentic saying of Jesus. But again, this is not what is at stake here. The refutation of such crude and positivistic historicity does not mean that the story does not reflect some kind of reality, more precisely some rabbinic awareness of Jesus and Christianity. The name of Jesus (Jesus ben Pandera/Jesus the Nazarene) is well attested in the manuscripts, and Maier's attempts to throw it out of the text or to declare it as later additions[31] are rather forced. It is therefore plausible to argue that the story has indeed something to do with Jesus (Jesus' teachings) and that R. Eliezer's heresy does refer to Christianity.

The real question, therefore, is: what precisely is this reality with regard to Christianity that the rabbinic sources reveal? According to Boyarin—who boldly and without further ado takes it for granted that R. Eliezer was arrested for Christianity[32]—our story reflects the early rabbinic discourse with the emerging Christianity (which was still regarded as part of Judaism), its simultaneous attraction to and repulsion from Christianity.[33] R. Eliezer is the "very figure of liminality," who personifies the tension between rabbinic Judaism and Christianity; through him the rabbis are "both recognizing and denying at one and the same time that Christians are us, marking out the virtual identity between themselves and the Christians

in their world at the same time that they are very actively seeking to establish difference."[34]

This is certainly correct, and Boyarin takes great pains to assure the
reader that he does not follow oversimplistic positivistic models but rather
"new methodologies," according to which R. Eliezer "no longer is a historical character in the first century, but a 'fictional' character in the third
century," and that he draws historical conclusions "not about events but
about ideologies, social movements, cultural constructions, and particularly repressions."[35] Nobody would want to object to such an approach today: not the event as the firm and provable historical "fact" is at stake but
what has developed around the event in all its complexity and historical
ramifications.[36] Yet we should not draw too firm a line between the "historical" and the "fictional" character, between the "event" and the "cultural construction." Both belong closely together, and even at the risk of
relapsing into the bad habits of positivism I want to posit that the rabbis
with their stories, including the present one, reveal more than just the
awareness (and recognition) of the breaking-off of Christianity from the
common ground of rabbinic Judaism. Rather, this awareness and recognition are not abstract constructs but deeply grounded in the *reality* and the
experience of what happened. Both can and need to be described in fuller
detail. As far as the stories about Jesus and his followers are concerned,
they indeed reveal some knowledge of the Christian sect and of its hero,
and this knowledge is not just a distorted and vague hodgepodge of this
and that, but a well-designed attack against what the rabbis experienced
as the reality of the Jewish-Christian message.[37]

Keeping these methodological considerations in mind, let us briefly review the Eliezer story again. It combines two strands that both in their
own way respond to the New Testament narrative.

(1) The first strand, the core of the story, is the charge against R. Eliezer,
the alleged Christian heretic, of prostitution/sexual orgies. This accusation fits in very well with what we have heard so far about Jesus himself:
that he was the illegitimate child of his mother Miriam's liaison with the
Roman soldier Pandera, that he himself led quite an indecent life and
that he was excommunicated by his teacher because of his frivolous
thoughts. Jesus and sexual offense seem to be a recurrent theme in the
(later) talmudic treatment of Christianity, and the Eliezer story is the ear-

liest evidence of this motif.[38] There, it is not directed, however, against Jesus himself but against his followers. We will see that this particular variation tallies with the fragments of anti-Christian polemics quoted by early Christian authors of the second century C.E.[39] In any case, this strand of the Eliezer story is very close to what was perceived as the historical reality of the emerging Jewish Christianity.

(2) The second strand—aptly emphasized by Boyarin, following Lieberman[40] and Guttmann[41]—is more indirect and becomes obvious only when we have a closer look at the rabbinic persona of R. Eliezer b. Hyrkanos. R. Eliezer is famous for his clash with his rabbinic colleagues regarding a complicated but relatively minor halakhic question, the structure of the Akhnai oven. When his colleagues disapprove of his argument, he resorts to some "unorthodox" methods:

It has been taught: On that day R. Eliezer used every imaginable argument, but they [his colleagues] did not accept them from him.

He said to them: "If the Halakha agrees with me, let this carob-tree prove it!" [Whereupon] the carob-tree was uprooted from its place a hundred cubits—others report, four hundred cubits. They retorted: "No proof can be brought from a carob-tree!"

Again he said to them: "If the Halakha agrees with me, let the stream of water prove it!" [Whereupon] the stream of water flowed backwards. They retorted: "No proof can be brought from a stream of water!"

Again he said to them: "If the Halakha agrees with me, let the walls of the schoolhouse prove it!" [Whereupon] the walls of the schoolhouse inclined to fall. But R. Yehoshua rebuked them, saying: "When the scholars are engaged in a halakhic dispute, what have you to interfere?" Hence they did not fall, in honor of R. Yehoshua, nor did they resume the upright, in honor of R. Eliezer; and they are still standing thus inclined.

Again he said to them: "If the Halakha agrees with me, let it be proved from heaven!" [Whereupon] a heavenly voice (*bat qol*) cried out: "Why do you dispute with R. Eliezer—because in all matters the Halakha agrees with him!" [Whereupon] R. Yehoshua arose and said: "She [the Torah] is not in heaven" (Deut. 30:12). What does it mean: She is not in heaven? R. Yirmeya said: "Since the Torah has already been given at Mount Sinai we pay no attention to a heavenly voice, because you [God] have long since written in the Torah at Mount Sinai: After the majority must one incline (Ex. 23:2)."[42]

What is going on here? An initially routine halakhic dispute among rabbis on a not particularly important question veers off course. R. Eliezer cannot assert himself in this dispute and resorts to the strongest means that he has at his disposal: magic.[43] He moves a carob tree, lets a stream of water flow backward, threatens to destroy the schoolhouse in which the rabbis are gathered, and finally gets an approval from heaven. But to no avail. His colleagues are not impressed by his magic and declare coolly that halakhic matters are not decided by magic. And as far as the heavenly voice is concerned, they declare even more coolly that God better does not interfere in these matters because he has given the Torah to his creatures — and the power to decide in case of conflict to the rabbis.[44]

So what is at stake here is sober halakhic reasoning according to the decision of the majority versus magic, and the message is: rabbinic authority rests on rabbinic rules of the game, not on magic, not even when approved by heaven. In trying to overrule the halakhic consensus of his colleagues with his magical tricks and the intervention of heaven, R. Eliezer infringes the essence of rabbinic authority. Accordingly, he is most severely punished with the worst punishment the rabbis have at their disposal (and which, as many scholars have observed, is completely out of proportion to the importance of the halakhic dispute) — excommunication: "It was said: On that very day all objects which R. Eliezer had declared clean were brought and burnt in fire (as unclean). Then they took a vote and excommunicated him."[45] The rabbis send R. Aqiva, one of the greatest scholars of his generation, to inform R. Eliezer of their horrible decision because someone less respected and tactful might provoke his unbridled wrath and cause him to release his magical powers and to destroy the world. R. Aqiva does a great job in carrying out his delicate mission, but still, when R. Eliezer realizes what his colleagues did to him,

he too rent his garments,[46] put off his shoes, removed [his seat], sat on the earth, and tears streamed from his eyes. The world was then smitten: a third of the olive crop, a third of the wheat, and a third of the barley crop. Some say, even the dough in women's hands swelled up.

It has been taught: Great was the calamity that befell that day, for everything at which [R. Eliezer] cast his eyes was burned up.[47]

Even in his defeat, R. Eliezer proved once more his magical power—and that the rabbis were right in excommunicating him unless they wanted to yield their authority to miracle workers and magicians. R. Eliezer's unruly magical power, which threatened the authority of the rabbis and *therefore* (in this sequence) the existence of the world, needed to be kept in check—and indeed was kept in check, until his death.[48] In portraying him as the dangerous arch-magician, the rabbis model R. Eliezer along the lines of the other arch-magician, who threatened their authority— Jesus. In other words: R. Eliezer becomes the rabbinic doppelgänger of Jesus. He combines in his person and life two major strands of the rabbinic perception of Jesus and his followers: sexual excesses and magical power. Hence, it is not just the painful process of the breaking-off of "Christianity" from "Judaism," which becomes apparent here; rather, we get a glimpse at the weapons that the rabbinic Jews used in order not only to demarcate themselves from Christian Jews but to fight against them with all the means at their disposal. And a fight to the death it was, because even the Roman governor acquitted R. Eliezer of the charge of sexual orgies and even heaven approved of his use of magic against rabbinic reasoning, of anarchic and destructive power against sober interpretation of the Torah, of "Christianity" against the rabbinic version of "Judaism"! Indeed, "the Christians are us," as Boyarin says, but, this is the message of the Eliezer story, they need to be unmasked and defeated once and for all.

5. Healing in the Name of Jesus

The mysterious heretic by the name of Jacob makes yet another appearance in a story preserved again in Palestinian as well as in Babylonian sources. This time he does not seduce a rabbi by his convincing Bible exegesis and expose the poor rabbi's hidden leanings toward Christianity but introduces himself as the proverbial miraculous healer who whispers a potent magical word or phrase over a wound/illness and, through the power of the word(s) used, heals the patient.

Rabbinic Judaism seems to be ambiguous about the custom of "whispering over a wound" for healing purposes. In the famous Mishna Sanhedrin 10:2,[1] R. Aqiva counts such miraculous healers among those who "have no portion in the world to come": "one who whispers over a wound and says: I will not bring upon you any of the diseases that I brought upon the Egyptians, for I the Lord am your healer (Ex. 15:26)." This sounds like a definite prohibition. The Tosefta, however, is much less strict. There it is stated clearly: "[It is permitted to] whisper over an eye, a serpent, and a scorpion (= over the bite inflicted by a serpent or a scorpion) and to pass [a remedy] over the eye on the Sabbath,"[2] and this tradition is repeated in both the Jerusalem and the Babylonian Talmud.[3] The Tosefta and the Talmudim take it for granted, therefore, that people whisper over wounds for healing purposes and even allow this practice on Sabbath. With a certain sense of irony, the Yerushalmi mentions

R. Aqiva, of all people, as someone over whose sick eye a (healing) object was passed.

The Talmudim do not resolve the contradiction between Aqiva's strict prohibition in the Mishna and the fact, documented in the Tosefta and related traditions, that such customs were not only (reluctantly) tolerated by the rabbis but commonplace and even explicitly permitted on Sabbath. An easy way out of this dilemma may be the suggestion made by Rashi (and followed by the Soncino translation of the Bavli): whispering over a serpent or a scorpion does not mean whispering over the bite inflicted by these venomous animals but rather whispering over the animals themselves (= charming them) in order to "render them tame and harmless";[4] accordingly, "passing an object over the eye (*ma'avirin keli 'al gav ha-'ayin*)" does not mean, literally, that an object (remedy) may be passed over the eye in order to heal it but rather that "an article may be placed over the eye on the Sabbath [to protect it]."[5] This is obviously a "tame" reading of the text in order to expurgate from it any magical implications.

A closer look at the Mishna suggests another solution. The Mishna first anonymously lists those who have no share in the world to come (those who do not believe in resurrection,[6] in the heavenly origins of the Torah, the Apikoros), and then Aqiva adds two further categories: one who reads noncanonical books and one who whispers over a wound; finally Abba Shaul (a teacher of the generation after Aqiva) includes also one who pronounces the divine name as it is spelled.[7] From this list it seems very likely that the Mishna does not deal here with ordinary Jews but with groups of heretics (*minim*), who are not regarded as belonging to "all of Israel" (*kol Yisrael*). Whereas all those who belong to Israel do have a share in the world to come, the heretics listed by the anonymous author, Aqiva, and Abba Shaul do not—because they do not belong (any longer) to Israel.[8] From this it becomes clear that the one who whispers over a wound, according to R. Aqiva, is not an ordinary Jew but a heretic. In other words, Aqiva does not prohibit the custom of healing by whispering secret names over a wound as such but only if it was practiced by a heretic who does not belong to the community of Israel (*kelal Yisrael*).

This is precisely the context to which our second narrative about the enigmatic Jacob belongs.[9] The Tosefta (Hul 2:20f.) states that the books of the heretics (*minim*) are deemed magical books[10] and that Jews are not

supposed to trade with heretics, to teach their sons a craft, or to seek healing from them, either in matters of their property or of their personal welfare.[11] Then a case story follows (Hul 2:22f.):[12]

> A case story (*ma'ase*) about R. Eleazar b. Dama[13] who was bitten by
> a snake. And Jacob of Kefar Sama[14] came to heal him in the name
> of Jesus son of Pantera.[15] But R. Ishmael did not allow him [Jacob]
> [to perform the healing].[16] They[17] said to him [Eleazar b. Dama]:
> "You are not permitted [to accept healing from Jacob], Ben Dama!"
> He [Eleazar b. Dama] said to him [Ishmael]:[18] "I shall bring you
> proof[19] that he may heal me!"[20] But he did not have time to bring the
> proof before he died.[21]
> Said R. Ishmael: "Happy are you, Ben Dama, for you have expired
> in peace[22] and did not break down the prohibition (*gezeran*) estab-
> lished by the Sages! For whoever breaks down the hedge (*gederan*)[23]
> erected by the Sages eventually suffers punishment, as it is said: He
> who breaks down a hedge (*geder*) is bitten by a snake" (Eccl. 10:8).

Not much is known about R. Eleazar b. Dama, the hero of this story who
dies such a tragic death: according to the Bavli,[24] he was the nephew of
R. Ishmael, the towering figure of early rabbinic Judaism, who affection-
ately called him "my son."[25] Since Ishmael seems to have died not long before the outbreak of the Bar Kokhba revolt (132 C.E.), his nephew's death
must have occurred sometime in the first third of the second century C.E.

Unlike most of the stories which we have discussed so far, in this particular case the possibility cannot be completely ruled out that the encounter between Eleazar b. Dama and his uncle Ishmael reflects some
kind of historical reality. Ishmael is well known for his harsh and uncompromising attitude not only toward heretics[26] but even to what is called in
rabbinic literature "Greek wisdom," the culture of the Greeks and Romans. And it is, again according to the Bavli, precisely poor Eleazar b.
Dama, who had to learn this the hard way:[27]

> Ben Dama, the son of R. Ishmael's sister, once asked R. Ishmael:
> May one such as I, who have studied the whole of the Torah, learn
> Greek wisdom? He [Ishmael] thereupon read to him the following

verse: This book of the Torah shall not depart out of your mouth, but you shall meditate on it day and night (Josh. 1:8). Go then and find a time that is neither day nor night and learn then Greek wisdom!

From this story it becomes clear that much as Ishmael disliked pagan culture, his nephew must have had some inclination toward it. This fits in very well with the story about his unfortunate death: Eleazar b. Dama keeps company with a heretic and wants to be healed by him and his potent charm, but his merciless uncle prefers the beloved nephew to die rather than to be healed by a heretic. The bitter irony of Ishmael's behavior can hardly be missed. Instead of justifying his refusal to accept the heretic's healing power with an appropriate verse from the Bible, Ishmael resorts to the authority of the rabbis: what a happy death did you die, Ben Dama—not because you did not transgress the commandments of the Torah, no, because you did not transgress the commandments of us, your fellow rabbis. For transgressing the hedge or fence that we erected around the Torah inevitably results in death. We, the rabbis, are much more powerful than any of these heretics because it is we who ultimately decide about life and death.

But the irony goes even further. The very verse from the Bible that Ishmael quotes to prove the bad destiny that awaits the transgressor of the rabbinic commandments (he will be bitten by a snake), exposes his hypocrisy: Eleazar b. Dama *was* bitten by a snake, before he had a chance to break down the hedge of the rabbis—he did not transgress the rabbinic commandments and nevertheless was bitten by a snake! The editors of our story in both the Yerushalmi and the Bavli did not miss the bitter irony but give different responses. The pious editor of the Yerushalmi answers the obvious question: "And did not a snake already bite him?" with referring to Eleazar's salvation in the world to come: Yes, it is true, he was bitten by a snake, but since he did not transgress the commandments of the rabbis "a snake will not bite him in the world to come."[28]

The Bavli gives a different and much more pungent answer:[29]

The master said: You did not transgress the words of your colleagues who have said: He who breaks down a hedge (*geder*) is bitten by a snake (Eccl. 10:8)?!

> But a serpent did indeed bite him! — [This is] the serpent of the rabbis, which can never be cured!
>
> Now, what is it that he might have said? — One shall live by them (Lev. 18:5), not that one should die by them![30]

The Bavli editor is clearly a match for R. Ishmael: not only does he notice the obvious contradiction in Ishmael's hypocritical reasoning (Eleazar b. Dama was already bitten by a snake), he exposes the real snake that bit poor Eleazar: the rabbis.[31] Not the bite of the snake caused his death but the bite of the rabbis who put their rulings above the Torah. The verse, which Eleazar did not have time to quote, states: "You shall keep my laws and my rules; by doing so one shall live: I am the Lord" (Lev. 18:5); in other words, the Torah provides life and the rabbis death. This is a devastating critique of the rabbis that ultimately holds R. Ishmael — one of the most respected heroes of tannaitic Judaism — accountable for his nephew's death. The rabbis, according to this critique, are only interested in their own importance, not in the Torah — and could not care less about the individual's destiny.

Moreover, the Bavli's[32] critique of R. Ishmael implies that R. Eleazar b. Dama, according to the true meaning of the Torah (as opposed to the hypocritical rabbinic "fence"), was correct and should indeed have been healed by the heretic Jacob. Hence, the Bavli editor disagrees with the view that only nonheretical Jews should be allowed to heal by "whispering over a wound": he pointedly includes the heretic.[33] Jacob's attempt to heal R. Eleazar was perfectly legitimate because in a life-threatening situation such as happened to the rabbi, it did not matter whether or not the healer was suspected to be a heretic. What only mattered was whether the word(s) he whispered were potent enough to save the patient. And obviously none of the players in our story ever doubted the effectiveness of the word to be used by Jacob: the name of Jesus ben Pantera/Pandera.

We encountered the name of Panthera as Jesus' father in Celsus' polemical treatise written in the second half of the second century C.E. and (as Pandera) in Bavli Shabbat/Sanhedrin; the Tosefta (with Pandera in the Qohelet Rabba parallel) is the earliest attestation of this name in rabbinic sources. As I have argued above, nothing prevents us from assuming that the name Jesus ben Pantera/Pandera refers to the Jesus of the

New Testament. The fact that the Bavli version of our story does not mention the name by which Jacob attempted to heal Eleazar is conspicuous but does not necessarily mean that another (earlier) version without the name of Jesus was circulating in Palestine and that it was this version which reached Babylonia[34]—after all, the Bavli does know the name Jesus ben Pandera, and there may have been other reasons for this particular omission. Moreover, Celsus' reference explicitly mentions the connection between Jesus and magical powers (acquired in Egypt) and concludes that because of these powers Jesus was convinced to be God: "He [Jesus] hired himself out as a workman in Egypt, and there tried his hand at certain magical powers on which the Egyptians pride themselves; he returned full of conceit, because of these powers, and on account of them gave himself the title of God."[35]

The identity of the magician with the god whom he conjures up is well known from Greek as well as from Jewish sources. In the Greek magical papyri from Greco-Roman Egypt(!), the magician secures for himself the power of the god Hermes by saying: "For you are I, and I am you; your name is mine, and mine is yours. For I am your image. . . . I know you, Hermes, and you know me. I am you, and you are I. And so, do everything for me, and may you turn to me with Good Fortune and Good Daimon, immediately, immediately; quickly, quickly."[36] Similarly, he invokes the magical power of the heptagramm, the name consisting of seven letters (part of which is the name Iao,[37] a common abbreviation of the tetragrammaton YHWH):[38] "For you are I, and I, you. Whatever I say must happen, for I have your name as a unique phylactery in my heart, and no flesh, although moved, will overpower me; no spirit will stand against me—neither daimon nor visitation nor any other of the evil beings of Hades, because of your name, which I have in my soul and invoke."[39]

In Jewish sources, it is above all the figure of the man-angel Enoch-Metatron, who is conspicuous for his close relationship with God through the power of his name. The antediluvian hero Enoch, who according to the Hebrew Bible did not die but was taken up into heaven (Gen. 5:24: "Enoch walked with God; then he was no more, for God took him"), was in fact—as the Third (Hebrew) Book of Enoch, one of the texts of Merkava mysticism, explains—physically transformed into the highest angel Metatron, seated on a throne similar to God's throne of

Glory, clothed in a majestic robe, crowned with a kingly crown, and called "The lesser YHWH" (*YHWH ha-qatan*), as it is written: "Since my name is in him" (Ex. 23:21).[40] This verse refers to the angel of the Lord,[41] who is identical with God because God's name is in him, that is, because he bears God's name. Whereas in the Bible the "angel of the Lord" is indeed God himself, Metatron in 3 Enoch becomes the highest being next to God, due to the power of God's name residing in his name.

But where do we find God's name in the name "Metatron"? Scores of scholars have tried to explain the enigmatic name "Metatron"[42] — the most likely explication is probably *(ho) meta thronon* = "(the throne) next to the (divine) throne" — but none of all the possible derivations explains the relationship between God's name and the name Metatron (unless we accept the not very likely explanation that "Metatron" contains the Greek *tetra* — "four," hence an allusion to the tetragrammaton). It seems safer to assume that the story as we have it in 3 Enoch and the Talmud reflects a later development and that an earlier version contained a name that more closely resembles the name of God. And, indeed, among the many names that Metatron has absorbed in the esoteric literature, appears most prominently the name "Yahoel,"[43] a name we know from other and earlier sources, independently of the Enoch-Metatron tradition. In the Apocalypse of Abraham, preserved only in Slavonic but written presumably in Hebrew sometime after 70 C.E.,[44] the angel Iaoel plays an important role. There, he says of himself: "I am Iaoel and I was called so by him who causes those with me [the other angels in the seventh heaven] . . . to shake, a power through the medium of his ineffable name in me."[45] This makes much better sense: the name "Iaoel/Yahoel" indeed contains the divine name "Iao/Yaho," the abbreviation of the tetragrammaton YHWH, which is also used in the Greek magical papyri. It seems, therefore, that it was originally the angel Iaoel/Yahoel to whom Exodus 23:21 was applied and who later, after Metatron had absorbed Yahoel, was replaced by the man-angel Metatron.[46]

The godlike magician, in assuming God's name, exercises power through the theurgical use of this name. Not by coincidence, it is the name of the Jewish God that appears quite prominently in the Greco-Roman magical texts of late antiquity.[47] The Jews were regarded as particularly powerful magicians (did not Moses already outdo the magicians of the Pharaoh in Egypt?), and what better name, then, could be used for magical purposes than the name of their God? The fact that the Jews themselves avoided pronouncing the tetragrammaton, the holiest name of God, may have contributed to this predilection for the name of the Jewish God. The Jewish historian Flavius Josephus refers to this prohibition in his *Antiquities*,[48] and according to rabbinic tradition the tetragrammaton was pronounced only once a year by the High Priest in the Holy of Holies during the service of the Day of Atonement.[49] Accordingly, Greek magical texts evoke the name that cannot be pronounced: "I call on you, eternal and unbegotten, who are one, who alone holds together the whole creation of all things, whom none understands, whom the gods worship, whose name not even the gods can utter,"[50] or: "I conjure you up with the holy name that cannot be uttered."[51]

This is the background against which the healing in the name of Jesus ben Pantera in our story must be seen. Jacob, the magical healer, regarded Jesus' name as a most powerful divine name and, as we have seen, not only Eleazar b. Dama followed him in this belief, but also Ishmael, the spokesman of those who prohibited the healing through a supposed heretic. Such a belief refers directly back to the New Testament or, to put it differently, the New Testament is an important source for the belief in the magical power of the divine name—and most likely the direct source for our story.[52] The Gospel of Mark relates the following exchange between the apostle John and Jesus:

> (38) John said to him: "Teacher, we saw someone casting out demons in your name (*en tō onomati sou*), and we tried to stop him, because he was not following us." (39) But Jesus said: "Do not stop him; for no one who does a deed of power in my name (*hos poiēsei dynamin epi tō onomati mou*) will be able soon afterward to speak evil of me. Whoever is not against us is for us."[53]

Casting out demons through the power of Jesus' name does not just mean through Jesus' authority (*exousia*),[54] but, literally, through using the power (*dynamis*) inherent in Jesus' name. The name "Jesus" was therefore believed to contain magical power that allowed the magician, who was in possession of this name, to cast out demons and thus to heal the possessed person. Moreover, it becomes clear from John's question and Jesus' answer that using the powerful name of Jesus had nothing to do with believing in Jesus. On the contrary, the magician, although not following Jesus, was nevertheless successful in casting out the demons by using his name. In other words, the magical use of the name of Jesus worked automatically, no matter whether or not the magician believed in Jesus. This is just the reversal of our rabbinical story where the follower of Jesus attempts to heal the nonbeliever. The healing power of the name does not depend on either the magician's or the patient's belief. Jesus, in explicitly allowing the use of his name even by nonfollowers, acknowledges the magical power inherent in his name.[55]

Hence, what our story is ultimately concerned about is not the healing power of Jesus' name—which is taken for granted—but again the question of authority. R. Ishmael (the hero of the emerging rabbinic elite), in erecting a hedge or a fence around the Torah, has a larger goal in mind: he not just fends off transgressions of the Torah by followers of his own group (the rabbis); rather, he aims at fending off people that do not belong to Judaism as defined by him and his fellow rabbis. In other words, what we have here is an (early) attempt to establish boundaries, to delineate Judaism by eliminating heretics—in this particular case clearly heretics belonging to a group that defined itself by its belief in Jesus of Nazareth.

It is only in Palestinian sources (Yerushalmi and Midrash Qohelet Rabba) that we find yet another healing story connected with Jesus. This time, the dramatis personae are R. Yehoshua b. Levi and his grandson:[56]

He [R. Yehoshua b. Levi] had a grandson, who swallowed (something dangerous). Someone (had)[57] came and whispered to him in the name of Jesus son of Pandera,[58] and he was healed.[59] When he [the magician] left, he [R. Yehoshua] said to him: "What did you say over him?"

He answered: "Such and such a word."[60]

He [R. Yehoshua] said to him [the magician]: "How much (better) would it have been for him[61] if he had died and had not heard this word!"[62]

And so it happened to him: like an error (*shegaga*) committed by a ruler (Eccl. 10:5).

R. Yehoshua b. Levi is one of the most important Palestinian rabbis, living in Lydda in the first half of the third century and famous for his aggadic teaching. His grandson, who was obviously close to suffocation, was healed by some anonymous heretic, a follower of Jesus. Hence, we have here the opposite of the Eleazar b. Dama story: whereas Eleazar b. Dama's healing was prevented (by R. Ishmael) and he was destined to die—but gained his life in the world to come, Yehoshua's grandson was healed—but lost his life in the world to come; his healing was inadvertent but nevertheless valid, like an error committed by a ruler, as the verse from Qohelet explains. A very unfortunate error, indeed, according to his grandfather, because it cost him his eternal life.[63]

Unlike in the Eleazar b. Dama story, where we hear only of the (attempted) healing "in the name of Jesus son of Pantera/Pandera," we learn here that the healing in the name of Jesus is accompanied by uttering, on the part of the magician, certain words: most likely verses or parts of verses from the Bible. Maier, in his usual zeal to play down the impact of Jesus' name on the magical procedure, puts the emphasis on the Bible verse(s) in which he sees the real offensive behavior rather than in the use of the name of Jesus.[64] This is again a reductionist interpretation that misses the point: it is the name of Jesus that gives the use of the Bible verse(s) the authority and efficacy; without Jesus' authority the whispering of the Bible verse(s) would have been meaningless and ineffective. So it was in the end Jesus who healed R. Yehoshua's grandson and not just the application of some verses from the Bible (and it is therefore also quite unimportant which precise verses the magician used). Again, we do not learn much about the historical Jesus as a person and a teacher, but we are affirmed— in concordance with the New Testament—that he was a potent magician whose magical power worked independently of the object to which it was applied. Once uttered, the magical charm took effect, and the poor grandfather was doomed to watching helplessly how his grandson kept his physical existence at the expense of his eternal life.

We can even go a step further. The story about Yehoshua b. Levi and his grandson is not just an affirmation of the automatic effectiveness of magic; rather, it presents an ironical critique of Jesus' and his followers' belief in their magical power. True, it argues, their magical power is undeniable: it works, and one cannot do anything against its effectiveness. But it is an unauthorized and misused power. It is just *shegaga*—a mistake, an unfortunate error.[65] Hence, our story ultimately conveys the message: this Jesus and his followers claim to have the keys to heaven,[66] to use their magical power with divine authorization—but they are dead wrong! The fact that heaven accepts what they do does not mean that it approves of it. On the contrary, they are tricksters and impostors who abuse their power. The real power and authority still rest with their opponents, the rabbis.

6. Jesus' Execution

That Jesus was condemned to death by the Roman governor Pontius Pilate, subsequently tortured and crucified, and on the third day after his crucifixion was resurrected and ascended to heaven is the foundation narrative of Christianity. His trial by the Roman authority and his death on the cross are described in all four Gospels, albeit with considerable variations (Mt. 27–28; Mk. 15–16; Lk. 22–24; John 18–21), and theologically interpreted by the apostle Paul. What familiarity do the rabbis, the heroes of rabbinic Judaism, show with the evangelists' interpretations of this event, or rather, more carefully formulated: what do they care to tell us about it in their literature?

The immediate and unambiguous answer is: very little. Within the vast corpus of rabbinic literature, we find but one reference to Jesus' trial and execution, and only in passing, as part of a broader halakhic discussion that has nothing to do with Jesus as a historical figure. Hardly unexpectedly (after the evidence discussed so far), this reference is preserved only in the Bavli. There, the Mishna in tractate Sanhedrin is discussed, which deals with the procedure of the capital punishment. The Bible knows four legal modes of executing the death penalty; namely, stoning, burning, hanging (the latter is actually a postmortem hanging of the person stoned to death, a form of publication that a capital sentence has been executed),[1] and slaying by the sword. The talmudic law drops hanging and adds strangling as an independent death penalty,[2] but the discussions in rabbinic literature are largely academic since the rabbis did not have the power of inflicting the death sentence.[3] With regard to stoning, the most common death penalty, the Mishna explains:[4]

> If they find him [the accused] innocent, they discharge him, and if not, he goes forth to be stoned. And a herald goes before him [heralding]:
>
> So and so, the son of so and so, is going forth to be stoned because he committed such and such a crime, and so and so are his witnesses. Whoever knows anything in his defense, may come and state it.

It is on this Mishna that the Bavli comments:[5]

> Abaye said: He [the herald] must also say: On such and such a day, on such and such an hour, and in such and such a place (the crime was committed),[6] in case there are some who know (to the contrary), so that they can come forward and prove (the original witnesses) to be false witnesses (having deliberately given false testimony).
>
> And a herald goes before him etc.:[7] indeed before him,[8] but not beforehand![9]
>
> However, (in contradiction to this) it was taught (*tanya*):
>
> On (Sabbath eve and)[10] the eve of Passover Jesus the Nazarene[11] was hanged (*tela'uhu*).[12] And a herald went forth before him 40 days (heralding): Jesus the Nazarene[13] is going forth to be stoned because he practiced sorcery (*kishshef*) and instigated (*hissit*) and seduced (*hiddiah*) Israel (to idolatry). Whoever knows anything in his defense, may come and state it. But since they did not find anything in his defense, they hanged him on (Sabbath eve and)[14] the eve of Passover.
>
> Ulla said: Do you suppose that Jesus the Nazarene[15] was one for whom a defense could be made? He was a *mesit* (someone who instigated Israel to idolatry), concerning whom the Merciful [God] says: Show him no compassion and do not shield him (Deut. 13:9).

With Jesus the Nazarene[16] it was different, for he was close to the government (*malkhut*).

This is a remarkable Bavli sugya. It starts with a comment by Abaye, a Babylonian amora of the early fourth century, arguing that the Mishna's vague "such and such a crime" must be made more precise: the herald should not just mention the crime but add the day, hour, and location of the crime. Only this more detailed description of the crime's circumstances guarantees the validity of the testimony of new witnesses who contradict the testimony of the original witnesses which had led to the defendant's condemnation.[17] The clear purpose of Abaye's statement is to facilitate the acquittal of the accused.

The Bavli then returns to the Mishna lemma that regulates the procedure undertaken by the herald. The anonymous Bavli author clarifies the unambiguous-looking "before him [the convicted]" and specifies: physically before the convicted on his way to the execution and not (chronologically) some other time before the day of the execution. This specification, which clearly conforms to the plain meaning of the Mishna, meets with a contradicting teaching which proves itself to be an early Baraita, introduced by the formula *tanya*: the precedent was set, it argues, of Jesus the Nazarene, in whose case the herald did not go out just before the execution but rather forty days beforehand (meaning either forty consecutive days before the day of his execution or just the fortieth day before the execution was carried out). Whatever the precise meaning of these forty days is (most likely the latter), it becomes clear that this Baraita contradicts the Mishna as it is understood by the anonymous author of the Bavli, allowing for a considerable interval between the announcement of the herald and the actual execution. This tension between the Mishna/Bavli and the Baraita is "solved" by an exchange between Ulla (also a Babylonian amora of the early fourth century) and his anonymous respondent(s): Since Jesus had friends in high places, the Jews took extra precautions before executing him: they went beyond the letter of the law so none of his powerful friends could accuse them of executing an innocent man.[18] Accordingly, this exchange seems to conclude, his case was not a halakhically valid precedent but rather a real exception;[19] in other words, the Baraita dos not contradict the Mishna.

It is within this halakhic discourse that some details of Jesus' condemnation and execution are reported:

- He was hanged on the eve of Passover which, according to one manuscript, happened to be Sabbath eve.

- The herald made the announcement required by the law forty days before the execution took place.

- Jesus was executed because he practiced sorcery and enticed Israel into idolatry.

- Nobody came to his defense.

- He was close to the government.

Several of these details can be easily explained against the background of the relevant Mishna in tractate Sanhedrin. There, the standard procedure according to the rabbinic law is explained as follows:[20]

All who are stoned are also hanged (*nitlin*) [afterwards] [on a tree]:[21] (these are) the words of R. Eliezer.

However the Sages said: only the blasphemer (*ha-megaddef*) and the idolater (*ha-ʿoved avodah zarah*) are hanged.

As to a man, they hang him facing the people, and as to a woman, (they hang her) facing the tree: (these are) the words of R. Eliezer.

However the Sages said: the man is hanged, but the woman is not hanged (at all). [. . .]

How do they hang him?

They drive a post into the ground, and a beam juts from it, and one ties together his two hands one upon the other, and thus does one hang him.

R. Yose says: the post leans against a wall, and one hangs him the way butchers do (it).

And they untie him immediately. Because, if he stays (on the tree) overnight, one transgresses a negative commandment on his account, as it is said: You must not leave his corpse on the tree [overnight], but you must bury him that same day, for he who is hanged (*talui*) is a curse against God (*qilelat elohim*), etc. (Deut. 21:23). That is to say, on what account has this [man] been hanged? Because he cursed[22] the Name, and the Name of Heaven[23] turned out to be profaned.

The Mishna systematically, and in its usual beautifully structured way, sets out to clarify the procedure of "hanging": who is hanged, how is he/she hanged, and for how long? The question of "who" is answered differently by R. Eliezer and the Sages: whereas R. Eliezer, as a rule, has everybody hanged who has been stoned to death, the Sages limit this procedure to the capital crimes of blasphemy and idolatry. Both R. Eliezer and the Sages, however, presuppose that "hanging" is a postmortem punishment (after the convicted criminal has been stoned to death), following the biblical instruction, which, after relating the stoning of the rebellious son, continues: "If someone is convicted of a crime punishable by death and is executed (namely by stoning), and you hang him on a tree" (Deut. 21:22, continuing with v. 23: "you must not leave his corpse on the tree"). In a similarly broader definition, R. Eliezer extends the hanging after stoning equally on men and women (distinguishing between the sexes only with regard to whether or not they face the crowd witnessing the execution), whereas the Sages exclude women from hanging altogether.

As to the "how," the Mishna defines the "tree" and the way the convicted criminal is hanged on it. The biblical "tree" is ambiguous and can mean a "pole" (e.g., Gen. 40:19) or "gallows" or even impalement upon a stake (e.g., Esth. 9:13). The Mishna gives two explanations of the "tree": the first (anonymous) description comes closest to gallows—a post driven into the ground and a beam jutting from it, presumably close to the top—whereas R. Yose has a post in mind, the lower end of which rests on the earth and the upper end leans against a wall. Accordingly, in the first case the criminal is hanged on the beam and in the second case he/she hangs on the post like butchers do with slaughtered animals—presumably hanging upside down, with their feet attached to the top of the post.

The third question, how long, is answered unequivocally and with reference to the biblical command: the public exposure of the corpse of the executed criminal must be terminated by the end of the day of the execution because he/she must be buried the same day; the corpse must not stay on the "tree" overnight. And then, in an interpretation of the second part of the biblical verse, the Mishna returns to the question of who is hanged and why. The phrase *qilelat elohim* is again ambiguous[24] and here interpreted as a "curse *against* God," in the sense that the criminal has uttered a curse against God by cursing God's name. In other words, he is the blasphemer (*megaddef*) who, according to the Sages (and of course also to R. Eliezer), deserves to be hanged.

Against this background, it is clear for the authors of our Bavli narrative that Jesus was first stoned and then hanged.[25] This is fully concurrent with the mishnaic Halakha. The same is true of the reason for his stoning and hanging: he was a sorcerer and enticed Israel into idolatry. Both crimes are explained in full detail in Mishna Sanhedrin: whereas the above-quoted Mishna mentions only the blasphemer and the idolater, later on the Mishna gives a much longer list of crimes that deserve the capital punishment, among them the *mesit*, the *maddiah*, and the *mekhashshef* (sorcerer)[26]—precisely as listed in our Bavli narrative. The *mesit* is someone who seduces an individual to idolatry,[27] whereas the *maddiah* is understood as someone who publicly entices many into idolatry.[28] Jesus, the Talmud tells us, was both: he not only enticed some individual but all of Israel to become idolaters. To make things worse, he was also a sorcerer in the sense defined more precisely in the Mishna: someone who really practices magic and not just "holds people's eyes" (*ha-'ohez et ha-'enayim*), that is, who deludes people by optical deception (which is permitted).[29] Finally, that a herald publicly proclaims his crime and asks for defense witnesses, follows the mishnaic rule, except for the fact, as we have seen, that the herald does so forty days before the execution takes place. What is not explicitly mentioned in the Bavli, however, is the provision—in the Bible as well as in the Mishna—that the corpse of the executed must not be exposed overnight.

Let us now compare the Bavli narrative with the testimony of the Gospels.[30] First, the *charge*: the Bavli mentions sorcery and idolatry/seduction (of all of Israel) into idolatry, but since the idolater is coupled with the blasphemer in the Mishna,[31] the charge of blasphemy may well be presupposed in the Bavli, too. The evangelists' depictions of the charge against Jesus are twofold: according to the trial both before the Council of the High Priest, the scribes, and elders (the Sanhedrin) and before the Roman governor Pontius Pilate, he pretended to be the Messiah, but the

Jews interpret this claim as his declaration to be the Son of God (and hence as blasphemy),[32] whereas Pilate concludes from it that Jesus wants to be the king of the Jews/of Israel (and hence is to be regarded as a political troublemaker).[33] The New Testament does not explicitly mention the charge of sorcery, but the first charge brought against Jesus by the (false) witnesses is the alleged claim that he is able to destroy the Temple and to rebuild it in three days:[34] this claim could easily be understood by the Talmud editors as sorcery. Moreover, Jesus' practice of casting out demons is explicitly connected with the messianic claim[35] and may indeed be presupposed in the trial before the High Court. Interestingly enough, when Celsus portrays Jesus as returning with "certain magical powers" from Egypt, he concludes that "because of these powers, and on account of them [he] gave himself the title of God,"[36] clearly connecting sorcery with the claim to be God. It is futile, therefore, to contrast too narrowly the charge of blasphemy (New Testament) with the charge of idolatry/sorcery (Bavli).[37] The narratives in both the New Testament and the Bavli are much more complex and "thicker" than so minimalist an approach is able to reveal. Again, it is not a (alleged) talmudic source for the trial of Jesus that is at stake here (and needs to be refuted) but the talmudic reading and interpretation of the New Testament narrative. As far as the charge is concerned, both are closer than one might expect at first glance.

As to the *procedure* of the execution, the Gospel narrative clearly agrees with the mishnaic procedure according to which the witnesses, particularly in criminal cases, must be investigated most thoroughly in order to avoid false testimony.[38] Both Matthew and Mark inform us that the Sanhedrin needed witnesses to proceed with the trial,[39] but that the legal procedure was a farce from the outset—and hence in disagreement with the Mishna—insofar as the Sanhedrin was deliberately looking for false witnesses.[40] Finally the members of the Sanhedrin did find two concurrent witnesses, as required by the law, who put forward the accusation of the destruction and rebuilding (within three days) of the Temple.[41] Since Jesus did not respond to this obviously fabricated accusation, the High Priest came up with the most devastating charge of the alleged blasphemy: Jesus' claim to be the Messiah and Son of God, which Jesus answered affirmatively (Mark)[42] or at least ambiguously (Matthew).[43] In view of this evident mistrial, it is a matter of course that the Gospel narrative leaves out the procedure of the herald seeking additional witnesses who might invalidate the testimony of the original witnesses that led to the conviction. The High Priest, only too happy with Jesus' acceptance of the charge of blasphemy, has the Sanhedrin condemn him to death[44] and, with no further ado, hand him over to the Roman governor to confirm and to execute the sentence—a procedure such as prescribed in the Mishna for the herald might only have disturbed this carefully orchestrated mistrial.

But why does the Talmud insist on the strange detail of the herald announcing the execution forty days before it takes place? The plain answer it gives is to leave enough time for prospective witnesses in Jesus' defense to come forward and to argue against the accusation. But there might be another subtext here that again subtly, or rather not so subtly, responds to the New Testament narrative.[45] There, Jesus foretells his disciples three times that he will be killed and resurrected within three days,[46] the last time on his way to Jerusalem before the Passion begins, that is shortly before Passover:

> (32) They were on the road, going up to Jerusalem, and Jesus was walking ahead of them; they were amazed, and those who followed were afraid. He took the twelve aside again and began to tell them what was to happen to him, (33) saying, "See we are going up to Jerusalem, and the Son of Man will be handed over to the High Priests and the scribes, and they will condemn him to death; then they will hand him over to the Gentiles; (34) they will mock him, and spit upon him, and flog him, and kill him; and after three days he will rise again."[47]

In emphasizing that the herald announced Jesus execution, and not just immediately before it took place but precisely forty days in advance, the Bavli directly contradicts Jesus' own prediction. Why all this fuss about him playing the prophet by dramatically prophesying his trial, sentence, and death—not only once but three times, the last time even a few days before it was about to happen? We all know, the Talmud counters, that he was going to be executed: because our (the Jewish) court had made this decision in public proceedings—as is customary in the Jewish law—and moreover had sent out a herald to proclaim this sentence publicly forty days before the execution (an unusually long period, not required in the Mishna), so that everybody could know it and, if necessary, had ample time to come up with exonerating evidence to prevent a wrong judgment. Hence, in providing the forty-day period the Bavli intends to expose Jesus once more as a swindler and false prophet who makes a fool of himself in claiming to predict what everybody already knew.

Now the *death penalty and execution.* Here we have a major discrepancy between the New Testament and the Talmud: according to the New Testament Jesus was crucified (obviously following Roman law),[48] whereas according to the Talmud he was stoned and subsequently hanged (following rabbinic law). The reason for this, of course, was the simple fact that the Sanhedrin could not impose and execute the death penalty but had to rely on the Roman authority, which followed Roman and not rabbinic law. So shall we conclude from this that the Talmud does not preserve any reliable evidence about the (historical) trial and execution of Jesus, and instead imposes on him later rabbinic law?[49] Yes, of course, but again, this is the wrong question. Not the historical execution—crucifixion versus stoning/hanging—is at stake here but the question of why the Talmud regards it as a matter of course, or rather insists, that Jesus was executed according to rabbinic law.

To answer this question, the rabbis were certainly aware that crucifixion was the standard Roman death penalty,[50] that Jesus was indeed crucified and not stoned and hanged. Hence, why their stubborn insistence on the latter? Because this is precisely the core of their polemical counternarrative to the Gospels. The author of our Bavli Baraita does not need to distort the New Testament report as such: the fact that Jesus was put on trial and executed like an ordinary criminal was devastating enough—such a story can hardly be made any worse. Instead, of the two (and indeed conflicting) stories about Jesus' trial in the New Testament he chooses the "Jewish" one and completely ignores the "Roman" one. Unlike Pilate, who emphasizes the political part of the charge against Jesus, our Bavli author adopts and interprets the version of the trial before the Sanhedrin, combining it with the mishnaic law: the accusation and condemnation of a blasphemer and idolater, who leads astray all of Israel. We, the Jews, he argues, have put him on trial and executed him for what he was: a blasphemer, who claimed to be God and deserved the capital punishment according to our Jewish law. With this deliberate "misreading" of the New Testament narrative, the Bavli (re)claims Jesus for the Jewish people—but only to fend off once and for all any claim by himself or his followers. Yes indeed, the Bavli admits, Jesus was a Jewish heretic, who was quite successful in seducing many of us. But he was taken care of according to the Jewish law, got what he deserved—and that's the end of the story.

The Baraita in our Bavli narrative about Jesus' execution adds yet another remarkable detail that needs closer inspection. All the uncensored manuscripts and printed editions of the Bavli reveal the precise day of his execution: he was hanged on the eve of Passover, that is, the day before Passover. The same is true for the only rabbinic parallel to our story (also in the Bavli), where it is said that the son of Stada was hanged in Lod/Lydda on the eve of Passover.[51] This conspicuously precise date is concordant with John, whose Gospel contradicts the three synoptic Gospels: Whereas Matthew, Mark, and Luke are quite vague about the date of the trial and execution but clearly state that Jesus eats the Passover meal (the "Last Supper") with his disciples *before* he is arrested (Mt. 26:3f. even states explicitly that the high priests and the elders of the people postpone Jesus' arrest until after Passover in order to avoid a riot among the people)[52] and was crucified on the first day of the feast (the fifteenth day of the month of Nisan), John declares that the Last Supper is not the Passover meal but takes place before Passover.[53] Instead, the trial before Pilate takes place about noon on the very day on which (in the evening) Passover begins (the fourteenth of Nisan).[54] Hence, whereas the synoptic Gospels agree that Jesus was executed on the fifteenth of Nisan (the first day of Passover), it is only John who says that the execution took place on the fourteenth of Nisan (the day *before* Passover).[55] Interestingly enough, it is the particular holiness of Passover falling on a Sabbath that John gives as the reason for the Jewish request to have Jesus and the two other criminals buried on that very Friday: the Jews did not want the bodies of the executed left on the cross over Sabbath.[56] This seems to be a (slightly distorted) reference to the biblical and rabbinic law that the body of an executed criminal must not remain on the tree/cross overnight (any night, not just the Sabbath night).[57]

Finally, the Bavli has preserved a further conspicuous detail that betrays an intimate knowledge of the New Testament Passion narrative: that

Jesus was close to the government (and therefore the herald went out forty days before the execution to ask for other witnesses); this detail does not belong to the Baraita but is the answer to Ulla's (later) objection. In all four Gospels, Pilate, the Roman governor, tries to save Jesus and to have Barabbas crucified instead of him.[58] Thus, one can indeed get the impression that Jesus had no less powerful a protector than the governor himself.[59] Pilate explicitly makes a great effort to convince the Jews that he hasn't found any case against him and wants to release him, but the Jews won't give in. It is again the Gospel of John that is particularly specific in this regard. There, when Pilate tries to release Jesus, the Jews cry out: "If you release this man, you are no friend of the emperor. Everyone who claims to be a king sets himself against the emperor!"[60] So the Jews play the Roman governor off against his master, the emperor—and that was the last thing in the world that Pilate needed: to be accused of disloyalty to the emperor. Jesus does not gain time, as the Talmud has it, but is immediately sentenced and executed.

The very fact that the Talmud's claim of Jesus' closeness to the Roman government reflects some knowledge—certainly not of the historical course of events[61] but of the New Testament narrative, particularly of John's version of it—does not come as a surprise anymore. What is more amazing is that this detail exonerates the Roman government from the blame of Jesus' condemnation and consequently, adopting the Gospels' message, puts the thrust of the accusation on the Jews. I have no definite answer to this rather odd conclusion, but it may well have to do with the fact that this element of our story is not part of the (early Palestinian?) Baraita[62] but of the fourth-century C.E. Babylonian discourse upon it. Could it be that the Babylonian Jews had a more relaxed attitude toward the Roman government in Palestine than their Palestinian brethren, who suffered increasingly from the Christian variety of Roman government? But the Jews in Babylonia must have known pretty well what was going on in Palestine in the early fourth century—Ulla, although a Babylonian amora, had moved from Palestine to Babylonia and frequently travelled back and forth between Babylonia and Palestine. Moreover, it is one thing to follow the New Testament version that Pilate tried very hard to rescue Jesus, but it is quite another to accept the message that—therefore—the Jews are to be blamed for his death. On the other hand, we should not forget that it was also the gist of the Baraita's narrative that the Jews took upon themselves the responsibility for Jesus' execution. So the later Babylonian discourse may not want to accept the Gospels' *blame* for Jesus' death; rather, like the Baraita but with different reasoning, it may want to convey the message: yes, the Roman governor wanted to set him free, but we did not give in. He was a blasphemer and idolater, and although the Romans probably could not care less, we insisted that he get what he deserved. We even convinced the Roman governor (or more precisely: forced him to accept) that this heretic and impostor needed to be executed—and we are proud of it.

What we then have here in the Bavli is a powerful confirmation of the New Testament Passion narrative, a creative rereading, however, that not only knows some of its distinct details but proudly proclaims Jewish responsibility for Jesus' execution. Ultimately and more precisely, therefore, it turns out to be a complete reversal of the New Testament's message of shame and guilt: we do accept, it argues, responsibility for this heretic's death, but there is no reason to be ashamed of it and feel guilty for it. We are not the murderers of the Messiah and Son of God, nor of the king of the Jews as Pilate wanted to have it. Rather, we are the rightful executioners of a blasphemer and idolater, who was sentenced according to the full weight, but also the fair procedure, of our law. If this interpretation is correct, we are confronted here with a message that boldly and even aggressively challenges the Christian charges against the Jews as the killers of Christ. For the first time in history, we encounter Jews who, instead of reacting defensively, raise their voice and speak out against what would become the perennial story of the triumphant Church.

7. Jesus' Disciples

One of the most characteristic features of the Gospels is the fact that Jesus gathered a circle of disciples around him. The selection of his disciples was a gradual process, which seems to have begun with four (Simon Peter and his brother Andrew, James son of Zebedee and his brother John)[1] and ultimately led to the number twelve, clearly alluding to the twelve tribes of Israel.[2] The twelve disciples accompanied him until his arrest in the garden of Gethsemane, celebrated the Last Supper with him, witnessed the betrayal of one of them (Judas) who delivered him to the authorities, and the remaining eleven saw him after his resurrection.[3]

It is therefore hardly surprising that the Bavli, immediately after the account of Jesus' execution, adds another story about his disciples. It is again transmitted as an (early) Baraita:[4]

Our Rabbis taught: Jesus the Nazarene[5] had five disciples, and these are they:

Mattai, Naqqai, Netzer, Buni, and Todah.

When they brought Mattai (before the court), he [Mattai] said to them [the judges]: Mattai shall be executed? It is written: When (*matai*) shall I come and appear before God? (Ps. 42:3). They [the judges] answered him: Yes, Mattai shall be executed, since it is written: When (*matai*) will he die and his name perish? (Ps. 41:6).

When they brought Naqqai (before the court), he [Naqqai] said to them [the judges]: Naqqai shall be executed? It is written: You shall not execute the innocent (*naqi*) and the righteous (Ex. 23:7). They [the judges] answered him: Yes, Naqqai shall be executed, since it is written: From a covert (*be-mistarin*)[6] he executes the innocent (*naqi*) (Ps. 10:8).

When they brought Netzer (before the court), he [Netzer] said to them [the judges]: Netzer shall be executed? It is written: An offshoot (*netzer*) shall grow forth out of his roots (Isa. 11:1). They [the judges] answered him: Yes, Netzer shall be executed, since it is written: You shall be cast forth away from your grave like an abhorred offshoot (*netzer*) (Isa. 14:19).

When they brought Buni (before the court), he [Buni] said to them [the judges]: Buni shall be executed? It is written: My son (*beni*), my firstborn is Israel (Ex. 4:22). They [the judges] answered him: Yes, Buni shall be executed, since it is written: Behold I will execute your firstborn son (*binkha*) (Ex. 4:23).

When they brought Todah (before the court), he [Todah] said to them [the judges]: Todah shall be executed? It is written: A psalm for Thanksgiving (*todah*) (Ps. 100:1). They [the judges] answered him: Yes, Todah shall be executed, since it is written: He who sacrifices the sacrifice of Thanksgiving (*todah*) honors me (Ps. 50:23).

This is a highly sophisticated fight with biblical verses, indeed a fight to the death. Whether the whole unit is an early tannaitic Baraita or a Babylonian fabrication, or whether only the list of the names is the Baraita and the following exegeses are a later Babylonian addition[7]—this does not really matter for our purpose.[8] We are clearly dealing here with a Babylonian tradition that may or may not rely on some earlier Palestinian elements. Nor should we be concerned with the fact that the Bavli lists only five students of Jesus whereas the New Testament has twelve. One could refer to the gradual process of Jesus acquiring his disciples and argue that the Bavli reflects an earlier stage, before the final number of twelve was reached,[9] or that a rabbi like Yohanan b. Zakkai had five prominent students[10]—but this would be a pseudo-historical explanation of a text[11] that has no intention of providing historical information about the historical Jesus and his disciples. What is important is only the message that the author/editor of our text wants to convey.

First of all, the Bavli takes it for granted that Jesus' disciples were executed like their master. There was, however, no meticulous trial, no charge, no conviction, and no formal death sentence—the five were simply put to death, and we aren't even told what kind of execution awaited them. We may just presume that they were charged with the same crime with which Jesus was charged: blasphemy and idolatry. And it may be safe to add that they were put to trial and executed immediately after Jesus' execution. These strange circumstances already suggest the suspicion that our author/editor somehow has deliberately blurred the boundaries between Jesus and his disciples: it seems as if they/their fate were/was just the same.

Except for Mattai, whose name may or may not allude to the apostle Matthew[12] (the alleged author of the Gospel bearing his name), the names of the remaining four disciples are not reminiscent of any of the twelve apostles. But this again should not be taken as historical information because it becomes immediately clear that all five names (including Mattai) are designed according to the Bible verses used for the disciples' defense and sentencing. Mattai is a play on words with the Hebrew word *matai* ("when") in the two verses, interpreting Psalm 42:3 (the defense) as "Mattai will come and appear[13] before the Lord" and Psalm 41:6 (the condemnation) as "Mattai will die and his name perish." The same is true for the other four disciples: For Naqqai, the defense verse Exodus 23:7 is interpreted as "You shall not execute Naqqai[14] and the righteous" and the condemnation verse Psalm 10:8 as "From a cover/in secret/in a mysterious way is Naqqai executed."[15] For Netzer, the defense verse Isaiah 11:1 is understood as "Netzer shall grow forth out of his roots," that is, he shall continue to flourish, and the condemnation verse Isaiah 14:19 as: "The abhorred Netzer will be cast forth from his grave." The name Buni is derived from the Hebrew word *beni* ("my son"), and whereas Buni applies Exodus 4:22 to himself (Buni is the firstborn of Israel and therefore cannot be executed), the judges quote the following verse Exodus 4:23, which refers to the firstborn of Egypt (Buni, Egypt's firstborn, must be executed). The defense verse Psalm 100:1 for Todah is understood as "A psalm for Todah" (hence Todah is going to be praised and not executed) and the condemnation verse Psalm 50:23 as "He who sacrifices = executes Todah honors me."

If we now look more closely at the Bible verses being used by the opponents, we discover some remarkable allusions. Mattai is most intriguing because he quotes Psalm 42, a text which could easily be applied to Jesus on the cross, desperately asking for God's help and being mocked by the people passing by. Compare Psalm 42:10f. ("I say to God, my rock: Why have you forgotten me, why must I walk in gloom because the enemy oppresses me? With a shattering in my bones [*be-retzah be-'atzamotai*][16] my oppressors revile me, taunting me always with: Where is your God?") with what the Gospels report about Jesus hanging on the cross: the passersby deride him and call upon him to come down from the cross if he is indeed God's son,[17] whereupon he calls out: "My God, my God, why have you abandoned me?!"[18] If the difficult *be-retzah be-'atzamotai* does refer to the crushing of the bones, one could easily see here a reference to John 19:31–34 (again, only in John), where the soldiers come to break the legs of Jesus and the two "robbers" (in order to hasten their death) but, when they discover that he is already dead, do not break Jesus' legs but instead pierce his side with a spear. Against this background, Mattai/Jesus in the Bavli story could be understood as saying: You can do with me whatever you want, and even if you execute me—I will soon appear before the face of God in heaven, in other words: I will rise from the dead! And the answer of the judges is: No, Mattai/Jesus will definitely die, and not only this—his name will perish, that is, he will be completely forgotten. There is no resurrection and accordingly no community of followers that will continue to believe in him. A most devastating verdict indeed.

Also Naqqai can easily be applied to Jesus: Pilate in his trial explicitly declares him innocent (*naqi*)[19] and does not want to execute him, but the Jews demand his death. So Naqqai is actually Jesus, claiming to be innocent and righteous, who is pleading for his life (quite in contrast to the Gospels where he does not defend himself). The Jews, however, do not accept his plea for innocence, arguing that he is not "innocent" but simply called by the name "Naqqai."

The messianic implication, and hence the reference to Jesus, becomes even stronger with regard to the following "disciples." As to Netzer, Isaiah 11:1ff. is one of the classical biblical texts interpreted as referring to the Davidic Messiah: the "offshoot" (*netzer*) growing forth from his roots is in fact David, the son of Jesse, and it is precisely this Davidic connection which the New Testament establishes (most prominently in Mt. 1, where Jesus' Davidic lineage is spelled out: Jesus, the Messiah, the son of David, the son of Jesse). Against this Davidic claim the judges set up quite another narrative: You, Netzer, are not from Davidic lineage, God forbid, but the "abhorred offshoot," who will be left unburied, "pierced with the sword"— another reference to the Gospels[20]—"like a trampled corpse" (Isa. 14:19). This is a direct allusion or rather counternarrative to the New Testament's claim of Jesus' resurrection. You will not only die, the judges argue, but you will be left unburied, the most horrible fate that can await someone because, as we know from the Mishna, even the worst criminal deserves to be taken from the tree/cross and to be properly buried. Jesus is worse than the worst criminal because, as Isaiah continues, "you destroyed your country, killed your people" (Isa. 14:20), that is, in the Bavli's reading, you blasphemed God and seduced your people into idolatry. And this destiny applies not only to Jesus himself but also to his followers. When Isaiah continues: "Prepare a slaughter for his sons because of the guilt of their father.[21] Let them not arise to possess the earth!" (Isa. 14:21), it becomes clear that, for the Bavli, Jesus' disciples are executed because of Jesus' guilt and that their hope to be resurrected is futile, as futile as Jesus' own expectation was. They will never arise and possess the earth as Matthew has Jesus promise his disciples after his resurrection: "All authority in heaven and on earth has been given to me. Go therefore and make disciples of all nations, baptizing them in the name of the Father and of the Son and of the Holy Spirit, and teaching them to obey everything that I have commanded you."[22] No, our Bavli narrative maintains, neither was Jesus the Messiah nor does his message live among his followers. They are all dead.

With regard to Buni's claim to be Israel, God's firstborn son, the implications are even bolder. First, Buni insists on being God's son. This is but another reference to a Bible verse with highly messianic overtones, namely Psalm 2:7: "He [the Lord] said to me: You are my son (*beni*), today I have begotten you." In the New Testament, when Jesus is baptized by John, the heavens open, the Holy Spirit descends as a dove, and a heavenly voice declares "You are my son, the beloved!"[23]—a clear allusion to Psalm 2:7. The same is true for Jesus' transfiguration on the mount, where a voice from heaven (clearly God's voice) declares: "This is my son, the beloved!"[24] Even more explicitly, when Paul, in the synagogue of Antioch in Pisidia,

summarizes the story of Jesus' life and death (the Jews asked Pilate to execute Jesus, although they did not find a cause for a death sentence; after he
was killed he was taken down "from the tree"[25] and buried in a tomb, but
God raised him from the dead),[26] he begins his series of biblical proof texts
with a full quotation of Psalm 2:7: "You are my son; today I have begotten
you!" Finally, the author of the epistle to the Hebrews, introducing Jesus as
God's son and hence superior to the angels, again quotes Psalm 2:7 to bolster his claim.[27]

Second, Buni insists on being God's firstborn. This is obviously an allusion to the claim, expressed frequently by Paul, that Jesus is the true firstborn of and before all creation: "He [Jesus] is the image of the invisible
God, the firstborn of all creation; for in him all things in heaven and on
earth were created, . . . all things have been created through him and for
him."[28] Since he is also the "firstborn from the dead,"[29] all his followers
will live through him: "But in fact Christ has been raised from the dead,
the first fruits of those who have died. For since death came through a human being, the resurrection of the dead has also come through a human
being; for as all die in Adam, so all will be made alive in Christ."[30] Jesus
and his followers form the new Israel, the "children of the promise" as opposed to the "children of flesh": "This means that it is not the children of
the flesh who are the children of God, but the children of the promise are
counted as descendants."[31] And Paul continues, quoting Hosea: "Those
who were not my people I will call my people, and the unloved I will call
beloved."[32] Therefore, when Buni maintains he is God's (beloved) son,
his (true) firstborn, he expresses the claim of the Christian Church to
have superseded the "old Israel" of the Jews. And it is to this supersession-
ist claim that the judges reply: You fool, you are not God's but the
Pharaoh's firstborn, the son of the wicked, who tried in vain to destroy Israel. The self-appointed Messiah turns out to be the descendant of the
worst of all of Israel's oppressors, the archenemy of Israel.

Finally, Todah, the last of Jesus' disciples. The Hebrew word *todah*
means "thanks" and "thanksgiving," more specifically also "thank offering," and it is this latter meaning with which our text plays. Todah, the
"disciple," maintains: "I am the thank offering for Israel and as such to be
praised rather than to be executed," but the judges counter with: "On the
contrary, your execution—which is by no means a sacrifice in the cultic

sense of the word—is unavoidable, and those who execute you fulfill God's will." Hence, the judges deny the New Testament's claim that Jesus is the sacrifice of the new covenant, the new Passover lamb, which "takes away the sin of the world."[33] Paul explicitly calls Jesus a "fragrant offering and sacrifice to God,"[34] presumably alluding to the burnt offering with a pleasing odor in Exodus 29:18, and a "sacrifice of atonement by his blood."[35] The burnt offering, more precisely the whole burnt offering (*'olah*)—because the animal is entirely consumed in the flame of the altar—is the most common sacrifice in the Hebrew Bible, and the sacrifice of atonement may refer to the biblical sin offering (*hattat*) or trespass/guilt offering (*asham*). The epistle to the Hebrews develops a full theory of Jesus as the new high priest, who "offers himself without blemish to God,"[36] but not "again and again, as the High Priest enters the Holy Place [the Holy of Holies in the Temple] year after year with blood that is not his own"—rather, Jesus "has appeared once for all at the end of the age to remove sin by the sacrifice of himself."[37]

To sum up, this battle with biblical verses is not (or only on the surface) a kind of mock trial, in which Jesus' disciples desperately fight to avoid the death penalty. In reality it is about Jesus, an exciting and highly sophisticated disputation between Jews and Christians about Jesus' fate and some of the most important principles of the Christian faith: Jesus' and his followers' claim that he indeed is the Davidic Messiah, that he is an innocent victim of the Jewish wrath, that he is the Son of God, resurrected after his horrible death, and that this death is the ultimate sacrifice of the new covenant, which supersedes the old and establishes the new Israel. As such, it is not just a bizarre and meaningless addition to the narrative of Jesus' trial and death; rather, it forms the climax of the Bavli's discussion about Jesus and Christianity. Moreover and most conspicuously, quite unlike the infamous disputations in the Middle Ages, in which the outcome was always a foregone conclusion in favor of the Christians, in this disputation the Jews prevail. As the last "disciple" learns: not the cultic sacrifice but the execution of Todah/Jesus honors God and becomes the ultimate vindication of the Jewish faith. Jesus was rightly killed, and there is nothing that remains of him and his teachings after his death.

8. Jesus' Punishment in Hell

According to the New Testament, Jesus was indeed resurrected on the third day after his crucifixion, as he had predicted, and appeared to his disciples. The synoptic Gospels do not relate what happened to him after his resurrection (in Luke he blesses the disciples and simply disappears),[1] and only the appendix in Mark adds that he was "taken up into heaven and sat down at the right hand of God" (Mk. 16:19). The introduction to the Acts of the Apostles, however, knows more details: There, Jesus presents himself alive after his Passion during forty days(!)[2] and, at his last appearance, promises them the power of the Holy Spirit to spread the new faith over the whole earth:

> (9) When he had said this, as they were watching, he was lifted up, and a cloud took him out of their sight. (10) While he was going and they were gazing up toward heaven, suddenly two men in white robes stood by them.[3] (11) They said: "Men of Galilee, why do you stand looking up toward heaven? This Jesus, who has been taken up from you into heaven, will come in the same way as you saw him go into heaven."[4]

In a reverse movement of the "Son of Man" in Daniel, who comes down with the clouds of heaven (Dan. 7:13), the resurrected Jesus ascends to heaven on a cloud, and the angels explain to the amazed disciples that he will later return from where he has gone, that is from heaven. Hence it is safe to assume that he will stay in heaven until his last and final appearance on earth.

It is again reserved to the Babylonian Talmud to tell a counternarrative to the New Testament's message, in fact the exact opposite of what the New Testament proclaims, namely a most graphic and bizarre story about Jesus' descent to and punishment in hell. The context is a large aggadic complex about the destruction of Jerusalem and the Temple during the first Jewish War and of Bethar, the last stronghold of the rebels, during the second Jewish War (the so-called Bar Kokhba revolt). The purpose of the story is to figure out why Jerusalem and Bethar were destroyed. Bethar is not our concern here, but with regard to Jerusalem, the argument goes as follows.[5]

A certain Bar Qamtza was offended at a banquet and, holding the rabbis partly responsible for this offense, denounces them to the authorities in Rome. He tells the Roman emperor that they are preparing a rebellion and offers, as a proof for this accusation, that they will refuse to offer the customary sacrifice for the emperor in the Temple.[6] When the emperor sends his animal for the sacrifice, Bar Qamtza renders it halakhically unfit (adducing a tiny bodily blemish) to be offered at the Temple. The rabbis are nevertheless inclined to sacrifice the unfit animal, in order not to offend the Roman government, but one of their colleagues convinces them that such a poor compromise wouldn't be acceptable. Hence, the Talmud concludes, because of this uncompromising halakhic rigidity the Temple was destroyed.

At first, and historically quite anachronistically, the Romans send the Emperor Nero against the Jews, but Nero, when he realizes that God wants to use him as his tool to punish his people, flees and becomes a proselyte (from whom, grotesquely enough, R. Meir is descendent). Then the Romans dispatch Vespasian, who, when he learns that he is elected emperor, sends Titus in his stead (historically quite correct). Titus defiles the Temple by entering the Holy of Holies (which is the privilege of the high priest only) and fornicating there with a whore on a Torah scroll. The burning of the Temple is not explicitly mentioned; only that Titus robs the utensils of the Temple for his triumph in Rome.[7] However, as a punishment for the arrogant and wicked emperor, God sends a gnat, which enters his brain through his nostril and feeds upon his brain for seven years.[8] When the poor emperor finally dies and they open his skull they find that the gnat had grown into something like a sparrow or even a young dove with a beak of brass and talons of iron. Before he dies, Titus decrees: "Burn me and scatter my ashes over the seven seas so that the God of the Jews will not find me and bring me to trial."[9] After this, the Bavli narrator proceeds with the story of a certain Onqelos the son of Qaloniqos who considers converting to Judaism, presumably following the example of Emperor Nero:[10]

> Onqelos the son of Qaloniqos, the son of the sister of Titus, wanted to convert to Judaism. He went and brought up Titus out of his grave by necromancy and asked him: Who is important in that world [in the world of the dead]?
>
> He [Titus] answered: Israel!
>
> He [Onqelos] answered: What then about joining them?
>
> [Titus:] Their (religious) requirements are many, and you will not be able to carry them (all) out. Go and attack them in that world [on earth] and you will be on top, as it is written: Her adversaries have become the head (Lam. 1:5), [meaning] whoever harasses Israel becomes head.
>
> [Onqelos:] What is your punishment [in the Netherworld]?
>
> [Titus:] What I decreed upon myself: Every day my ashes are collected and they pass sentence on me, and I am burned and my ashes are scattered [again] over the seven seas.
>
> He [Onqelos] went and brought up Balaam out of his grave by necromancy and asked him: Who is important in that world?
>
> He [Balaam] answered: Israel!
>
> [Onqelos:] What then about joining them?
>
> [Balaam:] You shall not seek their peace nor their prosperity all your days for ever (Deut. 23:7).
>
> [Onqelos:] What is your punishment?
>
> [Balaam:] With boiling semen.
>
> He [Onqelos] went and brought up Jesus the Nazarene (*Yeshu ha-notzri*)/the sinners of Israel (*posh'e Yisrael*)[11] out of his/their grave(s)

by necromancy and asked him/them: Who is important in that world?

He/they [Jesus/the sinners of Israel] answered: Israel!

[Onqelos:] What then about joining them?

[Jesus/the sinners of Israel:] Seek their welfare, seek not their harm. Whoever touches them is as though he touches the apple of his [God's] eye![12]

[Onqelos:] What is your punishment?

[Jesus/the sinners of Israel:] With boiling excrement.

For the master has said: Whoever mocks the words of the Sages is punished with boiling excrement.

Come and see the difference between the sinners of Israel and the prophets of the gentile nations![13]

It has been taught (*tanya*): R. Eleazar[14] said: Come and see how great is the power of humiliation. For the Holy One, Blessed be He, sided with Bar Qamtza and destroyed His house and burnt His Temple!

The story opens with Onqelos, who is well known as the alleged translator of the Hebrew Bible into Aramaic (and sometimes confused with Akylas/Aquila, the translator of the Bible into Greek). The Bavli makes him the son of Titus' sister, pondering whether he should convert to Judaism, presumably because Titus himself did not convert (unlike his "predecessor" Nero) but instead preferred to destroy the Temple of the Jews.[15] This Onqelos brings up by means of necromancy three arch villains of Jewish history out of their graves to get their informed advice: Titus, the destroyer of the second Temple; Balaam, the prophet of the nations; and Jesus the Nazarene, who is quite dubious, however, because in some versions of the Bavli he is replaced by the broad category of the "sinners of Israel." All three are obviously in the Netherworld (the biblical She'ol or Gehinnom) where they are punished for their grave misdeeds.

The background of our story is the famous passage in the Mishna that lists those terrible sinners who have no portion in the world to come.[16] Among them are certain heretics and Balaam as one of the four "commoners" (together with Doeg, Ahitophel, and Gehazi). As we have seen, the Bavli Berakhot story about the wicked disciple replaces Balaam with Jesus, insinuating by this bold move that Jesus, like Balaam, did not have a share in the world to come.[17] In our Bavli Gittin story, Jesus appears explicitly in this context of the afterlife, *together* with Balaam (and with Titus). The Tosefta parallel to the Mishna addresses the question, which is not dealt with in the Mishna and the Bavli (but probably presupposed in the latter), of how long these sinners are punished in the Gehinnom: the "sinners of Israel" and the "sinners of the nations" are supposed to stay in the Gehinnom for twelve months only: "after twelve months their souls perish, their bodies are burnt, Gehinnom discharges them, and they are turned into ashes, and the wind blows them and scatters them under the feet of the righteous." In regard to the various kinds of heretics, however, and the destroyers of the first and second Temples (the Assyrians and the Romans): "the Gehinnom is locked behind them, and they are judged therein for all generations."[18] So presumably the punishment in Gehinnom of Balaam (who belongs to the "sinners of the nations") and of Jesus/ the sinners of Israel is terminated—after twelve months they will cease to exist—whereas Titus (the destroyer of the second Temple) will be punished in Gehinnom forever: even "She'ol will perish, but they [the destroyers of the Temple] will not perish."[19]

All three sinners being punished in Gehinnom give the same answer to Onqelos' question of who is held in highest regard in the Netherworld: it is undoubtedly Israel. Now that these arch-villains finally are where they belong, they realize to whom they should have showed due respect on earth. Yet they diverge with regard to the subsequent question of whether one should strive to join Israel's fold as long as one enjoys living on earth. Titus, dismissing the model of his predecessor Nero, has decided for himself that there is no point in trying to emulate the Jews; instead, he opts for the other possibility, to persecute them, and hence to become the ruler of the world (if, sadly, only temporarily)—and this is the advice he gives to the son of his sister. Balaam, the prophet of the nations, gives quite a surprising answer: the verse that he quotes from the Bible (Deut. 23:7) does not refer to Israel at all but to the Ammonites and Moabites, the archenemies of Israel. The Ammonites and Moabites must forever be excluded from the "congregation of the Lord," the Bible demands (Deut. 23:4–7), because they hired Balaam to curse Israel. However, as we know from Numbers 22–23, Balaam did not curse Israel as requested by Balak, the king of Moab, but instead blessed them. Nevertheless, Balaam is held responsible for initially *wanting* to carry out Balak's request and to curse Israel.[20] Therefore, ironically, the author of the Bavli narrative puts the verse originally referring to Ammon and Moab into Balaam's mouth, turning it into an advice against Israel. So in the end Balaam gets what he always wanted: to curse Israel. And finally Jesus or the sinners of Israel, respectively: They are the only ones who actually advise Onqelos to seek Israel's welfare and not their harm, that is, in the present context, to indeed join them. The stark warning "Whoever touches them is as though he touches the apple of his eye" is an allusion to Zechariah 2:12, obviously interpreting "his eye" not as "his own eye" but as "His [God's] eye." Hence, Jesus/the sinners of Israel come out on top of this "contest" between the wicked of the wicked—but still, they are punished in the Netherworld for what they did in their lifetime.

What is it then that our arch-villains of Jewish history did, and how are they punished (because, obviously, the punishment stands in direct relationship to their crime committed against Israel)? Titus' case is the simplest of the three: He has burned the Temple to ashes and has fittingly decreed that after his death he shall be burned and his ashes be scattered over the seas. In an ironical enactment of his will, his punishment consists of his body being reassembled and burnt and his ashes being scattered over the seas over and over again—literally forever, as the Tosefta tells us. Balaam's sin, of course, is his attempt to curse Israel (unfortunately, he cannot take the credit for the fact that the curse failed and was transformed into a blessing), but what about his punishment in boiling semen? This can be inferred from the biblical account of Israel attaching itself to the Moabite god Baal-Peor, whose worship entailed, according to the Bible, whoring with Moabite women (Num. 25:1–3) and eating sacrifices offered to the dead (Ps. 106:28). The former is regarded as indulging in sexual orgies connected to the worship of Baal-Peor, and since Balaam enticed Israel into this sexual transgression (Num. 31:16), he is appropriately punished in the Netherworld by sitting in boiling semen.

Now Jesus/the sinners of Israel: We do not hear anything about his/their crime and cannot, therefore, explain the punishment (which is bizarre enough) as a consequence of any particular crime. The Talmud editor, in his first comment on the Jesus/sinners of Israel part of our narrative, encounters the same problem. The anonymous "master" alludes to the only parallel from the Bavli which mentions boiling excrement as a punishment:[21]

> And much study (*lahag*) is a weariness of the flesh (*yegiʿat baśar*) (Eccl. 12:12).
>
>   Rav Papa the son of Rav Aha bar Adda said in the name of Rav Aha bar Ulla: This teaches us that whoever ridicules (*malʿig*) the words of the Sages is punished [by immersion] in boiling excrement.
>
>   Rava objected: But is it written "ridicules" (*laʿag*)? Rather, what is written is "study" (*lahag*)! Hence (this is the correct interpretation): He who studies them [the words of the Sages] feels the taste (*taʿam*) of meat.

This exposition of the difficult verse from Qohelet, attributed to two Babylonian scholars from the early fourth and the mid fourth century, respectively, belongs to a series of statements that emphasize the importance of the teachings of the Oral Torah against (and even above) the teachings of the Written Torah. Immediately preceding is an exegesis of the first half of the verse from Qohelet: "And furthermore, my son, be admonished: Of making many books there is no end" (Eccl. 12:12), which concludes: "My son, be more careful (about observing) the words of the scribes[22] than the words of the Torah. For the words of the Torah contain both positive and negative commandments (which warrant varying punishments); but, as to the words of the scribes, whoever transgresses the words of the scribes incurs the death penalty."[23] Following this harsh verdict Aha bar Ulla declares that ridiculing the words of the Sages results in the death penalty of sitting (presumably forever) in boiling excrement. He reaches this quite eccentric conclusion by interpreting, first, the Hebrew word for "study" (*lahag*) as "ridicule" (*laʿag*)[24] and, second, the unusual expression "weariness of the flesh" as "excrement" (the weariness of the flesh results in excrement or rather, producing excrement results in the weariness of the flesh). Rava, the famous mid fourth century Babylonian amora, rejects this interpretation of *lahag* as *laʿag* and prefers a pre-digestion exposition: Studying the words of the rabbis is as enjoyable as tasting meat.[25]

We can hardly take for granted that the master's explanation of the crime (ridiculing the words of the Sages) is presupposed in our Bavli narrative[26] and hence that the crime committed by Jesus/the sinners of Israel was indeed ridiculing the Sages. Tempting as this interpretation may be—not least in view of the talmudic story portraying Jesus as a bad disciple[27]—it is more likely that our Talmud editor uses the parallel from Bavli Eruvin in order to explain a weird punishment for a crime the original circumstances of which were unknown to him.[28] Nor can we take it for granted that the second (anonymous) comment in the Bavli ("Come and see the difference between the sinners of Israel and the prophets of the gentile nations") belongs to the original core of our narrative or, more precisely, that it reflects the original core and that therefore the "sinners of Israel" were the original subject of our story and not Jesus.[29] No doubt that the final Bavli editor wanted the text to be understood this way, but he may have had his own agenda. Of course, he refers to the difference between the prophets of the gentiles (Balaam) and the sinners of Israel with regard to the advice they give Onqelos and not with regard to their punishment and their presumed crime: Balaam speaks against Israel, whereas the sinners of Israel speak in their favor. Their punishment, in contrast, is strikingly similar because it hardly makes much of a difference whether one sits in the Netherworld in boiling semen or in boiling excrement. Hence, despite their very different attitudes toward Israel, they are inflicted with almost the same punishment, or to put it differently and more precisely: the sinners of Israel's positive attitude toward Israel, acquired postmortem in the Netherworld, did not change their fate and did not affect their punishment in Gehinnom (they have to serve their time, no matter what they think of Israel *now*). It may well be that this irony is what the Bavli editor wants to convey with his remark.

Furthermore, if we consider the Tosefta's statement about the time the different categories of sinners spend in the Netherworld, the "sinners of Israel" and the "sinners of the nations" fall into one category (after twelve months in Gehinnom they cease to exist), and the heretics and the destroyers of the Temple into another (they are punished forever). So with regard to their punishment (and the presumed crime related to it) there is no difference between the sinners of Israel and the prophets of the nations (Balaam). This makes the Bavli's remark, with its emphasis on the advice given to Onqelos, even more obscure or forced. It is not at all incongruous, therefore, to argue that in an earlier editorial layer Jesus was indeed the third sinner, conjured up from the Netherworld by Onqelos, and that a later Bavli editor changed "Jesus" to the "sinners of Israel," adding the two comments by the "master" and the anonymous author. This also fits much better with the logic of the narrative with three individuals punished in Gehinnom (Titus, Balaam, Jesus) and the similar punishment for the latter two (sitting in boiling semen and excrement, respectively).

This conclusion, however, does not yet solve the enigma of the crime committed by Jesus and the deeper meaning of his punishment (presuming that there was one, as in the case of Titus and Balaam). If we follow again the Tosefta's categorization, we have Balaam as the representative of the sinners of the nations and Titus as the representative of the destroyers of the Temple. This leaves us with either the sinners of Israel or the heretics as the appropriate category for Jesus. If we forgo the Bavli's artificial and probably secondary identification of Jesus with the sinners of Israel, we can put Jesus into the category of the heretics and then have Titus for the destroyers of the Temple, Balaam for the sinners of the nations, and Jesus for the heretics (the first and the third punished in Gehinnom forever, the second released into nonexistence after twelve months). With this solution we finally arrive at a crime for Jesus: he has no portion of the world to come and is accordingly punished in Gehinnom because he is one of the worst heretics that the people of Israel have ever produced. Moreover, according to the Tosefta's taxonomy, he is punished in Gehinnom *forever* (like Titus). And this is clearly the essence of the Bavli's statement about Jesus: it claims (as in b Berakhot, but much more forcefully) that Jesus was not only never resurrected from the dead but that he still sits in Gehinnom, together with the other sinners who are denied an afterlife, and is punished there forever. This, of course, sends also a strong message to his followers, telling them that they better give up any hope for an afterlife for themselves: as with their hero, there is no afterlife reserved for them; they will be punished in Gehinnom forever.

But what then about the meaning of Jesus' punishment—if there is any connection with his crime and if it is not merely modeled along the line of Balaam's punishment with no deeper meaning? In Titus' case we have the link between burning the Temple and burning Titus' body, and in Balaam's case the link between enticing Israel into sexual orgies and sitting in hot semen. So what could be the link between Jesus' heresy and his sitting in hot excrement? Since the text does not give any clue (as in the case of Titus) and since we cannot use the Hebrew Bible to fill the gap left in the Bavli text (as in the case of Balaam), we can only speculate—and this is what I am prepared to do. We are looking for a connection between Jesus' heresy and his punishment (hot excrement), and I propose a connection as bizarre as the punishment. The Talmud does not tell us what the heresy was that Jesus propagated, but we can safely assume—with our knowledge of the other texts discussed—that it must have to do with idolatry and blasphemy. The first and obvious possibility that comes to mind is Jesus' discussion with the Pharisees in the New Testament when the Pharisees ask why Jesus' disciples do not wash their hands before they eat. Jesus explains to the crowd following him that "it is not what goes into the mouth that defiles a person, but it is what comes out of the mouth that defiles."[30] The disciples get the more detailed explanation:

> (17) Do you not see that whatever goes into the mouth enters the stomach, and goes out into the sewer? (18) But what comes out of the mouth proceeds from the heart, and this is what defiles. (19) For out of the heart come evil intentions, murder, adultery, fornication, theft, false witness, slander. (20) These are what defile a person, but to eat with unwashed hands does not defile.[31]

Hence, what Jesus apparently argues is that the Pharisaic purity rules do not really matter. What is important is not the purity of the hands and of the food—because food is processed within the body, and any inherent impurity will be excreted and ends up in the sewer—but the purity of the "heart" (because it is processed through the mouth and, when uttered, starts a fatal life of its own). In other words, not food is impure but human intentions and actions are impure. The rabbinic counternarrative about Jesus' punishment would then ironically invert his attack on the Pharisaic purity laws by having him sit in excrement and teaching him (as well as his followers) the lesson: you believe that only what comes out of the mouth defiles, well, you will sit forever in your own excrement and will finally understand that also what goes into the mouth and comes out of the stomach defiles.

It is certainly possible that our Bavli story refers to this particular New Testament discussion with the Pharisees. I would like, however, to go a step further and put up for discussion an (admittedly rather speculative) interpretation that focuses on the accusation of blasphemy and idolatry, in close parallel to Titus and Balaam (Jesus' attack on the rabbinic purity laws can hardly be understood as blasphemy and idolatry). Let us look again at the analogy to Balaam. Semen, in Balaam's case, is what sexual intercourse produces. Similarly, excrement is what eating produces: everyone who eats produces excrement. Balaam incited Israel to sexual orgies—and hence is punished by sitting in semen. Jesus incited Israel to eating—and hence is punished by sitting in what eating produces: excrement. And what is the "eating" that Jesus imposed upon his followers? No less a food than himself—his flesh and blood.[32] As he has told his disciples during the Last Supper:

(26) While they were eating, Jesus took a loaf of bread, and after blessing it he broke it, gave it to the disciples, and said: "Take, eat; this is my body." (27) Then he took a cup, and after giving thanks he gave it to them, saying: "Drink from it, all of you; (28) for this is my blood of the (new) covenant, which is poured out for many for the forgiveness of sins."[33]

What we have, then, in our Bavli narrative is a devastating and quite malicious polemic against the Gospels' message of Jesus' claim that whoever follows him and, literally, eats him becomes a member of the new covenant that superseded the old covenant with the Jews. How early the Eucharist was understood realistically as consuming the flesh and blood of Jesus is controversial, but it seems as if already Ignatius of Antioch (martyred soon after 110 C.E.?) attacks heretics who do not accept this view.[34] More important, the Gospel of John (composed around 100 C.E.) provides us with a discussion between Jesus and the Jews about precisely this problem of how to understand the eating of Jesus' flesh:[35]

(48) "I am the bread of life. (49) Your ancestors ate the manna in the wilderness, and they died. (50) This is the bread that comes down from heaven, so that one may eat of it and not die. (51) I am the liv-

ing bread that came down from heaven. Whoever eats of this bread will live forever; and the bread that I will give for the life of the world is my flesh."

(52) The Jews then disputed among themselves, saying: "How can this man give us his flesh to eat?" (53) So Jesus said to them: "Very truly, I tell you, unless you eat the flesh of the Son of Man and drink his blood, you have no life in you. (54) Those who eat my flesh and drink my blood have eternal life, and I will raise them up on the last day; (55) for my flesh is true food and my blood is true drink. . . . (57) Just as the living Father sent me, and I live because of the Father, so whoever eats me will live because of me. (58) This is the bread that came down from heaven, not like that which your ancestors ate, and they died. But the one who eats this bread will live forever."

Here we have it all. First, the clear equation of eating bread and eating the flesh of Jesus as well as drinking (presumably wine) and drinking the blood of Jesus. Second, the incredulous Jews contesting precisely this grotesque claim that Jesus can demand from his followers to eat his flesh: How can someone, who is not out of his mind, seriously offer his flesh to eat? Third, the unambiguous juxtaposition of the old and the new covenant: The Jews ate the bread from heaven, the manna; the followers of Jesus eat the real bread from heaven, his flesh. Moreover, and most conspicuously, eating the manna leads to death; eating Jesus' flesh (and drinking his blood) leads to life — not just to a prolongation of life but to eternal life.

It is this claim, not accidentally made explicit again in the Gospel of John, which our Bavli narrative attacks or rather parodies. No, it argues, Jesus is dead and remains dead, and eating his flesh won't lead to life. Not only that those who follow his advice and eat his flesh will not live *forever*, as he has promised; rather, he is punished in the Netherworld *forever* and not granted the milder punishment of those who will be released after twelve months into merciful nonexistence. And the peak of irony: the initiator of this bizarre heresy is appropriately punished by sitting in what his followers excrete, after allegedly having eaten him: excrement! With this explanation we finally have a crime (the heresy of the Eucharist) and a fitting punishment. And not least we have a case analogous to Balaam and to Titus.

One last remark: If my conclusion is correct that an earlier layer of the Bavli story indeed refers to Jesus (and not to the sinners of Israel), it is striking that the advice to Onqelos ("Seek their welfare, seek not their harm. Whoever touches them is as though he touches the apple of his eye") is put in the mouth of Jesus. Obviously, our author wants to convey the message: despite his horrendous and disgusting heresy, Jesus is still different from the destroyer of the Temple and from the prophet of the nations. He is still one of us, a sinner of Israel, and it may be that he has even come to his senses while being punished in Gehinnom. Although too late for him—he cannot be rescued, and he knows it, because of the gravity of his crime—by his advice to Onqelos he may want to give this message to his followers: do not believe any longer in my heresy, do not persecute(?) the Jews; repent and return to the "old covenant" because the alleged "new covenant" is fake and folly.[36] If this is the case, our Bavli editor not just parodies Jesus life and death and an essential aspect of the Christian faith; he addresses the contemporary Christians and calls upon them to follow the advice of their founder issued from the Netherworld.

9. Jesus in the Talmud

The Jesus passages in the rabbinic literature, most prominently in the Babylonian Talmud, reveal a colorful kaleidoscope of many fragments—often dismissed as figments—of Jesus' life, teachings, and not least his death. They are not told as an independent and coherent narrative but are scattered all over the large corpus of literature left to us by the rabbis. Even worse, only very rarely do they address Jesus, the object of our inquiry, directly; in many cases the immediate subject of the rabbinic discourse has nothing to do with Jesus and his life: he is mentioned just in passing, as a (minor) detail of an otherwise different and more important subject, or else he and his sect are carefully disguised behind some codes that need to be deciphered. Nevertheless, our close reading of the relevant texts yields a number of results that can be summarized and put in their appropriate context.

First and foremost, the fact must be emphasized that our texts, despite their scattered and fragmentary presentation, cannot be rejected as nonsense and sheer fiction, as the fantasies[1] of some remote rabbis who did not know and did not want to know anything about the Christian sect and its hero. Such a rash judgment can only be reached—and indeed has been reached much too often—if the wrong standard is applied, that is, if the rabbinic stories are combed for scraps of their historicity, for the historical truth concealed under the rubble and rubbish of lost or misunderstood information. Time and again I have argued that such an approach does not yield much (if anything at all), that it is simply the wrong question addressed to the wrong texts. Our rabbinic texts do not preserve, and did not intend to preserve, historical information about Jesus and Christianity that can be compared to the New Testament and that throws new (and different) light on the New Testament narrative. Such a naive attitude—which dominates most, if not all, of the relevant research literature, although to different degrees and with different conclusions—must be dismissed once and for all. This applies to the positivistic attempt to rediscover and justify the rabbinical texts as historical sources for the life of Jesus (for which stands, as the most prominent exponent, Travers Herford) as well as to the no less positivistic attempt to prove the opposite and to conclude from this that the rabbinic stories are worthless and in most cases do not even refer to Jesus at all (for which stands, as the most extreme proponent, Johann Maier)—neither approach leads very far and is a futile exercise in sterile scholarly erudition.

Moreover, either approach misjudges the literary character of both the New Testament and the rabbinic sources and underestimates the acumen of their authors. It has long been accepted in most camps of New Testament scholarship (except for its fundamentalist and evangelical branches) that the New Testament is anything but a report of "pure" historical facts, of what has "really" happened—although, of course, this does not mean that it presents just fiction. Rather, it is a retelling of "what happened" in its own way or, more precisely, in quite different ways by its different authors. And it has been equally accepted by most scholars of rabbinic Judaism that the same is true for rabbinic literature, namely that the rabbis were not particularly interested in "what happened"—for such a historistic and positivistic approach they reserved the disparaging judgment *mai de-hawa hawa* ("what happened happened")—but tell a story of their own: also, not just fiction but their interpretation of "what happened" in their peculiar and highly idiosyncratic way.[2]

This is precisely what takes place in our rabbinic stories about Jesus and the Christian sect. These stories are a deliberate and carefully phrased retelling—not of what "really" happened but of what has come to or captured the rabbis' attention. And the source to which they refer is not some independent knowledge of Jesus, his life, and his followers that has reached them through some hidden channels; rather, as I could show in detail, it is the New Testament (almost exclusively the four Gospels) as we know it or in a form similar to the one we have today. Hence, the rabbinic stories in most cases are a retelling of the New Testament narrative, a literary answer to a literary text.[3] Let us now summarize the major motifs that appear in the rabbinic sources and that the rabbis obviously regarded as representative of the Christian sect and its founder Jesus.

Sex

The most prominent characteristic that dominates quite a number of the rabbinic stories is sex, more precisely sexual promiscuity. Sexual promiscuity is already presented as the foundation story of the Christian sect: its hero is the son of a certain Miriam and her lover Pandera—a *mamzer*, born out of wedlock (because his mother was married to a certain Stada or Pappos b. Yehuda). The legal status of the bastard is defined in the Bible as such: "No bastard (*mamzer*) shall be admitted into the congregation of the Lord; even to the tenth generation shall he not be admitted into the congregation of the Lord" (Deut. 23:3), a fate that he shares with the eunuchs and the Ammonites and Moabites: he is excluded from the congregation of Israel for the foreseeable future.[4] His adulterous mother deserves—according to biblical and rabbinical law—the death penalty of stoning or strangulation, as the Bible decrees for our case, the adultery between a married woman and her lover: "If a man is found lying with another man's wife, both of them shall die, the man who lay with the woman as well as the woman; so you shall purge the evil from Israel" (Deut. 22:22).[5] Hence, under strict application of biblical law, Jesus' mother should have been stoned. The Talmud does not seem to be interested in her subsequent fate, but her son does fall under the other provision of the Mishna (idolatry) and will indeed be stoned. So in a highly ironical sense, Jesus' birth from an adulterous mother points to his own violent death.

As we have seen, this story of the adulterous mother and her bastard son is the perfect counternarrative to the New Testament's claim that Jesus was born from a virgin betrothed to a descendant of the house of David. Against the New Testament story (with its inherent inconsistency between "husband" and "betrothed") the Talmud concocts its drastic counternarrative of the adulteress and her bastard son (presumably from a Roman soldier), demonstrating the complete absurdity of any Davidic (and hence Messianic) claim. As a bastard, Jesus belongs to the community of Israel only in a limited sense. One of the restrictions of his status implies that he cannot enter a legitimate marriage with a Jewish woman and father Jewish children—let alone found a congregation that claims to be the "new Israel."

This scathing attack on the Christian claim of parthenogenesis may well explain the use of the strange name Panthera/Pantera/Pandera/Pantiri in most of its variations[6] for Miriam's lover and Jesus' real father (in Greek as well as in rabbinic sources). The last derivation among all the possibilities that Maier discusses, and that he finds "captivating at first glance" but nevertheless dismisses,[7] is the assumption of an intentional distortion of *parthenos* ("virgin") to *pantheros* ("panther"). This explanation, first suggested by F. Nitzsch[8] and followed by quite a number of scholars,[9] is indeed more plausible than the derivation from *porneia* ("fornication") which is philologically difficult (Panthera/Pandera as a corruption of *pornos/pornē/porneia?*).[10] In fact, it is the perfect deliberate distortion of the word *parthenos* since it is a reverse reading of the letters "r," "th," and "n": *pantheros*. So Boyarin is absolutely right in arguing that what we encounter here is the well-known rabbinic practice of mocking pagan or Christian holy names by changing them pejoratively,[11] such as *penei elah* ("face of god") that becomes *penei kelev* ("face of the dog").[12] But the punch line in our case is the reverse reading of the consonants within the Greek word—not by coincidence following the magical(!) practice of reading a word backwards (*le-mafrea*ʿ): by changing *parthenos* to *pantheros*, the rabbis do not just practice a case of "cacophemism";[13] rather, they utter a magical spell, or an exorcism, and "transform" Jesus' birth from a virgin to that of a common Roman soldier named Panther. Maier's major argument against this derivation (who could understand such a sophisticated pun?)[14] grossly underestimates the rabbis and their readers. All that we know from rabbinic as well as from pagan sources points to the fact that the unkind countermessage to the New Testament—Miriam/Mary was a whore and her son a bastard—was the Jewish answer to the Christian propaganda of the divine origin of Jesus.

The other allusions in our rabbinic texts to sexual promiscuity refer to the bad son, to the frivolous disciple, and to the understanding of Christianity as an orgiastic cult. The bad son who spoils his food by leading an indecent life turns out to be the true son of his adulterous mother, according to the motto: what else could be expected from him? Again, this accusation may have been upholstered with the New Testament story of Jesus' acquaintance with the immoral woman, later identified with Mary Magdalene—or else with the gnostic story of Jesus being the "lover" of Mary Magdalene, of all women.[15] With such a family history, no wonder that also the grown-up student (Jesus) of a pious rabbi (Yehoshua b. Perahya) gets silly ideas and insinuates to his teacher immodest thoughts (the notorious female hostess of an inn),[16] which the rabbi indignantly rejects and therewith unintentionally brings about the birth of the Christian sect.

And finally, the accusation against R. Eliezer b. Hyrkanos of clandestinely practicing Christianity which is understood as an orgiastic cult connected with prostitution. Here we enter different territory: we are no longer dealing with Jesus himself, his origins, behavior, and fate, but with a prominent rabbi who becomes, as it were, the rabbinic prototype of an early Christian, modeled along the lines of sexual promiscuity (and magic). Both sexual promiscuity and magic are often closely intertwined (I will return to the latter soon). The sexual misconduct brought up here is not that of an individual (Jesus) but, much worse, that of his followers who indulge in sexual mass orgies: the adherents of Jesus' sect follow his advice to such an extreme that sexual orgies have become, so to speak, the "trademark" of the believers in Jesus. This accusation can be found early on in the pagan and Christian literature, and it should not come as a surprise that R. Eliezer was charged with it by the Roman authorities. It appears already in the Christian apologist Justin Martyr's *Dialogue with Trypho*, written in Rome around the mid-second century C.E. There, Justin addresses his Jewish interlocutors as follows:

> My friends, is there any accusation you have against us other than this, that we do not observe the law, nor circumcise the flesh as our forefathers did, nor observe the Sabbath as you do? Or do you also

condemn our customs and morals? This is what I say, lest you, too, believe that we eat human flesh and that after our banquets we extinguish the lights and indulge in unbridled sensuality? Or do you only condemn us for believing in such doctrines and holding opinions which you consider false?[17]

Having first referred to the obvious and well-known distinction between the Jews and the new Christian sect (they do not circumcise themselves and do not observe the Sabbath), Justin gets to talking about the slanders spread about: that the Christians celebrate orgies during which they practice cannibalism and promiscuous sex. The Jew Trypho's brief answer ("This last charge is what surprises us, replied Trypho. Those other charges which the rabble lodge against you are not worthy of belief, for they are too repulsive to human nature") reveals that these horrible slanders are indeed widespread but that he does not take them very seriously: the subsequent discussion shows that he is mainly concerned about the Christian habit of not observing the Sabbath and the festivals and not practicing circumcision. Moreover, he seems to ignore the question of who is the originator of these slanders—or else takes the answer for granted—and simply dismisses them as repulsive. However, later in the dialogue Justin does not leave any doubt that he holds the Jews responsible for the slanders: "And you [the Jews] accuse him [Jesus] of having taught those irreverent, riotous, and wicked things, of which you everywhere accuse all those who look up to and acknowledge him as their Christ, their teacher, and the Son of God."[18]

No doubt, the "irreverent, riotous, and wicked things" refer to the orgies of cannibalism and sex mentioned earlier, and no doubt either that the Jews not only are presented here as the source of the slanders but as those who spread it about the whole civilized world, sending out "certain men chosen by vote" into every part of the empire as official representatives, "proclaiming that a godless and lawless sect has been started by a deceiver, one Jesus of Galilee."[19] But what precisely is this strange ritual of cannibalism and sex? Tertullian, Justin's younger colleague (second half of the second century C.E.) reports more graphic details. In his *Apology*, written 197 C.E., he writes:

We are said to be the most criminal of men (*sceleratissimi*), on the score of our sacramental baby-killing and the baby-eating that goes with it (*sacramento infanticidii et pabulo inde*) and the incest that follows the banquet, where the dogs are our pimps in the dark, forsooth, and make a sort of decency for guilty lusts by overturning the lamps. That, at all events, is what you always say about us; and yet you take no pains to bring into the daylight what you have been saying about us all this long time. Then, I say, either bring it out, if you believe all this, or refuse to believe it after leaving it uninvestigated.[20]

And even more drastic is Tertullian's malicious parody of the alleged Christian ritual in the following chapter, ironically inviting the Jewish interlocutor to join in with the Christians:

Come, plunge the knife into the baby, nobody's enemy, guilty of nothing, everybody's child; or, if that is another man's job, do you just stand by (that is all), by this human creature dying before it has lived; watch for the young soul as it escapes; catch the infant blood, steep your bread with it; eat and enjoy it. Meanwhile, as you recline on your couch, reckon the places where your mother, your sister, may be; make a careful note so that, when the darkness of the dogs' contriving shall fall, you can make no mistake. You will be guilty of a sin, unless you have committed incest. So initiated, so sealed, you live for ever. . . .

You must have a baby, still tender, that can know nothing of death, that can smile under your knife; item a loaf, to catch its juicy blood; add lampstands and lamps, a dog or two, and some sops to set the dogs tumbling the lamps over; above all, you must come with your mother and sister.[21]

This story, as Elias Bickerman has demonstrated in a famous article,[22] is nothing but the anti-Christian adaptation of an originally anti-Jewish propaganda narrative that accuses the Jews of ritualistic cannibalism. Its most prominent anti-Jewish propagandist is Apion, the Greek scholar of Egyptian origin in first century C.E. Alexandria, who, according to Josephus, relates the "malicious slander" about the Jews, capturing, fattening, slaughtering, and finally consuming the flesh of a foreigner (Greek) in a bizarre ritual.[23] In our anti-Christian version, the clandestine symposium consists of the two elements of cannibalism and sexual orgies among the participants, more precisely (in Tertullian) incestuous sexual orgies. The more detailed description in the second quotation from Tertullian, with the blood of the slaughtered child collected by the bread and then shared by all the participants, is clearly a parody of the wine and bread of the Eucharist.[24] And the incestuous sexual orgy seems to be an inversion of the Christian command to love one another.[25] Hence, according to the early Church Fathers, the Jews take up a propaganda narrative that was originally directed against them and turn it into a powerful anti-Christian weapon with the declared goal to discredit the new sect once and forever. Ironically, in our Eliezer b. Hyrkanos story, it is the Jewish rabbis who adopt this anti-Christian propaganda and apply (part of) it to one of them — to mark, and eliminate, him as the arch-heretic.

Magic

The other striking feature of the Christian sect and its founder is magic. Only in the Bavli (in the figure of the student of Yehoshua b. Perahya) it is connected directly with the person of Jesus: this student (Jesus) was not only indecent and prone to sex; he also set up an idolatrous brick worship and, as the Talmud explains, led Israel astray by his magical practices. The remaining allusions to magic are preserved in Palestinian sources: first indirectly, in R. Eliezer b. Hyrkanos' inclination to supporting his argument by miracles; and second and most prominently, in the two stories about the Christian magicians (Jacob of Kefar Sama and the anonymous healer) who heal in the name of Jesus.

That Jesus was a magician is, next to or (often) together with the accusation of sexual promiscuity, the other "trademark" of Christianity as reflected in the early pagan and Christian sources. As we have seen, the Neoplatonic philosopher Celsus has the son of the adulterous country woman acquire magical powers in Egypt and imagine, because of these powers, that he is God. Before him (in the middle of the second century) it is again Justin Martyr, who gives a full description, clearly inspired by the New Testament, of Jesus' magical deceit:

> As I said before, you [Jews] chose certain men by vote and sent them throughout the whole civilized world, proclaiming that a godless and lawless sect (*hairesis*) has been started by a deceiver (*apo . . . planou*), one Jesus of Galilee, whom we nailed to the cross, but whose body, after it was taken from the cross, was stolen at night from the tomb by his disciples, who now try to deceive men (*planōsi*) by affirming that he has risen from the dead and has ascended into heaven.[26]

Here we have the full thrust of the accusation of magic: a *hairesis*, literally a "school" or a "sect" that deviates from a common origin, caused by a "deceiver." The Greek word for "deceiver" or "impostor" (*planos*) is closely associated with magic, as becomes clear from the following quotation from Justin's *Dialogue*:

> The fountain of living water[27] which gushed forth from God upon a land devoid of the knowledge of God (that is, the land of the Gentiles) was our Christ, who made his appearance on earth in the midst of your people, and healed those who from birth were blind and deaf and lame. He cured them by his word, causing them to walk, to hear, and to see. By restoring the dead to life, he compelled the men of that day to recognize him. Yet though they [the Jews] witnessed these miraculous deeds with their own eyes, they attributed them to magical art; indeed they dared to call him a magician (*magos*), a deceiver of the people (*laoplanos*).[28]

The true Jesus, as Justin sees him, is the healer, who heals the cripples and revives the dead—but the incredulous Jews pervert his authentic healing power into deceiving magic. They claim—when he was crucified, died on the cross, and was put in a grave—that his followers (the deceivers of the deceiver) clandestinely stole his body from the tomb and asserted that he had risen from the dead and ascended into heaven. This is

clearly a reference to Matthew 27:63f., where the High Priests and the
Pharisees make the same argument to Pilate:

> (63) Sir, we remember what that deceiver (*planos*) said while he was
> still alive: After three days I will rise again. (64) Therefore command
> the tomb to be made secure until the third day; otherwise his disciples
> may go and steal him away, and tell the people: He has been raised
> from the dead, and the last deception would be worse than the first.

Pilate follows the advice of the High Priests and the Pharisees and sends
soldiers to guard the tomb. When the guards report to the High Priests
what they have seen (the empty tomb and an angel guarding it), the High
Priests bribe and instruct them:

> (13) You must say: His disciples came by night and stole him away
> while we were asleep. (14) If this comes to the governor's ears, we will
> satisfy him and keep you out of trouble. (15) So they took the money
> and did as they were directed. And this story is still told among the
> Jews to this day.[29]

The last remark by the evangelist ("this story is told among the Jews to this
day") makes two things clear. First, that the Jews, already according to
Matthew, were regarded as the originators of this defamatory version of
the events after the crucifixion, and second, that this counternarrative to
the New Testament had a long career because it was aggressively spread
by the Jews. No wonder that Justin dreads the question, obviously put into
the mouth of a Jew: "What excludes [the supposition] that this person
whom you call Christ was a man, of human origin, and did these miracles
you speak of by magic arts (*magikē technē*), and so appeared to be the Son
of God (*hyion theou*)?"[30]

It is certainly not by coincidence that here Justin, in exactly the same
way as Celsus, connects magical deception with the hubris of being the
Son of God. Magical deception leads to idolatry, and this is what is at
stake here.[31] Magic as such, although strictly forbidden in the Bible[32] but
nevertheless practiced,[33] was handled quite tolerantly by the rabbis, as a
matter of fact even practiced by some of them (not least by R. Eliezer

b. Hyrkanos).[34] Hence, it is not so much the practice of magic that disturbs the rabbis; rather, they attack the claim that comes with it: competing authority and power. Not by coincidence, the master in the Bavli story about Yehoshua b. Perahya and his student concludes from Jesus' brick worship that he "practiced magic and deceived *and led Israel astray.*"[35] And this is precisely the reproach that some Jews express against Jesus in the Gospel of John: "And there was considerable complaining about him [Jesus] among the crowds. While some were saying: He is a good man, others were saying: No, *he is leading the people astray!*" (John 7:12, 47).

A prime example of this magical power struggle between competing authorities is preserved in the New Testament story about Simon Magus:[36]

(9) Now a certain man named Simon had previously practiced magic (*mageuōn*) in the city and amazed the people of Samaria, saying that he was someone great. (10) All of them, from the least to the greatest, listened to him eagerly, saying: This man is the power of God called "Great" (*hē dynamis tou theou hē kaloumenē Megalē*). (11) And they listened eagerly to him because for a long time he had amazed them with his magic (*tais mageiais*). (12) But when they believed Philip,[37] who was proclaiming the good news about the kingdom of God and the name of Jesus Christ, they were baptized, both men and women. (13) Even Simon himself believed. After being baptized, he stayed constantly with Philip and was amazed when he saw the signs and great miracles that took place.

Simon, the great magician and, because of his magical powers, the direct outflow of divine power (some other candidate for the "Son of God") follows the message of the apostles and becomes baptized. Why? Not only because of the Christian message but also (and probably mainly) because he is convinced of the superior magical power of the apostles. Even after his baptism he continues to be impressed by their magical performances (which, of course, are miracles). The better magic "leads him astray," namely seduces him into the idolatry of the new Jewish sect.

The danger inherent in the exercise of magical power (idolatry) is the reason why the rabbis in the case of R. Eliezer b. Hyrkanos react so allergically and uncompromisingly to his magical intervention. R. Eliezer plays off his magical power against the authority of his fellow rabbis[38]—and loses this power struggle until his death: rabbinic authority cannot and must not be compromised by magic.[39] The same is true for Jacob of Kefar Sama and his anonymous colleague: their magical healing works, even better than the rabbis wish (they cannot prevent it, unless they forestall it by letting the poor victim die), but still, it is unauthorized magic and must be fought against at all costs. The magical power displayed by Jesus and his followers threatens the authority of the rabbis and their claim to lead the people of Israel. Hence, what is at stake here is the authority of the rabbis versus the authority of Jesus, reasoning—and deciding—among equal partners[40] versus unbridled individual power. For the rabbis, the keys to the kingdom of heaven have been given to them (through the Torah, which God did not want to remain in heaven but decided to hand over to them); for the Christians, the keys are now in the hands of the new Israel, who have access to God not least through their magical power.

Idolatry and Blasphemy

How closely magic and idolatry are connected in the Jewish perception of Jesus becomes apparent in the Bavli's story of Jesus' execution. There, the herald summarizes his crime: he practiced sorcery and instigated (*hesit*) and seduced (*hediah*) Israel. As we have seen, *mesit* and *maddiah* are technical terms for someone who seduces an individual secretly, or many publicly, into idolatry, and Jesus was explicitly accused of both: he did his disastrous and abhorrent work in secret as well as openly and hence deserves the death penalty even twice. His particular variety of idolatry affected—and threatened—the whole community of Israel.

The worst idolater is someone who propagates not just some pagan gods—horrible enough, but only too well known to the rabbis—but declares himself God or the Son of God.[41] This falls under the category of blasphemy, which, according to the Bible, deserves the death penalty of stoning: "And he who blasphemes (*noqev*) the name of the Lord, he shall surely be put to death, and all the congregation shall stone him; as well the stranger, as he who is born in the land, when he blasphemes the name of the Lord, shall be put to death" (Lev. 24:16). In the Mishna,[42] even uttering the name of God (the tetragrammaton) is punished by the death penalty of stoning—how much more does this apply to the blasphemer who uses the name of God for himself? Hence the great indignation of the High Priest, who tears his clothes upon hearing Jesus' blasphemy (Mt. 26:63–65):[43]

> (63) Then the High Priest said to him: I adjure you by the living God, tell us if you are the Messiah, the Son of God! (64) Jesus said to him: You have said so. But I tell you: From now on you will see the Son of Man seated at the right hand of Power [God] and coming on the clouds of heaven. (65) Then the High Priest tore his clothes and said: He has uttered blasphemy. Why do we still need witnesses? You have now heard his blasphemy.

Here, Jesus connects his expected resurrection and ascension to heaven with his claim to be the Son of God: the son will return to his original place, his throne next to his father's throne in heaven. This unthinkable blasphemy demands the immediate action of the Sanhedrin: the imposition of the death penalty.

The same is true for Jesus' "disciples," who, as I have argued, serve as codes for Jesus' claim to be the Messiah and Son of God. The rabbinic judges make sure that Jesus will not ascend to heaven and appear before God (Mattai), that he is not an innocent victim of the Jews (Naqqai), that he is not the Davidic Messiah (Netzer), that he is not God's son and first-born (Buni), and that he is not the sacrifice of the new covenant (Todah): rather, Jesus deserves to die, will be dead, and, most certainly, will not rise from the dead and guarantee his disciples-followers eternal life.

This devastating critique of Jesus' claim of divine origin is most explicit in the Babylonian Talmud, but it was not unique. Although we do not find in the rabbinic literature other sources that so directly and bluntly refer to Jesus, we do have a couple of texts that obviously allude to his blasphemous claim. One is preserved in the Jerusalem Talmud, where the following dictum is attributed to R. Abbahu, a Palestinian rabbi of the late third/early fourth century:[44]

If a man tells you:
I am **God** (*el ani*)—
he is a **liar**;
I am (the) **Son of Man** (*ben adam*)—
he will **regret** it;
I go up to the heavens—
he has said, but he shall not do it.[45]

This midrash is an interpretation of Balaam's oracle in Numbers 23:18–24: "**God** is not a **man**, that he should **lie**; nor a **son of man**, that he should **repent**. Has he said, and shall he not do it? Or has he spoken, and shall he not fulfill it?" In the original context of the Balaam oracle, this means that despite Balak's order to curse Israel, Balaam must follow God's command to bless Israel, a command that cannot be revoked. I have highlighted the relevant terms in the Bible verse and in R. Abbahu's interpretation, and we can easily see how well they correspond to each other (Bible : midrash):

(1) **God** is not a **man** who **lies** : a **man** who tells you that he is **God** is a **liar**;

(2) **God** is not a **Son of man** who **repents** (= revokes his decree) : a **man** who tells you that he is the **Son of Man** will **regret** it;

(3) **God** does what he says : a man who tells you that he goes up to heaven will not perform what he has promised.[46]

Maier has meticulously collected all the biblical and midrashic parallels to this text and wants to prove that in its original context it refers to the kings of the nations (most prominently Hiram), who elevated themselves to gods and were punished for their hubris.[47] This is no doubt correct. But is it equally correct that in the "original" midrash the term "son of man" does not represent a title but simply refers to a human being? True, in Ezekiel 28:2 Hiram, the king of Tyre, claims to be a god and is rebuked for this hubris ("yet you are a man [*adam*] and no god")—but what is wrong with claiming that he is a "son of man," and why will he regret telling us this?[48] Hiram is called a "man" and not a "son of man" (interest-ingly enough, in Ez. 28:2 it is the prophet who is called "son of man"), and the Hiram interpretation therefore belongs to the first part of our midrash (man-god) and not to the second part referring to the "son of man." If we take the sophisticated structure of the midrash seriously, "Son of Man" directly corresponds to "God": a man who tells you that he is God is a liar, and a man who tells you that he is the Son of Man will re-gret it.[49] Hence, R. Abbahu's midrash is indeed much more than just a re-flection of the well-documented Hiram traditions. It is very likely that it goes much further and does understand the "Son of Man" as a title refer-ring to Jesus, as frequently attested to in the Gospels[50] (I therefore capital-ized it in my translation). This interpretation goes well with the fact that R. Abbahu lived in Caesarea, the very center of Roman rule and Palestin-ian Christianity; some scholars even argue that he may well have been ac-quainted with the Church Father Origen (d. 253 C.E.) or at least with his teachings.[51]

Finally, the third and last part of the midrash. Here, the claim of going up to heaven is not covered by the biblical verse Numbers 23:19 (the Bible just confirms, without giving an example, that God always fulfills what he has promised). Again, one could argue that our midrash rejects (this time not Hiram's but) Nebuchadnezzar's hubris, of whom Isaiah says (Isa. 14:13f.): "For you have said in your heart: I will ascend to heaven, I will exalt my throne above the stars of God. . . . I will ascend above the heights of the clouds and will be like the most High," and who gets the de-served rebuff (Isa. 14:15): "Yet you shall be brought down to She'ol, to the sides of the pit."[52] But this is only part of the answer. Within the sequence God—Son of Man—ascent to heaven, it makes much more sense to con-clude that R. Abbahu uses a complex midrash tradition in order to apply it to Jesus and his movement: Jesus is a common human being, not God, not the Son of Man, and he certainly did not ascend to heaven to return to his divine father.

The other relevant midrash is also preserved in a Palestinian source, the homiletic midrash Pesiqta Rabbati. It is attributed to R. Hiyya bar Abba, a Babylonian-born amora, again of the late third/early fourth cen-tury, who, however, spent most of his life in Palestine:[53]

If the whore's son (*bera di-zeneta*) tells you:
There are two gods,
answer him:
I am the one from the sea—and I am the one from Sinai! [. . .]
And if the whore's son tells you:
There are two gods,
answer him:
It is not written here (in Deut. 5:4): "Gods[54] spoke (*dibberu elohim*) [to
   you] face to face," but "The Lord[55] spoke (*dibber YHWH*) [to you]
   face to face on the mountain."

As was the case with the previous midrash, the two answers given to the
heretical question are standard rabbinic theology. The first refers to the famous midrash about God who, despite his various historical manifestations (exemplified by his appearance at the Red Sea and on Mount
Sinai), always remains one and the same. Although at the Red Sea he appeared as a warrior, and hence a young man, and on Mount Sinai as the
wise and serene giver of the Torah, and hence an old man, God is and remains always the same God. He does not change, and one certainly cannot conclude from his various appearances that there is more than one
God.[56] Similarly, that God is referred to in the Bible verse about the revelation on Mount Sinai in the singular and not in the plural is clear proof
that he is one God and not two or more.[57]

However, this use of traditional midrashic material does not necessarily
mean that our text has nothing to do with Jesus.[58] Nor does the possibility
that we may instead be dealing with anti-gnostic polemics pose a persua-
sive counterargument.[59] Quite on the contrary, "gnosticism" is too vague a
label to be of much value—and should not be played off against "Christianity" anyhow, since often enough neither can be neatly separated in our
rabbinic sources. And the main argument in favor of anti-Jesus polemic, of
course, is the programmatic opening "If the whore's son tells you." Who
else could be the "son of the whore" other than Jesus, the bastard, born
from an adulterous mother, who distinguishes himself from his fellow rabbis by leading a life of sexual promiscuity and frivolity? The proposal that
this disparaging epithet refers, instead of to Jesus, just to pagan idolaters[60] is

an exceptionally feeble interpretation that does not explain anything. No doubt, it is Jesus whom R. Hiyya attacks as the "son of the whore" who claims to be God, of equal rank with the God of whom the Jews say that he is the only and single one.

Resurrection and Eucharist

The prerequisite for Jesus' claim to be the Son of God is the belief in his resurrection: it is only through his resurrection and subsequent ascent to heaven that the executed criminal can prove that he is indeed the Son of God. Our rabbinic texts, all in the Bavli, emphasize that Jesus, the new Balaam, does not have a portion in the world to come: his fate is that he must be punished in hell forever, with no chance of redemption—and the same is true for his followers: they better give up any hope of earning eternal life in his succession, as his apostles promise.

We have seen how Justin Martyr puts a similar attack on Jesus' alleged resurrection (it was a magical deceit concocted by his disciples) into the mouth of the Jews. But the Jews do not stand alone in such an assessment of the Christian belief in resurrection. Lucian of Samosata (ca. 120–ca. 180 C.E.), the great Greek satirist, ridicules the Christians' hope of being immortal. In his *Death of Peregrinus* Lucian exposes Peregrinus—a Cynic philosopher, for some time sympathetic to the cause of the Christians, who burned himself alive in order to demonstrate his indifference to pain—as a swindler, and in this context he gets to talking about a similarly stupid belief of the Christians: "You see, for one thing, the poor devils have convinced themselves they're all going to be immortal and live forever, which makes most of them take death lightly and voluntarily give themselves up to it."[61]

Whether or not this satirical answer to one of the core beliefs of Christianity is inspired by Jewish polemical sources (although this possibility cannot be ruled out: his native language was Syriac),[62] it clearly reflects how widespread it was in the Jewish as well as in the Greco-Roman world. It is left to the vicious acumen of Tertullian to summarize what the Jews think of Jesus. When he vividly imagines the last day of judgment—with the emperors who claimed to have been taken up to heaven, the governors of the provinces who persecuted the Christians, the philosophers, the poets, the tragedians, the wrestlers, and finally the Jews "whose fury vented itself against the Lord," all burning in the fire of hell—then he will give his triumphant answer to the Jews:[63]

> This is he, I shall say,
> that carpenter's or prostitute's (*quaestuaria*) son,
> that Sabbath-breaker,
> that Samaritan and demon-possessed!
> This is he, whom you bought from Judas!
> This is he, who was struck with reed and fist,
> who was defiled with spittle,
> who was given gall and vinegar to drink!
> This is he, whom his disciples secretly stole away that it might be said
>   he had risen,
> unless it was the gardener who removed him,
> lest his lettuces be damaged by the crowd of sightseers!

Most of these polemical invectives are directly taken from the New Testament,[64] with the exception of the Samaritan and the gardener: the former may be an attempt to identify Jesus with Simon Magus, who was located in Samaria (again emphasizing Jesus as magician),[65] the latter may refer to John 20:15, where Mary Magdalene mistakes the risen Jesus for the gardener who had carried Jesus' body away. No doubt, the climax of all the Jewish perversions of Jesus' life and fate, beginning with the insinuation that he was born as the son of a whore, is his disciples' plot to steal his body from the tomb in order to feign his resurrection. Tertullian is the first author who surpasses and ironically intensifies this New Testament motif by introducing the gardener so concerned about his vegetables.[66]

The Eucharist, the other central element of Christian practice, is mentioned in our rabbinical sources only once, and also only in the Bavli. Interestingly enough, the Talmud does not connect it with the nasty motif of cannibalism that was so prominent in the pagan and Christian sources. But what the Talmud does relate, reveals no less a wicked sense of humor:

Jesus is punished by forever sitting in hell in the excrement of his follow-ers, who believe that through eating his flesh and drinking his blood, they will live forever. This presents, as we have seen, a satirical inversion of Je-sus' promise to his disciples that he is the bread of life and that whoever eats his flesh and drinks his blood will earn eternal life. Already in the New Testament the Jews expressed their disbelief in such a bizarre claim; now, in the Talmud, this disbelief materializes itself in a bizarre story un-equaled in the Greco-Roman literature.

Palestinian versus Babylonian Sources

Let us now have a closer look at the rabbinic sources that offer us their view about Jesus and Christianity, more specifically, at the relationship between the Palestinian and Babylonian sources. Here the distribution is quite revealing: the texts that most graphically and bluntly refer to Jesus' life and fate are preserved only in the Bavli. This applies to

- Jesus the bastard, son of a whore: although Ben Stada/Satra does ap-pear in Palestinian sources (Tosefta, Yerushalmi)—not by accident as someone who imports sorcery from Egypt (Yerushalmi)—the identi-fication with the bastard (Jesus), and accordingly the counternarra-tive to the New Testament birth story, is reserved for the Bavli

- Jesus the bad son/disciple, guilty of sexual promiscuity

- Jesus the frivolous disciple who practices magic and becomes an idolater (the Yerushalmi parallel leaves out any reference to Jesus)

- the graphic and detailed description of Jesus' execution

- Jesus' disciples (as codes for his own destiny)

- Jesus' punishment in hell

This is an impressive list, which, most conspicuously, includes the two major counternarratives about the cornerstones of Jesus' life in the New

Testament—his birth and his Passion. No doubt, therefore, that the gist of the rabbinic Jesus narrative is preserved in the Babylonian Talmud. We can even go a step further: it is Rav Hisda, the Babylonian amora of the third generation (d. beginning of the fourth century C.E.), who transmits the traditions about both Jesus' adulterous mother and the bad son/disciple as well as adds, in the Eliezer b. Hyrkanos story, the instruction to keep away four cubits from the prostitute. Rav Hisda taught at the academy of Sura, and it may well be that this academy was a "center" of the Babylonian Jesus tradition (which by no means, however, was restricted to Sura since the rabbis of Pumbeditha take part in the discussion about Jesus' mother and her husband/lover).

By contrast, a very different picture emerges from the Palestinian sources. There, Jesus is not addressed directly; the main focus is put on the healing powers of his disciples (most prominently the enigmatic Jacob of Kefar Sekhaniah/Sama) and hence the heretical character of the sect founded by him. The Palestinian texts center around magic: the power inherent in magic, how it works, and the authority connected to it. On this background, R. Eliezer is portrayed as someone who sets up his magical authority against the authority of his fellow rabbis and who accordingly needs to be eliminated. The charges brought against him by the Roman government seem to refer to orgiastic rites that are well known from pagan and Christian sources.

Hence, the Palestinian sources are aimed at the origin of the Christian sect, emerging out of the common ground of Judaism—they reveal the threat that the Palestinian rabbis must have felt, their fear, but also the mechanisms of their defense. As such, they reflect the "simultaneous rabbinic attraction to and repulsion from Christianity,"[67] they describe the very beginning of the "parting of the ways"—a parting, however, that should take several more generations. But it needs to be emphasized that this "snapshot" is frozen, as it were, predominantly in Palestinian sources. There, the new sect seems to have been caught in the process of taking shape as a movement against the rabbis, the rabbinic form of Judaism, against rabbinic authority, a movement moreover that came under the suspicion of Christian libertinage.

In sum, whereas the Palestinian rabbis' (few) statements reveal a relative closeness to the emerging Christian sect, to its very origin and "local color," the Bavli's attention is focused on the *person* of Jesus, particularly his birth and death.[68] In other words, it is, amazingly enough, only the later source—and moreover the one that is geographically much further removed from the scene of action—that explicitly and openly deals with the main character of the events. This striking result deserves our attention, all the more so since it has been largely ignored by most of the scholars dealing with Jesus in the Talmud.

Why the Bavli?

First, the question needs to be addressed: why not the Palestinian sources? Why are the Yerushalmi and the midrashim so restrained with traditions about or reactions to the person of Jesus? The answer to this question is relatively easy. Palestinian Judaism was under the direct and continuously growing impact of Christianity in the Holy Land. When the emperor of the West, Constantine, defeated the emperor of the East, Licinius, in 324 C.E., it was the first time a Christian would become the ruler of Palestine—with profound and long-lasting consequences not least for the Jews. Already in 313 C.E., Constantine had issued the edict of Milan in which he granted legal status to Christianity, officially ending the persecution of Christians. Now, after the victory over his rival in the East, Constantine could promulgate—and carry through—the edict also in the east of his empire, including Palestine. Now began the inescapable and inexorable process that would lead to the eventual triumph of Christianity in Palestine, a triumph that clearly did not leave the Jews unaffected. Christian communities spread throughout Palestine, Christian churches were built, a Christian infrastructure was set up, and Christian pilgrims were attracted from all parts of the empire. Helena, the emperor's mother, visited Palestine in 327 C.E. and founded a number of churches, most important and magnificent among them the Church of the Holy Sepulchre in Jerusalem and the Church of the Nativity in Bethlehem (although the construction of the former had already began before she arrived in Jerusalem: no doubt, the emperor did not need much persuasion by his mother). Relics were found in great numbers, not least the relic of the cross, allegedly and timely discovered by the Queen herself, which served as the main attraction of the Church of the Holy Sepulchre.

The rise of Christianity in Palestine does not mean that the Jews were deprived of all their rights and under the constant threat of persecution; such a bleak picture[69] certainly does not do justice to the nevertheless flourishing religious and cultural Jewish life, predominantly in the Galilee after the Bar Kokhba revolt. But there can be no doubt, either, that the religious and political freedom of the Jews was more and more limited by a growing anti-Jewish legislation and that the Jews gradually became a minority against the increasingly aggressive majority of the Christians in Palestine. That such a climate was not propitious for an un-biased debate between Jews and Christians, let alone for a Jewish critique of the hero of the Christian faith, can hardly come as a surprise.

If we compare the situation of the Jews and the Christians in Palestine with the conditions under which both lived in Babylonia, we get a different picture. Under the dynasty of the Sasanians, which in the third century C.E. replaced the Parthian Arsacids, the Zoroastrian religion with its strong antagonism between good and evil and its fire worship became the uniting religious force in the vast and multiethnic Persian Empire. Whether or not Zoroastrianism can be described as a state religion, as some scholars suggest,[70] there can be no doubt that it was closely related to the claim to power of the Sasanian kings, who promoted it and used it mainly for their political purposes.[71] They gave the magians (*magi*), the priests of the Zoroastrian religion, almost unlimited power (when they saw fit politically), and from this higher point of view of national policy it did not make much of a difference to which deviant religion a victim of the magians' religious zeal belonged. A graphic example of this Zoroastrian fervor against any other religion can be found in the famous inscription put up by Katir, one of the most powerful magians during the reign of Bahram II (276–293):

And for the love of Ohrmazd[72] and the gods, and for the sake of his own soul, he [Bahram II] raised my [Katir's] rank and my titles in the empire. . . . And in all the provinces, in every part of the empire, the acts of worshipping Ohrmazd and the gods were enhanced. And the Zoroastrian religion and the Magi were greatly honored in the empire. And the gods, "water," "fire" and "domestic animals" attained great satisfaction in the empire, but Ahriman[73] and the idols suffered great blows and great damages. And the [false] doctrines of Ahriman and of the idols disappeared from the empire and lost credibility. And the Jews (*yahūd*), Buddhists (*šaman*), Hindus (*brāman*), Nazarenes (*nāsrā*), Christians (*kristiyān*), Baptists (*makdag*) and Manichaeans (*zandīk*) were smashed in the empire, their idols destroyed, and the habitations of the idols annihilated and turned into abodes and seats of the gods.[74]

This is a powerful declaration of the Zoroastrian faith—and a declaration of war against all the other major religions in the Persian Empire. Jews and Christians[75] are, together with the other heresies, on an equal footing as far as the chief magian's wrath is concerned, with no difference whatsoever (the Jews are even mentioned first). Yet this official attitude, or rather the desired ideal, of the Zoroastrian clergy does not convey the full picture. The reality was quite different.

In reality the Christians were much worse off than the Jews,[76] and this for very concrete political reasons: when Christianity became an officially recognized and patronized religion under Constantine and his successors, the major enemy of the Sasanian Empire suddenly turned out to be a Christian—and this did not leave the status of the Sasanians' Christian subjects unaffected. The Christians became suspected of being disloyal to the state and favoring the enemy, of being Rome's "fifth column" in the midst of the Sasanian Empire.[77] Large-scale persecutions of the Christians broke out, first under Shapur II (309–379), then under Yazdgard I (399–421), Bahram V (421–439), and Yazdgard II (439–457).

When Constantine, shortly before his death in 337 C.E., intervened in newly Christianized Armenia, Shapur II was forced into a direct confrontation with his Christian opponent. This threat just at the front door of the Sasanian Empire (with its barely controllable border) clearly did not remain unnoticed by the Sasanian Christians and may have aroused certain expectations. We do know that still in 337,[78] Aphrahat, the Syrian Church Father, triumphantly proclaimed in his *Demonstration* V the ultimate victory of Constantine and the Christians:

> The people of God have received prosperity, and success awaits the man who has been the instrument of that prosperity [Constantine]; but disaster threatens the army which has been gathered together by the efforts of a wicked and proud man puffed up with vanity [Shapur]. . . . The [Roman] Empire will not be conquered, for the hero whose name is Jesus is coming with his power, and his armor will uphold the whole army of the Empire.[79]

Such expectations certainly did not escape the attention of Shapur,[80] all the more so as Constantius, Constantine's son and successor in the East, continued to interfere in Armenia in favor of the pro-Christian party. When Shapur, in 338, unsuccessfully besieged the border city of Nisibis, he finally took action against his Christian subjects and started the first and prolonged persecution (of about forty years) of the Christians in the Sasanian Empire. We are well informed about this persecution by a large collection of texts in Syriac, dating from the time of Shapur II and called the Acts of the Martyrs.[81] They are of varying historical value but on the whole give a vivid picture of the situation.[82]

One of the most prominent texts, the martyrdom of Mar Simon, the Katholikos of the Oriental Church, sets the tone and displays the inextricable mixture of political and religious issues involved. When Shapur promulgated an edict imposing on his Christian subjects double taxes, Simon refused to obey and got caught, according to the Acts of the Martyrs, in a long debate with the king and his dignitaries that finally resulted in his martyrdom. Simon's refusal was duly recorded by the Persian officials and reported to the king, who, reacting with anger and fury, exclaimed: "Simon wants to make his followers and his people rebel against my kingdom and convert them into servants of Caesar (*kaisar*), their coreligionist. Therefore he does not obey my order!"[83] The "Caesar," of course, is the Christian emperor Constantius, and what is at stake here, at the very beginning of the controversy, is not so much a religious dispute (although, to be sure, this was to follow soon) but rather the loyalty of his Christian subjects to the king. Unlike the Jews, who had every reason to distrust the Christian emperor (because of his rule in Palestine) and to be loyal to their Sasanian king, the Christians aroused the suspicion of treason.

And this is precisely how the Acts of Simon continues. The Jews, it argues, are not only aware of the Christians' disloyalty to the king, they effectively take advantage of it and blacken the Christians' name before Shapur. Using the full arsenal of Christian anti-Jewish stereotypes (the Jews have always been against the Christians, they killed the prophets, crucified Jesus, stoned the apostles, and are thirsty for the Christians' blood), it claims that the Jews slander Simon as follows: when Shapur, the king of kings, sends long and wise missives to the Christian emperor (*kaisar*), together with resplendent gifts, they are received dismissively; but when Simon sends him a puny letter, the emperor immediately gets up to his feet, welcomes the letter with both hands and grants Simon's requests. "Moreover," the Acts continue, "you [Shapur] do not have a state secret that he [Simon] does not immediately write down and communicate to the Caesar!"[84] So that's what it is all about: even if they did not instigate the Sasanians' persecution of the Christians, the Jews, the perennial enemies of Jesus and his followers, actively supported it.[85]

If we look at the more concrete religious issues brought up in the Acts of the Martyrs, we find a number of themes that are frequently emphasized. First and foremost is the refusal of the Christians to worship the sun and the fire, the most holy objects of the Zoroastrian cult.[86] The earliest martyrdom described in the Acts, the martyrdom of the bishop Shapur and his coreligionists,[87] opens with the accusation of the magians that they cannot practice their religion because of the Nazarenes, who "despise the fire, revile the sun and do not honor the water."[88] Other accusations are that the Christians refuse to eat blood (i.e., ritually slaughtered meat), bury their dead in the earth, and often refuse to marry but instead proclaim the ideal of virginity.[89] Much as these Christian customs have been abhorrent to the Zoroastrians, most of them must have found the approval of the Jews; in other words, with regard to many of the Zoroastrian religious sensibilities, there cannot have been much of a difference between Christians and Jews (and Katir was therefore right to put both on an equal footing). The conspicuous exception is the ideal of virginity, which appears in almost all of the martyrdoms of women.[90] This is clearly something of which the Jews did not approve of, either, and which immediately reminds us of the Bavli's attack on the New Testament's birth narrative (Jesus born from a virgin). We do not know whether the Jews stand behind the Zoroastrian critique of the Christians' claim that God was born of a human woman (whose conduct moreover was not beyond any doubt),[91] but the possibility can certainly not be ruled out.

More important, the fate of the many Christian martyrs, beginning with the long persecution under Shapur II, did not escape the notice of the Sasanian Jews; in fact, as we have seen, they may have even played an active role in nourishing the suspicion of the Sasanian authorities with regard to the political implications connected with the dissident Christian sect. Jes Asmussen has pointed to the fact that the martyrologies preserved in the Acts of the Syrian Martyrs follow the ideal of a "conscious *imitatio Christi* to make the details of the martyr's death conform as much as possible to the Passion of Jesus,"[92] and of the various characteristics that he lists, two are particularly illuminating in our context: that Friday is the preferred day of martyrdom and that the corpse of the dead martyr is taken away in secret. As to the former, the Acts mentions explicitly that Simon and his friends were sentenced and killed on a Friday, between the sixth and the ninth hour, the very time that Jesus carried the cross and was finally crucified.[93] Interestingly enough, Guhashtazad, a high Persian official and Christian, who first denies his Christian faith and only in a second attempt accepts its consequences, is deemed worthy of being martyred only on Thursday, the thirteenth of Nisan;[94] and some later—and presumably less important—martyrs die just on any Friday, not the Friday of Jesus' execution.[95]

With regard to secretly taking away the corpse of the martyr, we are reminded of the New Testament narrative (only in Matthew) that the High Priests and Pharisees demand of Pilate to guard Jesus' tomb carefully for three days lest the Jews secretly steal his corpse and claim that he has risen from the dead after three days, as he had promised.[96] In a clear imitation of Jesus' fate, the Acts frequently mentions that the Christian coreligionists of the martyr secretly take away or "steal" the body and bury it. For example, after bishop Shapur was martyred, his Christian brethren came, "stole the body, and buried it secretly."[97] In Akebshema's case the torturers have his unburied body guarded, but after three days(!) an Armenian (hence Christian) hostage secretly takes it away.[98] Another martyr, by the name of Joseph, was taken away and, as the text explicitly says, "hidden—whether by God or a human being, we do not know because it [his corpse] was not seen and not known in the place."[99] Similarly, the corpse of the monk Mar Giwargis is displayed for three days and three nights on the cross, guarded by many soldiers, "lest the Christians come and secretly take away his pure and holy body."[100] This is not just an *imitatio Christi* but moreover an inversion of the Matthew narrative: what Matthew puts into the mouth of the Jews—the fear that Jesus' disciples or someone else might steal his body in order to claim that he was resurrected—is now adopted by the Christians and turned positively. Yes, the martyrologies argue, the corpses of the deceased martyrs are indeed secretly taken away, however by us Christians, in order not to fake but to facilitate resurrection (the case of Joseph is particularly revealing because the text bluntly hints at the possibility that he was immediately resurrected). So, in an ironic sense, the Jews finally prove to be right: even though the early Christians maintain that they did not steal the body of Jesus because he was (allegedly) resurrected, their Sasanian brethren admittedly do have the habit of stealing the bodies of their martyrs—to make precisely the same claim: that they are resurrected.

Since these and similar patterns appear in many of the martyrologies,[101] it is hard to avoid the conclusion that the Sasanian Jews must have been aware of them. To be sure, such patterns are—to different degrees—literary devices that belong to the genre of these particular martyrologies and not necessarily historical facts. Clearly, not all of the martyrs died on a Friday, but the pattern of the *imitatio Christi* is too prominent to be simply disregarded as fiction (let alone that nothing speaks against the possibility that the/some Sasanian Jews could and indeed read the Acts of the Martyrs, which after all was written in Syriac, an East Aramaic dialect very close to Babylonian Aramaic). And that the Christians were very eager to take away (and hide) the corpses of the martyrs to indicate their resurrection is an element of the martyrologies that even factually makes a lot of sense.

In sum, the increasingly precarious status of the Christians in the Sasanian Empire, with the waves of persecutions breaking out under Shapur II and continuing under some of his successors, makes it highly likely that a cultural climate could develop in which the Jews felt not only free but even encouraged to express their anti-Christian sentiments—and that they could expect to be supported in this endeavor by the Persian government.[102] Hence, it should not come as a surprise that we find the most graphic polemic against Jesus in the Babylonian Talmud (and not in Palestinian sources).[103] There, in the Bavli, a conflict emerges that is not a conflict any more between Jews and Jewish Christians or Christian Jews (i.e., Christianity in the making), but between Jews and Christians in the very process of defining themselves (i.e., the Christian Church). The polemic that the Bavli shares with us is scanty and has unfortunately been tampered with by Christian censors, but it nevertheless allows us a glimpse of a very vivid and fierce conflict between two competing "religions" under the suspicious eye of the Sasanian authorities.

The New Testament

Another striking result of our inquiry was that the rabbinic sources (again, particularly the Bavli) do not refer to some vague ideas about Jesus and Christianity but that they reveal knowledge—more often than not a precise knowledge—of the New Testament. In other words, they respond to a literary source, not to some vague or lost oral traditions. We cannot reconstruct what the New Testament looked like that the rabbis had in front of them and we even cannot be sure, of course, that they did have access to the New Testament at all. But still, the sometimes quite specific references presented in our sources make it much more feasible that they indeed had some version of the New Testament available.

What kind of New Testament might this have been? We do know that the "Harmony" of the four Gospels (Diatessaron) composed by Tatian in the second century C.E. became the authoritative New Testament text of the Syrian Church until it was replaced (in the fifth century) by the Syrian translation of the four separate Gospels (the New Testament Peshitta).[104] The Diatessaron provides a continuous narrative of the New Testament message, composed almost exclusively from the three synoptic Gospels and from John; its original language most likely was Syriac (and not Greek). In presenting his continuous narrative, instead of four different versions, Tatian could not leave the structure of the four Gospels untouched, but he begins, conspicuously, not only with the prologue in John but normally follows the order of the Gospel of John and inserts into it the passages from the synoptic Gospels.[105] Unfortunately, there hasn't remained any single full text of the Diatessaron, but it can largely be reconstructed through quotations from the Syrian Church Father Ephrem (especially in his Syriac commentary on the Diatessaron) and a number of translations into several languages.[106] In any case, it is highly probable that the Sasanian Jews had access to the New Testament through the Syriac Diatessaron and later on through the Peshitta.

If we review the allusions to the New Testament in detail, it becomes immediately clear that the rabbis must have been familiar primarily with all the four Gospels. The following picture emerges:[107]

- Jesus' family: behind the parody of Jesus' birth stands Matthew in particular, with the Davidic genealogy and the claim that he was born from a virgin. His mother Miriam, the long-haired woman, may refer to the later identification of Mary Magdalene with the "immoral woman" of Luke.

- Jesus the bad son/disciple: possibly also an allusion to Mary Magdalene/the immoral woman (Luke, but also John)

- Jesus the frivolous disciple: no parallel

- Jesus the Torah teacher: Sermon on the Mount (Matthew); Jesus teaching in the Temple (Luke, but also John)

- Healing in the name of Jesus: casting out demons in the name of Jesus (Mark and Luke)

- Jesus' execution: all four Gospels, but that Jesus' trial and execution took place on the fourteenth of Nisan, the day *before* the first day of Passover, is mentioned only in John
  Pilate tries to save Jesus: in all four Gospels, with specific emphasis on John
  Jesus on the cross: all four Gospels

- Jesus' disciples: all four Gospels, with particular emphasis on John (the crushing of the bones), Matthew (the Davidic Messiah), possibly

also Acts and Letter to the Hebrews (reference to Ps. 2:7), Paul
(God's firstborn, the sacrifice of the new covenant)

- Jesus' punishment: eating the flesh and drinking the blood of Jesus
  (John)

This is quite a colorful picture, but still, the familiarity of our (Babylonian) sources with John stands out.[108] So why this sometimes astonishing proximity to the Gospel of John in particular?

Why John?

To answer this question we need to have a closer look at the Gospel of John. As with all the New Testament writings, the elementary questions of authorship, time, place, and circumstances are hotly disputed. The details of this controversy do not affect our present discussion, but in order to put things straight I am prepared to reveal that I sympathize with those who see in John, who claimed to be Jesus' disciple, the head of a school that flourished between 70 and 100/110 C.E. in Asia Minor and that was responsible for the edition of the Gospel of John soon after 100 C.E.[109] No doubt, the Gospel of John is the last of the four Gospels that took shape. More important for our present investigation: it enjoyed wide circulation, it is the most unambiguous and as such the most "Christian," and, not least, the most strongly anti-Jewish Gospel of the four Gospels.

From its very beginning, the Gospel of John makes crystal clear whom it is talking about: the Word that "became flesh and lived among us" and that is no one else but the "only Son from the Father" (1:14). Hence, when John the Baptist sees Jesus, he immediately declares: "Here is the Lamb of God" (1:29, 36), who is the "Son of God" (1:34). That this Jesus, who is subsequently identified as the Messiah (1:41), this "Jesus of Nazareth, the son of Joseph" (1:45), is indeed the "Son of God" (1:49)—as well as the "King of Israel" (ibid.) and the "Son of Man" (1:51)—is solemnly proclaimed from the outset and becomes the leitmotif of the whole Gospel. Accordingly, the author of our Gospel does not wait until the bitter end of his narrative but reveals very early on that his hero was raised from the dead (2:22) and that he will ascend into heaven:

(13) No one has ascended into heaven except the one who descended from heaven, the Son of Man. (14) And just as Moses lifted up the serpent in the wilderness, so must the Son of Man be lifted up, (15) that whoever believes in him may have eternal life. (16) For God so loved the world that he gave his only Son, so that everyone who believes in him may not perish but may have eternal life (3:13–16).[110]

It is this eternal life, bestowed upon him by the Father, that Jesus constantly promises to those who follow him. When he heals the paralyzed man, he explicitly refers to the "Father":

(21) Indeed, just as the Father raises the dead and gives them life, so also the Son gives life to whomever he wishes. (22) The Father judges no one but has given all judgment to the Son, (23) so that all may honor the Son just as they honor the Father. Anyone who does not honor the Son does not honor the Father who sent him. (24) Very truly, I tell you, anyone who hears my word and believes him who sent me has eternal life, and does not come under judgment, but has passed from death to life (5:21–24).

This, he claims, is what Moses told the Jews in reality and which they stubbornly refuse to accept (5:46).[111]

A long series of miracles that Jesus performs is always aimed at proving his claim that he acts as the Son of God who provides eternal life. The miracle of feeding the five thousand with bread climaxes in the announcement that Jesus is the bread of life:

(51) I am the living bread that came down from heaven. Whoever eats of this bread will live forever; and the bread that I will give for the life of the world is my flesh. . . . (53) Very truly, I tell you, unless you eat the flesh of the Son of Man and drink his blood, you have no life in you. (54) Those who eat my flesh and drink my blood have eternal life, and I will raise them up on the last day (6:51–54).

After Jesus has healed him (again on a Sabbath), the blind man believes in the Son of Man, and, as John continues, "worship[s] him" (9:38). Similarly, when he awakes the dead Lazarus out of his "sleep," Jesus proclaims: "I am the resurrection and the life. Those who believe in me, even though they die, will live, and everyone who lives and believes in me will never die. Do you believe this?" (11:25f.)—whereupon Martha answers from the bottom of her heart: "Yes, Lord, I believe that you are the Messiah, the Son of God, the one coming into the world!" (11:27).

The approaching hour of his Passion and death is depicted not only as the fulfillment of his mission on earth but also as the return to his Father (12:23, 27f.; 13:1, 31f.), and this is also the leitmotif in his farewell speech to his disciples (chs. 14–16): "I came from the Father and have come into the world; again, I am leaving the world and am going to the Father" (16:28). Accordingly, he opens his prayer to the Father before he enters his Passion with the words:

"(1) Father, the hour has come; glorify your Son that the Son may glorify you, (2) since you have given him authority over all flesh, to give eternal life to all whom you have given him. (3) And this is eternal life, that they may know you, the only true God, and Jesus Christ whom you have sent" (17:1–3).

The counterpoint to this constant and dramatic insisting of Jesus being the Son of God is the no less constant and dramatic opposition of "the Jews" (as they are often called uniformly), an increasing exacerbation of their hatred for Jesus. At first they are curious, but the more they hear and understand from him and his claim—and the more he attracts a growing number of their fellow Jews—the more impatient and furious they get with him. The healing of the paralyzed man is offensive in their eyes not only because it took place on a Sabbath but also and mainly because it is an immediate consequence of his claim to be the Son of God: "For this reason the Jews were seeking all the more to kill him, because he was not only breaking the Sabbath, but was also calling God his own Father, thereby making himself equal to God" (5:18). The feeding of the five thousand impresses "the people" (whoever this is, but obviously a large number of the Jews)—who acknowledge him as a prophet and want to install him as their king (6:14f.) — but "the Jews" remain skeptical and ask: "Is not this Jesus, the son of Joseph, whose father and mother we know? How can he now say: I have come down from heaven?" (6:42). And then follows the heated exchange regarding Jesus' flesh and blood, which is hard to swallow not only for "the Jews" (6:52) but even for his disciples (6:60). Similarly, when he teaches in the Temple and impresses the crowd listening to him, it is the Pharisees and the High Priests (the "authorities") who turn out to be his chief enemies and who actively seek to arrest and kill him (7:32ff.).

Some of the confrontations are portrayed as direct discussions between Jesus and "the Jews" or the Pharisees. When Jesus prevents the stoning of the adulterous woman, the Pharisees argue that it is only his testimony that acquits the woman (instead of the halakhically required two witnesses). His answer — "In your law it is written that the testimony of two witnesses is valid. I testify on my own behalf, and the Father who sent me testifies on my behalf" (8:17f.) — must have sounded in the ears of the Jews like a parody of this Halakha. The discussion gains almost unparalleled bitterness when they quarrel over the Jews' claim to be descendants of Abraham. "I know that you are descendants of Abraham," Jesus retorts, "yet you look for an opportunity to kill me, because there is no place in you for my word. I declare what I have seen in the Father's presence; as for you, you should do what you have heard from the Father" (8:37f.). Abraham, this is his daring argument, did not seek to kill someone; hence, in their attempt to kill him, they cannot be the children of Abraham but must be the offspring of a different father. Who can this be? His Jewish opponents seem to have a premonition of what he is after, because when he accuses them: "You are indeed doing what your father does," they reply: "We are not illegitimate children; we have one father, God himself!" (8:41). But Jesus does not give up and finally reveals whom he has in mind:

> (43) Why do you not understand what I say? It is because you cannot accept my word. (44) You are from your father the devil, and you choose to do your father's desires. He was a murderer from the beginning and does not stand in the truth, because there is no truth in him. When he lies, he speaks according to his own nature, for he is a liar and the father of lies (8:43f.).

Jesus, the Son of God, with his followers, the children of God, versus the Jews, the children not of Abraham but of Satan—this is the message of the Gospel of John (which, not surprisingly, is concordant with the Book of Revelation—attributed also to John—where those who claim to be Jews are exposed as the "synagogue of Satan").[112] Accordingly, the Jews not only try to stop Jesus, the deceiver of their people, and to kill him; they moreover begin the process of eliminating his followers from their synagogue.[113]

The resurrection of the dead Lazarus was to become the last straw in Jesus' encounter with "the Jews" according to John. When they hear of this new provocation, the Pharisees and the High Priests gather and discuss the situation, which threatens to get out of control. Whereas the majority fears that "If we let him go on like this, everyone will believe in him, and the Romans will come and destroy both our holy place [the Temple] and our nation," Caiaphas, the incumbent High Priest, rebukes them: "You know nothing at all! You do not understand that it is better for you to have one man die for the people than to have the whole nation destroyed" (11:48–50). This was the death sentence, and Jesus' fate should take its course: "So from that day on they planned to put him to death" (11:53). Jesus must and will die because he is a blasphemer and "has claimed to be the Son of God" (19:7).

There exists hardly any other New Testament text that is more unambiguous and firm in Jesus' mission on earth and his divine origin, indeed his identification with God,[114] and that is sterner in its attitude toward the Jews than the Gospel of John. Having been written in the Jewish Diaspora of Asia Minor, it bears all the characteristics of a bitter struggle between the established Jewish and the emerging Christian communities, a struggle moreover that was waged by both sides with the gloves off. The Christians are unsparing with nasty invectives (the Jews have Satan as father), and the Jews answer with the last and most cruel resort at their disposal: they persecute the "would-be God" and force the Roman governor to execute him against the evidence and against the governor's own will. There is every reason to believe that the Gospel of John was spread and well known in Babylonia, if not separately then in the version of Tatian's Diatessaron with its predilection for John.[115] With its strongly anti-Jewish bias it presents the perfect Christian narrative against which another

Jewish Diaspora community could argue—a new and self-confident Diaspora community, far removed in time and place from both the turmoil of the emerging Christianity in Asia Minor in the late first and early second centuries C.E. and of the continuously strengthening Christian power in the Palestine of the fourth and fifth centuries. The Babylonian Jews in the Sasanian Empire, living in a non-Christian and even progressively anti-Christian environment, could easily take up, and continue, the discourse of their brethren in Asia Minor; and it seems as if they were no less timid in their response to the New Testament's message and in particular to the anti-Jewish bias that is so prominent in the Gospel of John. They fought back with the means of parody, inversion, deliberate distortion, and not least with the proud proclamation that what their fellow Jews did to this Jesus was right: that he deserved to be executed because of his blasphemy, that he will sit in hell forever, and that those who follow his example up until today will not, as he has promised, gain eternal life but will share his horrible fate. Taken together, the texts in the Babylonian Talmud, although fragmentary and scattered, become a daring and powerful counter-Gospel to the New Testament in general and to John in particular.

Appendix: Bavli Manuscripts and Censorship

We are still far away from a complete history of the textual transmission of the Babylonian Talmud, but considerable progress has been made recently, thanks to the new technology of collecting huge amounts of data and putting them electronically at the research community's disposal. Most notable in this regard are the Saul Lieberman Institute for Talmudic Research at the Jewish Theological Seminary of America in New York that provides scholars with a computerized databank (the Sol and Evelyn Henkind Talmud Text Data Bank) of talmudic manuscripts[1] and the on-line databank of talmudic manuscripts maintained, together with the Hebrew University's Department of Talmud, by the Jewish National and University Library in Jerusalem (the David and Fela Shapell Family Digitization Project).[2] I have been able to utilize the following Bavli manuscripts and printed editions (arranged according to the presumed date of the respective manuscripts):[3]

Firenze II-I-7-9: Ashkenazi, 1177

Oxford Heb. d. 20 (Neubauer-Cowley 2675): Sephardic, Geniza, 13th century(?)

Karlsruhe Reuchlin 2: square Ashkenazi, 13th century

New York JTS Rab. 15: Sephardic, 1291

Vatican ebr. 487/9: square Ashkenazi, 13th century(?)

Vatican ebr. 108: Sephardic, 13th–14th century

Munich Cod. Hebr. 95: Ashkenazi, 1342[4]

Vatican ebr. 110: square Ashkenazi, 1380

Vatican ebr. 130: square Ashkenazi, 1381

Vatican ebr. 140: square Ashkenazi, 14th century

Oxford Opp. Add. fol. 23: square Sephardic, 14th–15th century

Paris heb. 1337: square Sephardic, 14th–15th century

Paris heb. 671/4: Byzantine, 15th century

Herzog 1: Yemenite, after 1565

Soncino printed edition: printed in Soncino, Barco, and Pesaro between 1484 and 1519

Vilna printed edition: 1880–1886

According to this list, the earliest available evidence for our Jesus texts is the Firenze manuscript from the late twelfth century. The latest manuscript is a Yemenite manuscript from the second half of the sixteenth century. Altogether, the transmission history of the Bavli text is hampered by the fact that many of the earlier manuscripts are lost because of the aggressive policy of the Catholic Church against the Talmud, which culminated in many burnings of the Talmud ordered by the Church (at first 1242 in Paris). Moreover, after the (in)famous Christian-Jewish disputation of Barcelona in 1263, the Church began (often relying on the "expertise" of Jewish converts) to censor the Talmud text and to eliminate (erase, blacken, etc.) all the passages that the experts found objectionable or offensive to the Christian doctrine. It goes without saying that passages referring to Jesus became the prime victim of such activity. In later printed editions, many such supposedly incriminating passages were left out by the Jewish printers themselves in order not to jeopardize the publication of the Talmud (or of other Hebrew books).

In the following charts, I have summarized the references about Jesus as they appear in the manuscripts and some printed editions, arranged according to the topics and the sequence in which they are discussed in the book.

1. Jesus' family

b Shab 104b/Sanh 67a

b Shab 104b

Oxford 23
> Was he the son of Stara (and not) the son of Pandera?

Vatican 108
> Was he the son of Stada (and not) the son of Pandera?

Vatican 487
> son of Siteda[5]

Munich 95
> Was he the son of Stada (and not) the son of Pandera?

Soncino
> Was he the son of Stara (and not) the son of Pandera?

Vilna
> Was he the son of Stada (and not) the son of Pandera?

b Sanh 67a

Herzog 1
> Was he the son of Stara (and not) the son of Pandera?

Munich 95
> Was he the son of Stada (and not) the son of Pandera?

Firenze II.1.8–9
> Was he the son of Stada (and not) the son of Pandera?

Karlsruhe 2
> Was he the son of Stara (and not) the son of Pandera?

Barco
> Was he the son of Stara (and not) the son of Pandera?

Vilna
> Was he the son of Stada (and not) the son of Pandera?

b Shab 104b

Oxford 23   husband Stara, lover Pandera
Vatican 108   husband Stada, lover Pandera
Munich 95   husband Stada, lover Pandera
Soncino   husband Stara, lover Pandera
Vilna   husband Stada, lover Pandera

b Sanh 67a

Herzog 1	husband Stara, lover Pandera
Munich 95	husband Stada, lover Pandera
Firenze II.1.8–9	husband Stada, lover Pandera
Karlsruhe 2	[husband Stara, lover Pandera][6]
Barco	husband Stara, lover Pandera
Vilna	husband Stada, lover Pandera

b Shab 104b

Oxford 23	husband Pappos, mother Stara, father Pandera
Vatican 108	husband/lover[7] Pappos, mother Stada, [he is Jesus the Nazarene][8]
Munich 95	husband Pappos, mother Stada
Soncino	husband Pappos, mother Stara
Vilna	husband Pappos, mother Stada

b Sanh 67a

Herzog 1	husband Pappos, mother Stara
Munich 95	husband Pappos, mother Stada
Firenze II.1.8–9	husband Pappos, mother Stada
Karlsruhe 2	lover/husband[9] Pappos, mother Stara
Barco	husband Pappos, mother Stara
Vilna	husband Pappos, mother Stada

b Shab 104b

Oxford 23	his mother Miriam who let grow (her) women's (hair)
Vatican 108	[his mother Miriam and his father Prince/Naśi?][10]
Munich 95	his mother was letting grow (her) women's (hair)
Soncino	his mother Miriam who let grow (her) women's (hair)
Vilna	his mother Miriam who let grow (her) women's hair

b Sanh 67a

Herzog 1	his mother Miriam who let grow (her) women's (hair)

Munich 95	his mother Miriam who let grow (her) women's (hair)
Firenze II.1.8–9	his mother Miriam who let grow (her) women's (hair)
Karlsruhe 2	his mother Miriam who let grow (her) women's (hair)
Vilna	his mother Miriam who let grow (her) women's (hair)

2. The son/disciple who turned out badly

b Sanh 103a/b Ber 17b

b Sanh 103a

Herzog 1	that you will not have a son or disciple . . . like Jesus the Nazarene
Munich 95	that you will not have a son or disciple . . . like Jesus the Nazarene
Firenze II.1.8–9	that you will not have a son or disciple . . . like Jesus the Nazarene
Karlsruhe 2	that you will not have a son or disciple . . . like Jesus the Nazarene
Barco	that you will not have a son or disciple . . . like Jesus the Nazarene
Vilna	that you will not have a son or disciple . . . [censored]

b Ber 17b

Oxford 23	that we will not have a son or disciple . . . like Jesus the Nazarene
Munich 95	that we will not have a son or disciple . . . [text erased]
Firenze II.1.7	that we will not have a son or disciple . . . [text erased]
Paris 671	that there will not be a son or a disciple . . . like Jesus the Nazarene

Soncino	that we will not have a son or a disciple . . . [not legible; censored]
Vilna	that we will not have a son or a disciple . . . [censored]

3. The frivolous disciple

b Sanh 107b/b Sot 47a

b Sanh 107b

Herzog 1	not as Yehoshua b. Perahya who pushed Jesus the Nazarene away
Munich 95	not as Yehoshua b. Perahya who pushed [text erased] away
Firenze II.1.8–9	not as Yehoshua b. Perahya who pushed Jesus away
Barco	not as Yehoshua b. Perahya who pushed Jesus the Nazarene away
Vilna	not as Yehoshua b. Perahya who pushed Jesus the Nazarene away

b Sot 47a

Oxford 20	not as Yehoshua b. Perahya who pushed Jesus the Nazarene away
Vatican 110	not as Yehoshua b. Perahya who pushed Jesus the Nazarene away
Munich 95	not as Yehoshua b. Perahya who pushed Jesus the Nazarene away
Vilna	not as Yehoshua b. Perahya who pushed one of his disciples away

b Sanh 107b

Herzog 1	Jesus said to him: Rabbi, her eyes are narrow
Munich 95	He said to him: Rabbi [text erased] her eyes are narrow
Firenze II.1.8–9	He said to him: Rabbi, her eyes are narrow
Barco	He said to him: Rabbi, her eyes are narrow
Vilna	He said to him: Rabbi, her eyes are narrow

b Sot 47a

Oxford 20	Jesus the Nazarene said to him: Rabbi, her eyes are narrow
Vatican 110	He said to him: Rabbi, her eyes are narrow
Munich 95	He said to him: Rabbi, her eyes are narrow
Vilna	One of his disciples said to him: Rabbi, her eyes are narrow

b Sanh 107b

Herzog 1	The master said: Jesus the Nazarene goes out to be stoned because of magic . . .
Munich 95	The master said: he practiced magic . . .
Firenze II.1.8–9	The master said: Jesus the Nazarene practiced magic . . .
Barco	The master said: Jesus the Nazarene practiced magic . . .
Vilna	The master said: Jesus practiced magic . . .

b Sot 47a

Oxford 20	As they said: Jesus the Nazarene practiced magic . . .
Vatican 110	As the master said: because he practiced magic . . .
Munich 95	The master said: Jesus the Nazarene because he practiced magic . . .
Vilna	As the master said: he practiced magic . . .

4. The Torah teacher

b AZ 17a/t Hul 2:24/QohR 1:8 (3)

b AZ 17a

Munich 95	One of the disciples of Jesus the Nazarene found me
Paris 1337	One of the disciples of Jesus the Nazarene found me
New York 15	One of the disciples of Jesus the Nazarene found me

t Hul 2:24	He told me a word of heresy in the name of Jesus son of Pantiri
QohR 1:8 (3)[11]	
Vatican 291	He told me a word in the name of Jesus son of Pandera
Oxford 164	He told me a word in the name of the son of Pandera
Pesaro 1519	He told me a word in the name of Jesus son of Pandera
Constantinople 1520	He told me a word in the name of Jesus son of Pandera
Vilna	He told me a word in the name of [empty space]
Jerusalem	Her told me a word in the name of so-and-so
b AZ 17a	
Munich 95	Thus was I taught by Jesus the Nazarene
Paris 1337	Thus was I taught by Jesus the Nazarene
New York 15	Thus taught him Jesus his Master

5. Healing in the name of Jesus

t Hul 2:22f./y AZ 2:2/12/y Shab 14:4/13/QohR 1:8 (3)/b AZ 27b

t Hul	Jacob . . . came to heal him in the name of Jesus son of Pantera
y AZ	Jacob . . . came to heal him. He said to him: we will speak to you in the name of Jesus son of Pandera[12]
y Shab	Jacob . . . came in the name of Jesus Pandera[13] to heal him
QohR[14]	
Vatican 291	Jacob . . . came to heal him in the name of Jesus son of Pandera
Oxford 164	Jacob . . . came to heal him in the name of Jesus son of Pandera
Pesaro 1519	Jacob . . . came to heal him in the name of Jesus son of Pandera

Vilna	Jacob . . . came to heal him in the name of [empty space]
Jerusalem	Jacob . . . came to heal him in the name of so-and-so

b AZ 27b

New York 15	Jacob . . . came to heal him[15]
Munich 95	Jacob the heretic . . . came to heal him
Paris 1337	Jacob . . . came to heal him[16]
Pesaro	Jacob . . . came to heal him[17]
Vilna	Jacob . . . came to heal him[18]

y AZ 2:2/7/y Shab 14:4/8/QohR 10:5

y AZ	someone . . . whispered to him in the name of Jesus son of Pandera[19]
y Shab	a man . . . whispered to him in the name of Jesus Pandera[20]
QohR[21]	he went and brought one of those from the son of Pandera

6. Jesus' execution

b Sanh 43a–b

b Sanh 43a–b

Herzog 1	on the eve of Passover they hanged Jesus the Nazarene
Munich 95	on the eve of Passover they hanged [name erased]
Firenze II.1.8–9	on Sabbath eve and the eve of Passover they hanged Jesus the Nazarene
Karlsruhe 2	on the eve of Passover they hanged Jesus the Nazarene
Barco	on the eve of Passover they hanged [???][22]
Vilna	[whole passage deleted by censor]

b Sanh 43a–b

Herzog 1	Jesus the Nazarene is going forth to be stoned
Munich 95	[name erased] is going forth to be stoned
Firenze II.1.8–9	Jesus the Nazarene is going forth to be stoned
Karlsruhe 2	Jesus the Nazarene is going forth to be stoned
Barco	[???][23] is going forth to be stoned
Vilna	[deleted by censor]

b Sanh 43a–b

Herzog 1	Do you suppose Jesus the Nazarene was one for whom a defense could be made?
Munich 95	Do you suppose [name erased] was one for whom a defense could be made?
Firenze II.1.8–9	Do you suppose Jesus the Nazarene was one for whom a defense could be made?
Karlsruhe 2	Do you suppose Jesus the Nazarene was one for whom a defense could be made?
Barco	Do you suppose [???][24] was one for whom a defense could be made?
Vilna	[deleted by censor]

b Sanh 43a–b

Herzog 1	With Jesus the Nazarene it was different
Munich 95	[name erased] it was different
Firenze II.1.8–9	With Jesus the Nazarene it was different
Karlsruhe 2	With Jesus the Nazarene it was different
Barco	[???][25] it was different
Vilna	[deleted by censor]

7. Jesus' disciples

b Sanh 43a–b

b Sanh 43a–b

Herzog 1	Jesus the Nazarene had five disciples
Munich 95	[text erased]

Firenze II.1.8–9	Jesus the Nazarene had five disciples
Karlsruhe 2	Jesus the Nazarene had five disciples
Barco	[???][26] had five disciples
Vilna	[whole passage deleted by censor]

8. Jesus' punishment in hell

b Git 57a

b Git 57a

Vatican 130	he went and brought up Jesus the Nazarene
Vatican 140	he went and brought up Jesus
Munich 95	he went and brought up Jesus
Soncino	he went and brought up[27]
Vilna	he went and brought up the sinners of Israel

From this overview a number of conclusions can be drawn:

(1) The son of Stada/Stara–son of Pandera passage in b Shabbat/ Sanhedrin (chapter 1) is very stable. Most remarkably, this is the only passage in the Bavli which mentions these two names in relation to Jesus (the copyist of Ms. Vatican 108, therefore, feels compelled to explain that we are indeed talking about Jesus). Hence, it seems very likely that the Talmud *responds* to a *Palestinian* tradition about Jesus' names (son of Stada and son of Pandera respectively). All the other son of Pandera/Pantera/Pantiri references appear solely in Palestinian sources: t Hullin and Qohelet Rabba in chapter 4; and t Hullin, y Avodah Zarah, y Shabbat, and Qohelet Rabba in chapter 5. Here again the textual tradition is very stable: whereas the Palestinian sources have son of Pandera, etc., this time clearly identified as Jesus,[28] the Bavli manuscripts have exclusively Jesus the Nazarene.[29] Moreover, none of the Bavli manuscripts mentioning Jesus the Nazarene is censored. The only conspicuous result of this overview is the fact that the Bavli in chapter 5, unlike the Palestinian sources, does not say explicitly that Jacob came to heal in the name of Jesus: according to the Bavli pattern, we would expect its editor to substitute "in the name of Jesus the Nazarene" for the Palestinian "in the name of Jesus son of Pandera" (as in chapter 4). But this certainly cannot be taken as proof that the Bavli did

not know of the Jesus connection in this passage—on the contrary, it may
have taken it for granted (and note that Ms. Munich makes clear that Jacob is a "heretic").

(2) The "Jesus/Jesus the Nazarene" tradition in the stories unique to
the Bavli is surprisingly stable, although here the intervention in the text
by the censors becomes more visible. In chapter 2 all the b Sanhedrin
manuscripts have "Jesus the Nazarene," including the old Firenze manuscript, but the name is left out, not surprisingly, in the late Vilna edition.
In the b Berakhot parallel, the censor was at work (or was preempted by
the Jewish printers) not only in the printed editions Soncino and Vilna
but also in the Firenze and Munich manuscripts.

A similar picture emerges from chapter 3 (b Sanh and b Sot). All manuscripts in both Talmud passages agree that "Jesus the Nazarene"[30] was
pushed away by R. Yehoshua; but interestingly enough, the name is erased
in Ms. Munich 95 only in the b Sanhedrin version and not in the b Sota
parallel (clear indication of how sloppily the censor worked). Again, only
the printed edition Vilna has instead of "Jesus the Nazarene" the obviously
emended phrase "one of his disciples." However, in the encounter between R. Yehoshua and Jesus in the inn, it is only Ms. Oxford 20 and Ms.
Herzog that explicitly identify the disciple as "Jesus"; the other manuscripts
as well as the printed editions have "he/one of his disciples." Yet it is worth
emphasizing that Ms. Oxford Heb. d.20 seems to belong to the earliest
manuscripts we possess and confirms the rule that the Yemenite manuscript tradition (to which Ms. Herzog belongs), despite being rather late,
preserves older textual evidence that has often not survived in the other
(and earlier) manuscripts. In any case, in the concluding statement by the
master most manuscripts return to "Jesus the Nazarene" (again, Ms. Munich 95 in b Sanh has just "he," whereas in b Sota the same manuscript
has no trouble in spelling out "Jesus the Nazarene").

Finally, as to the narratives about Jesus' execution, the fate of his disciples, and Jesus' punishment in hell, there can be no doubt that they are
talking about Jesus/Jesus the Nazarene. In b Sanhedrin (chapter 6) it is
only Ms. Munich that deletes "Jesus the Nazarene." The printed editions
Barco and Vilna clearly reflect the intervention of censorship or rather
preempting self-censorship: Vilna has left out the whole passage, and
Barco shows a (nonlegible) later addition, obviously of the previously

deleted name of Jesus. A similar picture emerges from the story about Jesus' disciples (chapter 7): Munich has larger parts of the story erased, Vilna leaves the whole passage out, whereas Barco tries to mend the intervention of the censorship. With regard to Jesus' punishment in hell (chapter 8), all the manuscripts have Jesus/Jesus the Nazarene (including Munich 95), as opposed to the printed editions, which simply leave the name out (Soncino) or prefer the reading "sinners of Israel" (Vilna).

(3) From this it can be concluded that the unabashed "Jesus/Jesus the Nazarene" tradition is absent in the Palestinian sources and unique to the Babylonian Talmud. Instead, the Palestinian sources refer to Jesus as "Jesus son of Pandera/Jesus Pandera/son of Pandera" (and this rather infrequently as well as indirectly: only in the story about R. Eliezer and in the two healing stories). In the only passage in which the Bavli mentions the "son of Stada/Stara" and the "son of Pandera," it takes up Palestinian nomenclature and discusses it in the typical Babylonian way. In other words, the manuscript evidence supports the claim that it is the Bavli, and solely the Bavli, that takes the liberty of discussing Jesus and his fate freely and unimpeded by the exertion of Christian power.

To be sure, however, the manuscript evidence of the Bavli does not lead us back in time any closer to the historical origin of our narratives. The earliest available manuscript was written, as we have seen, in the second half of the twelfth century. The question arises, therefore, whether the uncensored manuscripts reflect, not an urtext of the Bavli (any attempts to reconstruct such an urtext are as impossible as they are fruitless because such an ideal construct never existed), but an early form of the text of our narratives, as close as possible to the time of their origin or at least to the time when the Talmud was regarded as a more or less finally edited work (around the eighth century). One major result of our survey of the talmudic manuscripts was the finding that the Jesus passages abound in the manuscripts not only before the implementation of Christian censorship but even thereafter. This evidence strongly suggests that indeed Jesus of Nazareth is the original hero of our Bavli stories and that the available manuscripts do reflect the earliest possible form of our stories.

This rather natural conclusion was contested by Maier, in his zeal to cleanse the "original" Bavli stories of any reference to Jesus and to postpone the (sometimes indisputable) intrusion of Jesus into the Talmud text to the Middle Ages. Instead of a two-tiered transmission history of the Bavli stories (Jesus, at first an integral part of the Talmud narratives, was later gradually removed, due to the involvement of Christian censorship), he suggests a three-tiered transmission history: (1) an original stage, Talmud stories without any reference to Jesus; (2) gradual and late intrusion of Jesus into the stories as part of the textual history of the Bavli before the implementation of censorship but not as part of the "original" Bavli text; (3) removal of the Jesus passages by Christian censorship.[31]

This reconstruction of the Bavli's textual history is hard to comprehend. Maier starts from oversimplified assumptions when he seems to suggest that there is no manuscript evidence for Jesus at all for the time before the implementation of Christian censorship (there is) and that the majority of the manuscripts that were exposed to the censorship deleted Jesus (they do not). The textual tradition of the Bavli is far more complex than Maier wants to admit. True, we do not have much manuscript evidence for the pre-censorship period, but we do have some. More important: To take it for granted that *all* the pre-censorship manuscripts did not contain Jesus[32] is a much bolder claim than to conclude from the manuscript evidence we possess (and some of which does go back to the pre-censorship period) that the lost earlier manuscripts also included Jesus. The latter assumption proposes an essentially unbroken text history with regard to Jesus that starts within the earlier stages of the Bavli transmission, whereas Maier's reconstruction presupposes a major break in the early Middle Ages, when some later editors suddenly felt free to sneak Jesus into the Talmud—only to be repudiated, almost simultaneously, by their Christian censors. This does not make much sense. I therefore propose to hold on to the traditional view that the Bavli's manuscript transmission, so far as we can presently reconstruct it, reflects *the Bavli's* discussion with the founder of Christianity.

Notes

Introduction

1. When using the term "New Testament" here and throughout the book, I do not imply that the specific traditions discussed are characteristic of "the" New Testament as a whole; rather, I am aware that the New Testament is a quite diverse collection of writings and I will be more specific when necessary and where applicable.

2. Although, within the Talmud, there are obvious clusters in the tractate that deals with capital punishment, the tractate Sanhedrin.

3. The history of the *Toledot Yeshu* and its relationship with the talmudic literature needs to be reevaluated; see the book by Krauss mentioned below. Princeton University's library has acquired a collection of some of the relevant manuscript, and we are preparing a new edition with English translation and commentary.

4. A very good summary of the state of the art is provided by Annette Yoshiko Reed and Adam H. Becker in their introduction to the Princeton conference volume edited by them: *The Ways that Never Parted: Jews and Christians in Late Antiquity and the Early Middle Ages*, Tübingen: J.C.B. Mohr (Paul Siebeck), 2003, pp. 1–33.

5. See the survey in Johann Maier, *Jesus von Nazareth in der talmudischen Überlieferung*, Darmstadt: Wissenschaftliche Buchgesellschaft, 1978, pp. 18–41.

6. The University of Altdorf (a German city not far from Nuremberg) was founded in 1623 and became one of the most famous European universities in the seventeenth and eighteenth centuries. It was closed in 1809; the Wagenseil collection of Hebrew writings is now located at the Friedrich-Alexander University of Erlangen-Nuremberg (founded 1743).

7. A similar work, written in German, is Johann Schmid's *Feuriger Drachen-Gifft und wütiger Ottern-Gall*, Augsburg, 1683.

8. Submitted in two parts: *Jesus in Talmude, Sive Dissertatio Philologica Prior/Posterior, De iis locis, in quibus per Talmudicas Pandectas Jesu cujusdam men-*

tio injicitur, Altdorf, 1699. The second part even carries the Hebrew abbreviation בע"ה (*be-'ezrat ha-shem*, "in the name of God") above the title. Meelführer must have been a colorful figure: he fostered close contacts with rabbinic authorities and even communicated with them in Hebrew letters, but nevertheless was involved in inquisitions of Hebrew books ordered by the government and even informed against the Jews, pointing to the allegedly anti-Christian elements in their books. On him see S. Haenle, *Geschichte der Juden im ehemaligen Fürstentum Ansbach*. Vollständiger Nachdruck der Ausgabe von 1867 bearbeitet und mit einem Schlagwortregister versehen von Hermann Süß, Hainsfarther Buchhandlung, 1990 (Bayerische Jüdische Schriften, 1). I owe this information and some other references about Meelführer as well as a copy of Meelführer's dissertation to Hermann Süß.

   9. The full title is: *Entdecktes Judenthum, oder Gründlicher und Wahrhaffter Bericht, welchergestalt die verstockte Juden die Hochheilige Drey-Einigkeit, Gott Vater, Sohn und Heil. Geist, erschrecklicher Weise lästern und verunehren, die Heil. Mutter Christi verschmähen, das Neue Testament, die Evangelisten und Aposteln, die christliche Religion spöttisch durchziehen, und die ganze Christenheit auff das äusserste verachten und verfluchen [. . .].* The work was first printed at Frankfurt (Main) in 1700—and Eisenmenger subsequently was appointed Professor of Oriental Languages at the University of Heidelberg—but the Frankfurt Jews, fearing outbursts of anti-Jewish riots, succeeded in having it confiscated and banned by the government; after Eisenmenger's death in 1704, his heirs secured from the Prussian king a second edition, which was printed in Berlin in 1711 (for legal reasons, the title page gives Königsberg as the place of publication, which was outside the boundaries of the German empire). On the Eisenmenger controversy, see Anton Theodor Hartmann, *Johann Andreas Eisenmenger und seine jüdischen Gegner, in geschichtlich literarischen Erörterungen kritisch beleuchtet*, Parchim: Verlag der D. E. Hinstorffschen Buchhandlung, 1834.—Interestingly enough, Meelführer did know Eisenmenger's book, although by 1699 it was not yet published. He calls Eisenmenger his "most pleasant friend" (*amicus noster suavissimus*) and refers to his *Entdecktes Judenthum* as *Judaismus detectus* (*Jesus in Talmude*, p. 15).

   10. No attempt at a comprehensive summary of the history of research is made here. For details see Maier, *Jesus von Nazareth*, pp. 25ff.

   11. Samuel Krauss, *Das Leben Jesu nach jüdischen Quellen*, Berlin: S. Calvary, 1902.

   12. London: Williams & Norgate, 1903 (reprint, New York: Ktav, 1975).

13. Herford, *Christianity in Talmud and Midrash*, pp. 344ff. (see in particular p. 347: although the historical Jesus is definitely referred to in talmudic literature, "it is remarkable how very little the Talmud does say about Jesus"), as emphasized also by Maier, *Jesus von Nazareth*, p. 28.

14. First published under the title *Einleitung in Talmud und Midrasch* in 1887, and subsequently in many editions; first English edition 1931.

15. Leipzig: J. C. Hinrichs'sche Buchhandlung, 1910. Almost twenty years earlier, Heinrich Laible published *Jesus Christus im Thalmud*, Berlin: H. Reuther's Verlagsbuchhandlung, 1891, to which Strack added a brief preface; deeply imbued with the certainty of Christianity's superiority to Judaism (but not anti-Semitic), Laible provides a thematically structured narrative, full of creative and by no means just absurd or far-fetched suggestions. It is obvious that Strack's sober and reserved approach finds much more favor in Maier's eyes than Laible (Maier, *Jesus von Nazareth*, pp. 27f.), but Laible should not be underestimated.

16. An even more reductionist approach can be found in Kurt Hruby, *Die Stellung der jüdischen Gesetzeslehrer zur werdenden Kirche*, Zürich: Theologischer Verlag, 1971.

17. Joseph Klausner, *Yeshu ha-Notzri* ("Jesus the Nazarene"), Jerusalem: Shtibl, 1922; English translation, *Jesus of Nazareth: His Life, Times, and Teaching*, trans. Herbert Danby, New York: Macmillan, 1925. The entry "Jesus von Nazareth" in *EJ* 9, 1932, cols. 52–77, is written by Joseph Klausner, but does not refer to the rabbinic sources; they are dealt with in a brief and quite balanced appendix, written by Jehoschua Gutmann (cols. 77–79). The popular book about Jesus by the Israeli New Testament scholar David Flusser (*Jesus in Selbstzeugnissen und Bilddokumenten*, Hamburg: Rowohlt, 1968) does not mention the Jewish references to Jesus. Interestingly enough, the entry "Jesus" in *EJ* 10, 1971, cols. 10–14, is written by Flusser, but the appendix "In Talmud and Midrash" (cols. 14–17) is translated from Joseph Klausner's article in the *Encyclopedia Hebraica* (vol. 9, 1959/60, cols. 746–750).

18. Morris Goldstein, *Jesus in the Jewish Tradition*, New York: Macmillan, 1950.

19. Jacob Z. Lauterbach, "Jesus in the Talmud," in *Rabbinic Essays*, Cincinnati: Hebrew Union College Press, 1951 (reprint, New York: Ktav, 1951), pp. 473–570.

20. Darmstadt: Wissenschaftliche Buchgesellschaft, 1978. It was followed by a companion: Johann Maier, *Jüdische Auseinandersetzung mit dem Christentum in der Antike*, Darmstadt: Wissenschaftliche Buchgesellschaft, 1982. For a cautious yet firm critique, see William Horbury, *Jews and Christians in Controversy*, Edinburgh: T&T Clark, 1998, pp. 19f., 104ff.

21. *Jesus von Nazareth*, p. 34; see also p. 32.

22. Accordingly, I use "talmudic literature" synonymously with "rabbinic literature."

23. I strongly believe that any serious reevaluation of this question must start with an evaluation of the full manuscript evidence and a literary analysis of the text.

24. See his results, *Jesus von Nazareth*, pp. 268ff. (especially p. 273).

25. Methodologically, therefore, I am interested solely in what is called the *Wirkungsgeschichte* ("reception history") of the New Testament's narratives, i.e., how they are mirrored in the talmudic sources and how the rabbis might have read and understood them. In other words, I am neither concerned about the complex question of the historicity of the New Testament stories as such nor about the possible contribution of the rabbinic texts to the historical evaluation of the events described in the New Testament (although I do agree that the latter is nil).

Chapter 1
Jesus' Family

1. b Shab 104b; b Sanh 67a.

2. Lit. "who scratches (a mark) on his flesh/incised his flesh (*ha-mesaret 'al beśaro*)."

3. Tattooing one's body is generally forbidden, even when it is not on a Sabbath. Hence, the Talmud isn't talking about permanent tattoos but rather about whether or not tattooing constitutes a violation of the Sabbath.

4. t Shab 11:15.

5. This is the version in b Shab 104b; y Shab 12:4/3, fol. 13d: "But did not Ben Stada bring forth witchcraft from Egypt precisely through this (namely through scratching or inscribing letter-like signs on skin)?" Hence, the Yerushalmi does not speak just about tattoos on the skin of one's body but about all kinds of skin.

6. The Ben Satra version of his name seems to be more original (at least here) since *Satra* is obviously a play on words with *le-saret*—"to scratch, incise."

7. The parallel in b Sanh 67a is almost identical but put in a different context, namely the *mesit*, i.e., the person who seduces someone to idolatry (see below, ch. 6).

8. Interestingly enough, some manuscripts (Ms. Oxford Opp. Add. fol. 23 in Shab 104b and Mss. Yad ha-Rav Herzog 1 and Karlsruhe Reuchlin 2 in Sanh 67a) as well as printed editions (Soncino in Shab 104b and Barco in Sanh 67a) continuously call him/the husband/his mother "Stara" instead of "Stada." The word *stara* can also be vocalized as *sitra* (lit. "side"), and *sitra* could be a play on words with *seritah*, the "scratches/tattoos" through which Ben Stada brought his witchcraft from Egypt. I do not want to suggest that "Sitra" could be an allusion to the kabbalistic notion of *sitra ahra*, the "other side" of evil, particularly in the Zohar. The Karlsruhe manuscript (13th century) might be too early for such a kabbalistic reading of the Jesus story.

9. *ela hu ela immo* in Ms. Munich is clearly a dittography; the other Mss. of Shab 104b read as follows:

> Ms. Oxford 23: "the husband was this Pappos ben Yehuda, and rather his mother was Stada and his father Pandera";
>
> Ms. Vatican 108: "the husband [variant reading: the cohabiter] was Pappos ben Yehuda, (and) his mother was Stada [addition: (and) he is Jesus the Nazarene]";
>
> Ms. Vatican 487: after the name "Ben Siteda" the following part is missing;
> printed edition Soncino: "the husband was Pappos ben Yehuda and his mother was Stada."
>
> The Mss. of Sanh 67a: Ms. Munich 95: "the husband was Pappos ben Yehuda, but rather say: Stada was his mother";
>
> Ms. Firenze II.1.8–9: "the husband was Pappos ben Yehuda, but rather say: his mother was Stada";
>
> Ms. Karlsruhe (Reuchlin 2): "the husband/cohabiter was Pappos ben Yehuda, but rather say: his mother was Stada";
>
> Ms. Yad ha-Rav Herzog 1: "the husband was Pappos ben Yehuda, but rather say: his mother was Stada."

10. "Miriam" in most manuscripts and printed editions, but in Ms. Munich only in Sanh 67a.—Ms. Vatican 108 has the unique and strange addition: his mother was Miriam "and his father (? *avoya/e* ?) Prince/Nasi (? *naśi/neśiya*?)."

11. "Hair" (*se'ar*) is missing in all the manuscripts and appears only in the Vilna printed edition. See on this passage the illuminating article by Burton L. Visotzky: "Mary Maudlin among the Rabbis," in idem, *Fathers of the World: Essays in Rabbinic and Patristic Literatures*, Tübingen: J.C.B. Mohr (Paul

Siebeck), 1995, pp. 85–92. Visotzky compares our passage with the one in b Hag 4b (see below, n. 19) and argues that se‘ar made it into the Ashkenazi Talmud editions through Rashi's explanation and that the "original" phrase was just megadla neshayya, lit. "raiser of women." Whatever this strange phrase could mean, he proposes that a confusion or more likely a deliberate pun on Mary Magdalene and Mary, the mother of Jesus, was at work (see also below, n. 22).

12. Or "Miriam who plaits women's [hair]" (see Michael Sokoloff, A Dictionary of Jewish Babylonian Aramaic of the Talmudic and Gaonic Periods, Ramat-Gan: Bar Ilan University Press, 2002, s.v. gedal # 2).—The whole phrase is vocalized in Ms. Yad ha-Rav Herzog.

13. The preceding ela in Ms. Munich 95 (only Shab 104b) is again a dittography.

14. "About her" only in Ms. Munich Shab 104b.

15. On the variations of the latter name, see below.

16. I understand the first sentence as a question and not as a statement that anticipates the result of the following clarification.

17. With the wonderful Hebrew play on words ba‘al: bo‘el.

18. The result that the name "ben Stada" would accordingly be a matronymic instead of the customary patronymic does not seem to bother the rabbis of Pumbeditha.

19. The only direct parallel is b Hag 4b, where a story is told about the angel of death who by mistake took Miriam "the children's nurse" (megadla dardaqe) instead of the long-haired Miriam (megadla se‘ar neshayya).

20. Lilith is the notorious demon who seduces men and endangers pregnant women.

21. roshah parua‘ = "bareheaded."

22. It may even be that the Talmud conflates the two most important Marys in the New Testament: Mary, the mother of Jesus, and Mary of Magdala (Magdalene), one of Jesus' female followers. Furthermore, the "immoral woman" in Luke (7:36–50), who was later identified with Mary Magdalene (see below) and who dried Jesus' feet with her hair, must have had very long hair.

23. This is made explicit in Ms. Oxford Opp. Add. fol. 23 (366): "the husband was this Pappos ben Yehuda, and rather his mother was Stada and his father Pandera."

24. More precisely, during the reign of Marcus Aurelius (161–180 C.E.); see John Granger Cook, The Interpretation of the Old Testament in Greco-Roman Paganism, Tübingen: Mohr Siebeck, 2004, p. 55 with n. 1.

25. This "Jew" is an important link between the Gospel traditions, the Talmud, and the later *Toledot Yeshu*, and the traditions that he presents are clearly older than the sixties and seventies of the second century C.E.

26. Origen, *Contra Celsum* I:28; translation according to *Origen: Contra Celsum*, trans., introd., and notes by Henry Chadwick, Cambridge: Cambridge University Press, 1953, pp. 28–31.

27. Ibid. I:32. See also Eusebius, *Eclogae propheticae* III:10 (*Eusebii Pamphili Episcopi Caesariensis Eclogae Propheticae*, ed. Thomas Gaisford, Oxford 1842, p. 11): the Jews argue maliciously that Jesus "was fathered from a panther (*ek panthēros*)."

28. Only Ms. Vatican 108 identifies the child as "Jesus the Nazarene" (see above, n. 9).

29. t Hul 2:22 (y Shab 14:4, fol. 14d; y AZ 2:2, fol. 40d); t Hul 2:24; see below, pp. 42, n. 9, 54.

30. Hence it does not come as a surprise that Ernst Haeckel in his notorious *Welträthsel* uses Jesus' non-Jewish father as "proof" that he was not "purely" Jewish but partly descended from the "superior Aryan race" (Ernst Haeckel, *Die Welträthsel. Gemeinverständliche Studien über Monistische Philosophie*, Bonn: Emil Strauß, 9th ed., 1899, p. 379).

31. Another almost contemporary author, the Christian theologian Tertullian (second and early third century C.E.), calls Jesus the son of a carpenter and a prostitute (*quaestuaria*: De Spectaculis, 30); see above, p. 112.

32. Adolf Deissmann, "Der Name Panthera," in *Orientalische Studien Th. Nöldeke zum Siebzigsten Geburtstag*, vol. 2, Gießen: A. Töpelmann, 1906, pp. 871–875; idem, *Licht vom Osten*, Tübingen: J.C.B. Mohr (P. Siebeck), 4th ed., 1923, p. 57.

33. Maier, *Jesus von Nazareth*, pp. 243, 264ff.

34. As Maier, *Jesus von Nazareth*, p. 265, seems to suggest.

35. A tradition that obviously starts with the Egyptian magicians contending with Moses (Ex. 7–12). On ancient Egyptian magic, see Jan Assmann, "Magic and Theology in Ancient Egypt," in *Envisioning Magic: A Princeton Seminar and Symposium*, ed. Peter Schäfer and Hans G. Kippenberg, Leiden—New York—Köln: Brill, 1997, pp. 1–18. The epitome of syncretistic, Greco-Egyptian magic are the magical papyri from Egypt; see Hans Dieter Betz, ed., *The Greek Magical Papyri in Translation: Including the Demotic Spells*, Chicago and London: University of Chicago Press, 1986, and his introduction, pp. xlivff. On the Talmud's assessment of Egyptian magic see b *Qid* 49b: "Ten kabs [measure of capacity] of

witchcraft (*keshafim*) descended to the world: nine were taken by Egypt and one by the rest of the world."

36. See Morton Smith, *Jesus the Magician*, San Francisco: Harper & Row, 1978, especially pp. 21–44.

37. See below, ch. 5.

38. In Mk. 6:3, Jesus is called a carpenter.

39. In Greek *ton andra* (lit. "the man"), which in this context can only mean "the husband."

40. The evangelist Mark, who does not report about Jesus' birth, mentions just in passing that he has brothers and sisters, in other words, belongs to a completely "normal" family (Mk. 6:3).

41. Who is again anachronistically called "her husband" (1:19).

42. Martin Hengel reminds me that Matthew puts the emphasis very much on Joseph, unlike Luke with his emphasis on Mary. If we accept the dating of Matthew about fifteen–twenty years later than Luke, namely between 90 and 100 C.E. (see Hans-Jürgen Becker, *Auf der Kathedra des Mose. Rabbinisch-theologisches Denken und antirabbinische Polemik in Matthäus 23,1–12*, Berlin: Institut Kirche und Judentum, 1990, p. 30 with n. 155), we might find in Matthew's account of the story of Jesus' birth a response to Jewish reproaches with regard to the doubtful origins of Jesus.

43. Apart, of course, from the *Toledot Yeshu*, which does not belong to the established canon of rabbinic Judaism.

44. R. Yehoshua b. Hananya is famous for these dialogues, and the emperor very often is Hadrian; see Moshe David Herr, "The Historical Significance of the Dialogues between Jewish Sages and Roman Dignitaries," *Scripta Hierosolymitana* 22, 1971, pp. 123–150 (which is still useful, despite its rather positivistic tendency).

45. b Bekh 8b.

46. Mt. 5:13.

47. This has been suggested already by Moritz Güdemann, *Religionsgeschichtliche Studien*, Leipzig: Oskar Leiner, 1876, pp. 89ff., 136ff.; and Paul Billerbeck, "Altjüdische Religionsgespräche," *Nathanael* 25, 1909, pp. 13–30, 33–50, 66–80 (p. 68); see also Hermann L. Strack and Paul Billerbeck, *Kommentar zum Neuen Testament aus Talmud und Midrasch*, vol. 1: *Das Evangelium nach Matthäus*, Munich: Beck, 1922, p. 236. Maier even did not consider the stories worthy of being included in his *Jesus von Nazareth*. However, he does dis-

cuss them briefly in its sequel, *Jüdische Auseinandersetzung mit dem Christentum in der Antike*, pp. 116–118 (of course, to reject any connection with the New Testament, let alone with Jesus).

Chapter 2
The Son/Disciple Who Turned out Badly

1. I follow again the Munich manuscript with variant readings from other manuscripts where necessary.

2. The word "doubtful" is missing in Ms. Munich but can be added according to most of the other manuscripts and printed editions.

3. In a state in which it is doubtful whether she is menstruating or not.

4. The reference to "Jesus the Nazarene" is in all the manuscripts and printed editions that I could check (see the chart below, p. 135).

5. Either still by Rav Hisda or anonymous.

6. b Ber 34a; Er 53b.

7. b Bes 29a.

8. The latter is Maier's interpretation (*Jesus von Nazareth*, p. 65) on the basis that *davar* means also "word." This meaning may play a role here, but Maier overemphasizes it.

9. Abba is the real name of Rav.

10. b Ber 62a; cf. b Hag 5b.

11. A much simpler explanation of the phrase would be that the son spoils his food in the sense that he disregards the education received from his parents and accordingly that the disciple spoils his food in the sense that he disregards the teaching received from his teachers. But the strong sexual connotation of "food/dish" in the Bavli makes this easy way out not very likely.

12. See also John 11:2, 12:1–8 (Mary of Bethany). The identification is first mentioned in Ephraim the Syrian's bible commentary (373 C.E.) and was endorsed by Pope Gregory the Great in the sixth century C.E., who furthermore identifies the two Marys with Mary of Bethany (John 12:1–8); see Karen King, *The Gospel of Mary of Magdala: Jesus and the First Woman Apostle*, Santa Rosa, CA: Polebridge, 2003, pp. 151f.

13. Dan Brown, *The Da Vinci Code*, New York: Doubleday, 2003.

14. "The Gospel of Mary (BG 8502,*1*)," trans. G. W. MacRae and R. McL. Wilson, ed. D. M. Parrott, in *The Nag Hammadi Library in English*, ed. James M. Robinson, San Francisco: Harper, 1990, p. 525 (BG 7, 10:1–3); King, *Gospel of Mary of Magdala*, p. 15 (6:1).

15. "The Gospel of Philip (II,3)," introd. and trans. Wesley W. Isenberg, in *Nag Hammadi Library*, p. 145 (II 59, 9).

16. Ibid., p. 148 (II 63, 35).

17. Cf. ibid., p. 145 (II 59, 1–4).

18. See King, *Gospel of Mary of Magdala*, p. 146: "Kissing here apparently refers to the intimate reception of spiritual teaching."

19. I am aware that the terms "gnosis" and "gnostic" have fallen out of favor in recent scholarship. When I use them, I do not intend to make a statement about some kind of unified "gnostic religion" or "worldview" as opposed to other "religions" and "worldviews"; rather, I want to set up a certain (more or less well defined) body of literature against other bodies of literature, such as "New Testament" or "rabbinic literature."

20. Here *alluf* is understood as "scholar," hence "our scholars are well loaded" (with your teachings).

21. Derives *mesubbalim* from *saval* "suffer."

22. "Like Jesus the Nazarene" in Mss. Oxford Opp. Add. 23 (366) and Paris Heb. 671. In Mss. Munich 95 and Firenze II.1.7, after "in public" follows an erased passage that may have contained the words "like Jesus the Nazarene." In the Soncino and Vilna printed editions, the text has been tampered with by the censor (see the chart below, pp. 135f.).

23. Maier's treatment of this passage (*Jesus von Nazareth*, pp. 64ff.) is a good example of how his most detailed literary analysis misses the major point of the story: he explains Jesus away as a late addition but does not ask himself *why* he is included/added here.

24. m Sanh 10:2.

25. This heading is missing in the important Kaufmann manuscript of m Sanh 10:1 and was obviously later added.

26. "In the Torah" is missing in many manuscripts, among them the Kaufmann manuscript.

27. The proverbial heretic.

28. Noncanonical books.

29. The tetragrammaton YHWH.

30. Sifre Deuteronomy, 357:10 (ed. Finkelstein, p. 430); Seder Eliyahu Zuta, ed. Friedmann, p. 191; b BB 15b; BamR 20:1; Tanhuma, Balaq 1.

31. Targumim (Codex Neofiti, Fragment-Targums, Pseudo-Jonathan) on Num. 24:25; y Sanh 10:2/25–29, fol. 28d; b Sanh 106a; Sifre Numbers, 131 (ed. Horovitz, pp. 170f.). See on Balaam, Peter Schäfer, "Bileam II. Judentum," in *TRE* 6, 1980, pp. 639f.

32. The same problem should apply, however, to Doeg as well because he is an Edomite.

Chapter 3
The Frivolous Disciple

1. b Sanh 107b and b Sot 47a. I follow the version in Sanhedrin and refer to the variant readings in the manuscripts.

2. b Sanh: Yehoshua b. Perahya/Jesus are preserved in Mss. Yad ha-Rav Herzog 1, Firenze II.1.8–9 and in the Vilna printed edition; Ms Munich 95 erases "Jesus the Nazarene" (*le-Yeshu* is still faintly visible). b Sot: Yehoshua b. Perahya/Jesus are preserved in Mss. Oxford Heb. d. 20 (2675), Vatican 110, and this time also Munich 95, whereas the Vilna printed edition reads: "and not as Yehoshua b. Perahya, who pushed one of his disciples away with both hands."

3. b Sot adds: "Shimon b. Shetah was hidden by his sister" (who happened to be, according to rabbinic tradition, king Yannai's wife).

4. Vilna printed edition: "and Jesus."

5. "Jesus (the Nazarene)" in Mss. Yad ha-Rav Herzog 1 (b Sanh) and Oxford Heb. d. 20 (2675) (b Sot).

6. Or "bleared, dripping" (*terutot*); cf. Jastrow, *Dictionary*, s.v. "tarut."

7. Mss. Munich 95 (Sanh 107b), Vatican 110, and the Vilna printed edition (Sot 47a) have only "He [the disciple]."

8. For a detailed analysis of the story and its Christian parallels, see Stephen Gero, "The Stern Master and His Wayward Disciple: A 'Jesus' Story in the Talmud and in Christian Hagiography," *JSJ* 25, 1994, pp. 287–311; also the brief treatment in Daniel Boyarin, *Dying for God: Martyrdom and the Making of Christianity and Judaism*, Stanford, CA: Stanford University Press, 1999, pp. 23–26.

9. See my *The History of the Jews in the Greco-Roman World*, London and New York: Routledge, 2003, p. 75 (with references).

10. m Avot, ch. 1.

11. A possible motif for connecting him with Alexandria might be a halakhic statement attributed to him, namely that wheat coming from Alexandria was impure because of the watering device used by the Alexandrians (t Makh 3:4). On his connection with magic, see below.

12. y Hag 2:2/3 and 4, fol. 77d; y Sanh 6:9/1, fol. 23c.

13. For an attempt to explain the message from Shimon b. Shetah to Yehoshua b. Perahya/Yehuda b. Tabbai historically, see my article "'From Jerusalem the Great to Alexandria the Small': The Relationship between Palestine and Egypt in the Graeco-Roman Period," in *The Talmud Yerushalmi and Graeco-Roman Culture*, vol. 1, ed. Peter Schäfer, Tübingen: Mohr Siebeck, 1998, pp. 129–140.

14. For the slightly different version in the Yerushalmi see ibid., pp. 130ff.

15. The Aramaic word used here, *akhsanya*, can mean both "inn" and "innkeeper."

16. In the Yerushalmi version, the student's thoughts are worsened by the fact that he makes the master an accomplice of his risqué remark.

17. The master wanted him to wait because he could not interrupt the Shema prayer.

18. See Schäfer, "From Jerusalem the Great to Alexandria the Small," p. 130, n. 11.

19. This is what Maier, *Jesus von Nazareth*, constantly confuses.

20. Richard Kalmin emphasizes the Bavli's tendency to portray Jesus as a rabbi (see "Christians and Heretics in Rabbinic Literature of Late Antiquity," *HTR* 87, 1994, pp. 156f.). This is true, but the teacher-student relationship is already present in the Yerushalmi version of our story (without, however, identifying the disciple with Jesus). The most "rabbinic" Jesus is the one in t Hul/QohR/b AZ (below ch. 4), but here, too, does the portrayal of Jesus as a Torah teacher belong to the Palestinian stratum of the story (QohR).

21. Meticulously listed by Maier, *Jesus von Nazareth*, p. 123.

22. Whatever the exact nature of this worship was (it may even be a literary motif rather than a real custom). However, that brick worship is a distinctively Babylonian motif/custom becomes clear from the fact that the (originally Palestinian) discussion whether or not an egg that has been worshipped may subsequently be consumed by a Jew is expanded in the Bavli (AZ 46a) by a brick: if a

Jew has set up a brick in order to worship it (but in the end did not carry out this abhorrent deed) and then an idolater comes and does carry it out—is this brick permitted for subsequent use by a Jew (e.g., building)?

23. See Joseph Naveh and Shaul Shaked, *Amulets and Magic Bowls: Aramaic Incantations of Late Antiquity*, Jerusalem: Magnes; Leiden: Brill, 1985, pp. 17f. On the practice of magic in general see Michael G. Morony, "Magic and Society in Late Sasanian Iraq," in *Prayer, Magic, and the Stars in the Ancient and Late Antique World*, ed. Scott Noegel, Joel Walker, and Brannon Wheeler, University Park: Pennsylvania State University Press, 2003, pp. 83–107.

24. James A. Montgomery, *Aramaic Incantation Texts from Nippur*, Philadelphia: University Museum, 1913, nos. 8 (1. 6, 8), 9 (1. 2f.), 17 (1. 8, 10), 32 (1. 4), and 33 (1. 3), pp. 154f., 161, 190, 225 (with Montgomery's commentary on pp. 226–228), and 230; Naveh and Shaked, *Amulets and Magic Bowls*, Bowl 5, pp. 158–163; Shaul Shaked, "The Poetics of Spells: Language and Structure in Aramaic Incantations of Late Antiquity 1; The Divorce Formula and Its Ramifications," in *Mesopotamian Magic: Textual, Historical, and Interpretive Perspectives*, ed. Tzvi Abusch and Karel van der Toorn, Groningen: Styx, 1999, pp. 173–195; Dan Levene, *A Corpus of Magic Bowls: Incantation Texts in Jewish Aramaic from Late Antiquity*, London: Kegan Paul, 2003, pp. 31–39 (Bowls M50 and M59).

25. Samuel Krauss, *Das Leben Jesu nach jüdischen Quellen*, Berlin: S. Calvary, 1902, pp. 185f.; Louis Ginzberg, *Ginze Schechter: Genizah Studies in Memory of Doctor Solomon Schechter*, vol. 1: *Midrash and Haggadah*, New York: Jewish Theological Seminary of America, 1928 (reprint, New York: Hermon, 1969), p. 329; William Horbury, "The Trial of Jesus in Jewish Tradition," in *The Trial of Jesus: Cambridge Studies in Honour of C.F.D. Moule*, ed. Ernst Bammel, London: SCM, 1970, pp. 104f.; Maier, *Jesus von Nazareth*, p. 295, n. 291; Ze'ev Falk, "Qeta' hadash mi-'Toledot Yeshu,'" *Tarbiz* 46, 1978, p. 319; Daniel Boyarin, "Qeriah metuqqenet shel ha-qeta' he-hadash shel 'Toledot Yeshu,'" *Tarbiz* 47, 1978, p. 250.

26. Montgomery, *Aramaic Incantation Texts*, bowl 34 (1. 2), p. 23: *Yeshua' asya*—"Jesus the healer."

27. Dan Levene, "'. . . and by the name of Jesus . . .': An Unpublished Magic Bowl in Jewish Aramaic," *JSQ* 6, 1999, pp. 283–308.

28. See below, ch. 9.

29. The translation follows the *editio princeps* of the bowl provided by Levene, "and by the name of Jesus," p. 287 (text) and p. 290 (translation).

30. See on this Levene, "and by the Name of Jesus," p. 301 (he suggests that this spelling, with an initial Aleph, "possibly represents a transcription of the Christian Syriac form not as it is spelled . . . but as it is pronounced").

31. The plural "holy spirits" is most likely a misunderstanding on part of the (Jewish) writer of the bowl, as has been observed also by Shaul Shaked: "Jesus in the Magic Bowls: Apropos Dan Levene's '. . . and by the name of Jesus . . .'," *JSQ* 6, 1999, p. 314.

32. The bowl, however, is not the only bowl text written in Jewish Babylonian Aramaic that makes an explicit allusion to Jesus, as Shaked claims (ibid., p. 309); the first bowl mentioning Jesus is the one published by Montgomery (above, n. 26).

33. Shaked, "Jesus in the Magic Bowls," p. 315.

34. The connection with magic has also been emphasized by Elchanan Reiner: "From Joshua to Jesus: The Transformation of a Biblical Story to a Local Myth; A Chapter in the Religious Life of the Galilean Jew," in *Sharing the Sacred: Religious Contacts and Conflicts in the Holy Land, First-Fifteenth Centuries CE*, ed. Arieh Kofsky and Guy G. Stroumsa, Jerusalem: Yad Izhak Ben Zvi, 1998, pp. 258–260.

Chapter 4

The Torah Teacher

1. See also Lk. 21:37; Mt. 26:55; Mk. 14:49; John 7:14–16, 18:20.

2. t Hul 2:24; QohR 1:24 on Eccl. 1:8 (1:8 [3]).

3. Also in the sense of "trustworthy," "right."

4. Or "right."

5. The Bavli and all the parallels use here the Latin word in Hebrew characters (*dimus*).

6. This is the reading in t Hul (*matzati*, lit. "I found"); QohR has "and . . . came to me"; the Talmud manuscripts: "one of the disciples of . . . found me (*metza'ani*)."

7. The explicit reference to Jesus in Mss. Munich 95, Paris Suppl. Heb. 1337, and JTS Rab. 15.

8. Or "Sikhnaya."

9. t Hul: "He told me a word of heresy (*minut*) in the name of Jesus ben Pantiri/Pandera" (the following exegesis of Deut. 23:19 and Mic. 1:7 is missing in

t Hul); QohR: "He told me something (lit. a certain word) in the name of So-and-So" (however, some manuscripts and printed editions of QohR read "in the name of Jesus ben Pandera": see Maier, *Jesus von Nazareth*, p. 296, n. 305, and the chart below, pp. 137f.).

10. Mss. Munich 95 and Paris Suppl. Heb. 1337; Ms. JTS Rab. 15: "thus taught him Jesus his Master."

11. Reading *qubbtzsah* instead of *qibbatzsah*.

12. The money, in the Hebrew plural.

13. QohR has only "heresy."

14. QohR: "prostitution" (*zenut*).

15. On Eliezer b. Hyrkanos, see Jacob Neusner, *Eliezer Ben Hyrkanus: The Tradition and the Man*, 2 vols., Leiden: Brill, 1973. For Neusner's analysis of our story see vol. 1, pp. 400–403, and vol. 2, pp. 366f.; Neusner is certain that Eliezer "cannot have been a *min*," although "it seems difficult to say whether the account before us reports something which actually happened" (vol. 2, p. 367).

16. In all the three versions; only t Hullin leaves out "idle."

17. This is Neusner's translation in *The Tosefta Translated from the Hebrew, Fifth Division: Qodoshim (The Order of Holy Things)*, New York: Ktav, 1979, p. 74, and, almost identical, in *Eliezer Ben Hyrkanus*, vol. 1, p. 400; see also Saul Lieberman, "Roman Legal Institutions in Early Rabbinics and in the Acta Martyrorum," *JQR*, n.s., 35, 1944/45, pp. 20f.

18. The version in QohR does not help, either, because it reads: "Is it possible that these rabbinic schools (*yeshivot hallalu*) should err in such matters?" (Lieberman, p. 20, n. 129, finds in QohR the corrupt word *šyšyšbwt*, which he emends to *she-ševot*, but the emendation *she-yeshivot*, as in fact the printed edition reads, is much more plausible). It is, of course, possible that R. Eliezer's colleagues bribed the governor and that he uses R. Eliezer's grey hair = old age and sign of wisdom as an "excuse" for his acquittal, but such an explanation is not very convincing. Richard Kalmin (in a written remark on my manuscript) and one of the anonymous readers draw my attention to the fact that the missing letter in *šhsybw*[t] is not so strange for the Tosefta or for Hebrew manuscripts altogether. This is certainly correct, but still, why no indication of an abbreviation (*šhsybw'*) and why such a crucial letter in a crucial phrase? Also, the "grey hair" is clearly influenced by the translation of *zaqen* as "old man," but this is not imperative. As Solomon Zeitlin reminds us ("Jesus in the Early Tannaitic Literature," in *Abhandlungen zur Erinnerung an Hirsch Perez Chajes*, Wien: Alexander

Kohut Memorial Foundation, 1933, p. 298), *zaqen* can also mean "scholar, sage" and does not necessarily refer to old age and grey hair.

19. Maier, *Jesus von Nazareth*, pp. 152–154. Maier does not understand the first part as a question but rather as a statement, but the meaning is the same. The weakness of this interpretation, as Richard Kalmin rightly points out, is that the governor suddenly refers not just to R. Eliezer but to a whole group of suspects and that it remains open why the accusers were mistaken. One could respond that it was only R. Eliezer who was caught or that the governor wanted to make an example of (the old and respected) R. Eliezer—and that the Tosefta did not intend anyway to give a record of the court's proceedings.

20. Justin, *Dialogue with Trypho*, 10:1; Tertullian, *Apology*, 7 and 8; (see below, pp. 99ff.). That the accusation of sexual promiscuity as a prominent feature of Christians/Jewish Christians was well known also in rabbinic literature becomes evident from a story about R. Yonathan, a Palestinian amora of the first generation, in QohR 1:25 on Eccl. 1:8 (1:8 [4]), immediately following our story about R. Eliezer (translation according to Visotzky, *Fathers of the World*, p. 80, which is based on the critical edition of Marc G. Hirshman: "One of R. Yonathan's students fled to them [the Jewish Christians?]. He went and found that he had [indeed] become one of those evil ones. The heretics sent [a message to R. Yonathan]: Rabbi, come share in deeds of loving-kindness for a bride. He went and found them occupied [sexually] with a young woman. He exclaimed: This is the way Jews behave?! They replied: Is it not written in the Torah: Throw in your lot among us, we will have one purse (Prov. 1:14)? He fled and they hurried after him until he got to the door of his house and slammed it in their faces. They taunted him: R. Yonathan, go boast to your mother that you did not turn and you did not look at us. For had you turned and looked at us, you'd be chasing after us more than we have chased after you."

21. QohR 1:24 on Eccl. 1:8 (1:8 [3]).

22. Presumably a metaphor for a male prostitute.

23. The Soncino translation suggests that the Halakha not to listen to the words of a *min* escaped him, but it is much more likely that R. Eliezer refers to the Halakha regarding income gained from prostitution.

24. In the biblical context, Temple prostitution, but here used in the wider context of money gained from any (female and male) prostitution.

25. It concludes, however, the unit with Eliezer's own dictum: "One should always flee from what is ugly (*ki'ur*) and from whatever appears to be ugly." The

"ugly" he refers to presumably has to do with sexual uncleanness; see Maier, *Jesus von Nazareth*, p. 158.

26. The Bavli interpretation is more complex: it first relates the first part of the verse to heresy and the second part to the Roman authority, and in a second (anonymous) interpretation relates the first part to heresy *and* the Roman authority and the second part to prostitution.

27. Or, rather, the anonymous interpretation has R. Eliezer admit.

28. See the exhaustive references in Maier, *Jesus von Nazareth*, p. 159, n. 327.

29. See Herford, *Christianity*, pp. 137ff. (around 109 C.E.); Rudolf Freudenberger, "Die *delatio nominis causa* gegen Rabbi Elieser ben Hyrkanos," in *Revue internationale des droits de l'antiquité*, 3rd ser., 15, 1968, pp. 11–19; Boyarin is convinced, with no further discussion, that it was part of the Trajanic persecutions of Christianity (*Dying for God*, p. 26), obviously following Lieberman, "Roman Legal Institutions," p. 21.

30. *Jesus von Nazareth*, p. 163; see also Boyarin, *Dying for God*, p. 31.

31. Maier, *Jesus von Nazareth*, p. 165.

32. Boyarin, *Dying for God*, p. 27 with n. 22.

33. Ibid., p. 27.

34. Ibid., p. 32.

35. Ibid., p. 31

36. However, to implement this approach is not an easy task. Even in Boyarin's presentation, there appears a conspicuous gap between the intention and the implementation: his interpretation quite often reads like the paragon of a positivistic reconstruction of reality and one wonders whether he sometimes simply forgets his methodologically correct intentions.

37. About the important distinction between Palestinian and Babylonian sources see below, pp. 113ff.

38. Interestingly enough, the same R. Hisda who concludes our story (in the Bavli and in QohR) with the ironical statement that one has to stay away four cubits from the harlot, plays a prominant role in a number of the Bavli's Jesus narratives.

39. See below, pp. 99ff.

40. In his unpublished lectures.

41. Alexander Guttmann, "The Significance of Miracles for Talmudic Judaism," *HUCA* 20, 1947, pp. 374ff.; idem, *Studies in Rabbinic Judaism*, New York: Ktav, 1976, pp. 58ff.

42. b BM 59b.

43. Another magical performance by R. Eliezer is preserved in b Sanh 68a. There, upon the request of his colleague R. Aqiva to teach him the art of the magical planting of cucumbers, Eliezer has a field covered with cucumbers by one magical word, and the cucumbers collected into one heap by another.

44. The prooftext used by R. Yirmeya is anything but convincing: in its original biblical context it just says the opposite.

45. Lit. "they blessed him," a euphemism for "excommunicated him."

46. Aqiva appeared before him dressed in the black garments of the mourner (this was his "discreet" hint at what had happened).

47. b BM 59b.

48. b Sanh 68a.

Chapter 5
Healing in the Name of Jesus

1. See above, p. 32.

2. t Shab 7:23 (following Ms. Erfurt in the Zuckermandel edition; Ms. Vienna reads "they pass [a remedy] over the belly (*me'ayin*)."

3. y Shab 14:3/5, fol. 14c; b Sanh 101a (as a Baraita).

4. Soncino translation; Rashi even assures his readers that such a charm over the snakes does not imply hunting which, of course, is forbidden on Sabbath.

5. Soncino translation.

6. Or, with the addition "in the Torah," that the belief in resurrection is not mentioned in the Torah.

7. Lit. "according to its letters" = one who pronounces the tetragrammaton.

8. This is how the later editor who added the programmatic heading "*All* of Israel have a share in the world to come" (which is missing in the best manuscripts; emphasis added) obviously understood the Mishna's list of those who have no share in the world to come: they are heretics and *therefore* do not belong to Israel. All of those who do belong to Israel (*kelal Yisrael*) have a share in the world to come. On this Mishna see Israel Yuval, "All Israel Have a Portion in the World to Come" (in preparation).

9. The parallel in b AZ 27b introduces the story as follows: "No man should have any dealings with *heretics,* nor is it allowed to be healed by them even [in risking] an hour's life" (emphasis added).

10. This may refer to Aqiva's noncanonical books in the Mishna.

11. Interestingly enough, the Mishna (AZ 2:2) not only distinguishes between healing of property (permitted) and of individuals (prohibited); it also speaks unambiguously about non-Jews (*goyim*) and not about heretics (*minim*).

12. Parallels y AZ 2:2/12, fol. 40d–41a; y Shab 14:4/13, fol. 14d–15a; QohR 1:24 on Eccl. 1:8 (1:8 [3]); b AZ 27b.

13. In QohR and the Bavli he is the son of R. Ishmael's sister.

14. QohR and Bavli: Kefar Sekhaniah/Sikhnaya, as in the first Jacob story (see above). The "Kefar Sama" version is not only a pun with "Eleazar b. Dama," but also with *sam/samma* — literally "medicine" or "poison."

15. y Shab: "and Jacob . . . came in the name of Jesus Pandera to heal him"; y AZ: "and Jacob . . . came to heal him. He [Jacob] said to him: We will speak to you in the name of Jesus son of Pandera" (QohR has also Pandera); the explicit reference to Jesus is missing in the Bavli (in all the manuscripts that I could check), but in Ms. Munich 95, Jacob is called "Jacob the heretic (*min*) from Kefar Sekhaniah/Sikhnaya." Jacob Neusner (*The Talmud of the Land of Israel: An Academic Commentary to the Second, Third, and Fourth Divisions,* vol. 26: *Yerushalmi Tractate Abodah Zarah,* Atlanta, GA: Scholars Press, 1999, p. 50) tacitly omits the reference to Jesus. One may only speculate why: most likely because it is not in some of the traditional editions of the Yerushalmi, and Neusner did not bother to check the Leiden manuscript and the *editio princeps* where it does appear. To make things worse, Neusner claims to have checked his translation against the German translation by Gerd Wewers and to have found only minor differences (ibid., p. xv). In fact, however, Wewers was fully aware of all the variants in the available manuscripts and the *editio princeps* and translates according to Leiden and the *editio princeps*; see Gerd A. Wewers, *Avoda Zara. Götzendienst,* Tübingen: J.C.B. Mohr (Paul Siebeck), 1980, p. 49.

16. Or "But R. Ishmael did not allow him (Eleazar b. Dama) [to accept the healing]."

17. y AZ and QohR: "He [R. Ishmael] said to him. . . ."

18. In the Bavli the following sentence is preceded by: "R. Ishmael, my brother, let him, so that I may be healed by him!"

19. QohR and Bavli: "from the Torah."

20. QohR and Bavli: "that he is to be permitted."

21. Bavli: "before his soul departed and he died."

22. Bavli: "for your body [remained] pure and your soul left you in purity."

23. A play on words with *gezerah* (decree, prohibition) and *geder* (hedge/fence).

24. b Ber 56b; b Men 99b.

25. t Shevu 3:4.

26. b Ber 56b; b Shab 116a.

27. b Men 99b.

28. Same answer in QohR.

29. b AZ 27b.

30. This last sentence with the quotation from Leviticus appears also in the Yerushalmi version.

31. Hence it seems that the Bavli, in contrast to the Yerushalmi, identifies the flesh-and-blood snake by which Eleazar b. Dama was bitten with the rabbis. According to the Yerushalmi, Eleazar b. Dama was *not* bitten by the metaphorical snake of the rabbis (which punishes the transgression of their commandments), but according to the Bavli the real snake that bit him *is* the metaphorical snake of the rabbis (because they prevented him from being cured).

32. And probably also the Yerushalmi's.

33. That in a next step another (or even the same) Bavli editor harmonizes this conclusion with R. Ishmael's strict approach (Ishmael would have allowed the heretic's healing only in private but not in public) does not detract from the boldness of his argument.

34. Maier, *Jesus von Nazareth*, pp. 188, 191.

35. Origen, *Contra Celsum* I:28; see above, p. 19.

36. PGM VIII, 35–50, in Betz, *Greek Magical Papyri*, p. 146.

37. "Iao" is the Greek form of Hebrew "Yaho." On the name see R. Ganschinietz, "Iao," in *Paulys Real-Encyclopädie der Classischen Altertumswissenschaft*, Neue Bearbeitung, begonnen von Georg Wissowa, . . . hrsg. v. Wilhelm Kroll, Siebzehnter Halbband, Stuttgart: Metzler, 1914, cols. 698–721.

38. See Hugo Odeberg, *3 Enoch; or, The Hebrew Book of Enoch*, Cambridge: Cambridge University Press, 1928 (reprint, New York: Ktav, 1973), pp. 188–192 (with parallels from the gnostic literature).

39. PGM XIII, 795–800, in Betz, *Greek Magical Papyri*, p. 191.

40. Peter Schäfer, ed., *Synopse zur Hekhalot-Literatur*, Tübingen: J.C.B. Mohr (Paul Siebeck), 1981, § 15 and parallels; also in b Sanh 38b.

41. The full biblical context reads: "I am going to send an angel in front of you, to guard you on the way and to bring you to the place that I have prepared. Be attentive to him and listen to his voice. Do not rebel against him, for he will not pardon your transgression, since my name is in him" (Ex. 23:20f.).

42. See the summary in Philip Alexander, "3 (Hebrew Apocalypse of) Enoch," in *OTP*, vol. 1, p. 243.

43. In *Synopse zur Hekhalot-Literatur*, § 76, Yahoel is the first of the seventy names of Metatron.

44. Ryszard Rubinkiewicz, "Apocalypse of Abraham," in *OTP*, vol. 1, p. 682.

45. Apocalypse of Abraham 10:8 (see also 10:3); translation by Rubinkiewicz in *OTP*, vol. 1, pp. 693f.

46. This has been suggested already by Gershom Scholem, *Major Trends in Jewish Mysticism*, New York: Schocken, 1961 (reprint, 1995), p. 68; and see Philip Alexander, "The Historical Setting of the Hebrew Book of Enoch," *JJS* 28, 1977, p. 161; idem, "3 (Hebrew Apocalypse of) Enoch," p. 244.

47. Cf. Ganschinietz, "Iao," cols. 709–713; Johann Michl, "Engel II (jüdisch)," in *RAC*, vol. 5, Stuttgart: Hiersemann, 1962, col. 215, n. 102.

48. *Ant.* 2, 276.

49. Cf. m Yoma 6:2 (where, however, the priests and the people in the Temple court could hear him pronouncing the name); m Sot 7:6 (according to which the priests in the Temple, when reciting the priestly blessing, did pronounce the name). See on the rabbinic evidence Ephraim E. Urbach, *The Sages: Their Concepts and Beliefs*, Jerusalem: Magnes, 1979, vol. 1, pp. 127–129.

50. PGM XIII, 840–845, in Betz, *Greek Magical Papyri*, p. 191.

51. Auguste Audollent, *Defixionum tabellae*, Luteciae Parisiorum: A. Fontemoing, 1904, no. 271/19 (p. 374). See also Papyrus Berol. 9794, in *Abrasax. Ausgewählte Papyri religiösen und magischen Inhalts*, vol. 2, ed. Reinold Merkelbach and Maria Totti, Opladen: Westdeutscher Verlag, 1991, pp. 124–125, no. 13.

52. Healing in the name of Jesus is a common early Christian custom; see Acts 3:6, 16; 4:7, 10, 30; cf. Rom. 10:13. According to Acts 19:13 "some itinerant Jewish exorcists tried to use the name of the Lord Jesus over those who had evil spirits," but the evil spirit responded "Jesus I know, and Paul I know; but who are you?" (19:15).

53. Mk. 9:38–40; see also Lk. 9:49–50.

54. As in Mk. 3:15.

55. Morton Smith, *Jesus the Magician*, pp. 114f.

56. y AZ 2:2/7, fol. 40d; y Shab 14:4/8, fol. 14d; QohR 10:5. I follow y AZ and refer to the important variants in the notes.

57. y Shab: "a man" (bar nash).

58. The name of Jesus is deleted in the Leiden manuscript and added again by the second glossator; QohR: "he went and brought one of those from the son of Pandera to relieve his choking." Neusner, in his Yerushalmi translation, again omits Jesus.

59. The successful healing is not explicitly mentioned in QohR but presupposed.

60. Read (with y Shab) millat instead of le-millat. QohR: "such and such verses" or "one verse after another."

61. y Shab: "it would have been better for him. . . ."

62. QohR: "better that he had been buried and you had not quoted this verse over him."

63. Richard Kalmin (commenting on my manuscript; but see also his "Christians and Heretics," p. 162) draws my attention to an even more devastating reading: the "error committed by a ruler" is not the error resulting from the heretic's magic (the healing) but rather the grandfather's error. R. Yehoshua's rash and furious statement "How much (better) would it have been for him if he had died" came true, although he did not (fully) intend this terrible result. Hence, the heretic's magic did work, but the grandfather undid (or rather outdid) it! According to this interpretation R. Yehoshua b. Levi was not one bit better than R. Ishmael in the Eleazar b. Dama story.

64. Maier, Jesus von Nazareth, p. 195.

65. Or, if the shegaga refers to R. Yehoshua's ultimately granted wish that the grandson is better off dying: the rabbi's wish can even undo powerful, yet unauthorized, magic.

66. We may even see here another allusion to and inversion of a New Testament narrative. When Peter acknowledges Jesus as the Messiah, Jesus responds with his famous statement: "And I tell you, you are Peter (Petros), and on this rock (petra) I will build my Church, and the gates of Hades will not prevail against it. I will give you the keys of the kingdom of heaven, and whatever you bind on earth will be bound in heaven, and whatever you loose on earth will be loosed in heaven" (Mt. 16:18f.; see also Mt. 23:14, where the scribes and Pharisees are accused of locking people out of the kingdom of heaven). Binding and loosing are not only technical terms referring to the rabbinic authority of forbid-

ding and permitting in halakhic matters; they are also technical terms used in magical texts and expressing magical powers. See the magical use of the verbs *asar* ("to bind with a spell") and *sherei* ("to release from a spell") in Sokoloff, *Dictionary of Jewish Babylonian Aramaic*, pp. 150f., 1179; idem, *A Dictionary of Jewish Palestinian Aramaic of the Byzantine Period*, Ramat-Gan: Bar Ilan University Press, 1990, pp. 68, 567; Giuseppe Veltri, *Magie und Halakha. Ansätze zu einem empirischen Wissenschaftsbegriff im spätantiken und frühmittelalterlichen Judentum*, Tübingen: J.C.B. Mohr (Paul Siebeck), 1997, pp. 32, 78, 123. See also Smith, *Jesus the Magician*, p. 114.

Chapter 6

Jesus' Execution

1. Hanging as an actual mode of execution is regarded in the Bible as a non-Jewish law (Gen. 4:22; Josh. 8:29; 2 Sam. 21:6–12; Ezra 6:11; Esth. 7:9). On the death penalty, see Haim Cohn, *The Trial and Death of Jesus*, New York: Harper and Row, 1971, pp. 211–217, and the summary in Haim Hermann Cohn and Louis Isaac Rabinowitz, "Capital Punishment," in *EJ*, 1971, vol. 5, cols. 142–147.

2. m Sanh 7:1: stoning (*seqilah*), burning (*śerefah*), slaying (*hereg*), and strangling (*heneq*).

3. Paul Winter in his classic *On the Trial of Jesus* (Berlin: de Gruyter, 1961, pp. 70–74) suggests, rather unconvincingly, that the death penalty of strangling was introduced by the rabbis in order to secretly exercise jurisdiction even in capital cases, although they were deprived of this authority after 70 C.E.

4. m Sanh 6:1.

5. b Sanh 43a. I follow the Firenze (II.1.8–9) manuscript with reference to the other available manuscripts.

6. Or (a different interpretation): "On such and such a day, on such and such an hour, and in such and such a place (the criminal will be executed)," announcing the precise time of the execution.

7. This is the Mishna lemma, which is commented upon in the following.

8. Literally before him, on his way to the execution.

9. Chronologically, sometime before the execution.

10. Only in Ms. Firenze.

11. The name is erased in Ms. Munich.

12. Lit. "they hanged him."

13. The name is erased in Ms. Munich.

14. Again only in Ms. Firenze.

15. The name is again erased in Ms. Munich.

16. Same.

17. If we understand Abaye's comment as the herald referring to the precise time of the execution, he contradicts the following interpretation of the Mishna lemma ("not beforehand"), which is certainly possible but does not go well with the structure of the sugya: Abaje would agree with the Baraita, which contradicts the anonymous interpretation of the Mishna lemma.

18. I owe this clarification to a remark by Richard Kalmin.

19. This has also been argued by Maier, *Jesus von Nazareth*, p. 223.

20. m Sanh 6:4; see also Sifre Deuteronomy, 221 (ed. Finkelstein, pp. 253–255). On m Sanh 6 see now Beth A. Berkowitz, *Execution and Invention: Death Penalty Discourse in Early Rabbinic and Christian Cultures*, Oxford: Oxford University Press, 2006, pp. 65–94.

21. That the hanging is performed on a tree is evident from Deut. 21:22f.; on the Mishna's interpretation of "tree," see the following discussion.

22. Lit. "blessed" (a euphemism for "cursed").

23. The name of God.

24. It can also mean (literally): "a curse of God."

25. In conspicuously leaving out the stoning and mentioning only the hanging, the Talmud is obviously influenced by the New Testament narrative and identifies hanging with "hanging on the tree = cross" = being crucified.

26. m Sanh 7:4.

27. m Sanh 7:10.

28. Ibid., end of the Mishna; see also ibid., 10:4.

29. m Sanh 7:11.

30. For a summary of the Gospels' accounts of Jesus' trial (neatly distinguishing between primary and secondary traditions and editorial accretions), see Winter, *Trial of Jesus*, pp. 136–148; much more thorough is Raymond E. Brown, *The Death of the Messiah: From Gethsemane to the Grave; A Commentary on the Passion Narratives in the Four Gospels*, 2 vols., New York: Doubleday, 1994. For a critique of what he calls "critical ignorance" of some of recent New Testament scholarship, see Martin Hengel, *Studies in Early Christology*, Edinburgh: T&T Clark, 1995, pp. 41–58. Much as these analyses may (or may not) contribute to

our understanding of the historical event, this is *not* my concern here: I am concerned with the (possible) *talmudic reading* of the Gospels, not with the historical reality. Also, Winter's brief analysis of our talmudic Baraita (p. 144) is solely interested in the narrowly defined question of its historicity and, of course, proves its "unhistorical character."

31. m Sanh 6:4 and 7:4.

32. Mt. 26:62–65; Mk. 14:61–64; Lk. 22:66–71; John 19:7.

33. Mt. 27:17, 22, 29, 37, 39–43; Mk. 15:2, 12, 18, 26, 32; Lk. 23:2–5, 35, 37, 39; John 18:33, 37; 19:3, 12, 14f., 19, 21.

34. Mt. 26:61; Mk. 14:58.

35. Mt. 12:23f. (Mk. 3:22; Lk. 11:15).

36. See above, p. 19.

37. Maier, *Jesus von Nazareth*, p. 227. On this, see the critique by Horbury, *Jews and Christians*, p. 104.

38. m Sanh 4 and 5. To avoid a misunderstanding: I am not suggesting here (and with similar phrases) that the Gospels are based on the Mishna. Rather, I am arguing that the Halakha presupposed here in the Gospels is similar to the Halakha (later) codified in the Mishna.

39. Mt. 26:59; Mk. 14:55.

40. Explicitly only in Mark.

41. The concurrent testimony only in Matthew (26:60); Mark insists that even here the two witnesses did not agree on the circumstances of the crime (14:59).

42. "I am" (Mk. 14:62).

43. "You have said so" (Mt. 26:64).

44. Mt. 26:65f.; Mk. 14:63f.

45. This has been suggested to me by my graduate student Moulie Vidas, when we were reading the texts together in a private reading course.

46. (1) Mt. 16:21; Mk. 8:31; Lk. 9:22; (2) Mt. 17:22f.; Mk. 9:30f.; Lk. 9:44; (3) Mt. 20:17–19; Mk. 10:32–34; Lk. 18:31–33.

47. Mk. 10:32–34.

48. See, e.g., Martin Hengel, *Crucifixion in the Ancient World and the Folly of the Message of the Cross*, London: SCM, and Philadelphia: Fortress, 1977, especially pp. 33ff.

49. Maier, *Jesus von Nazareth*, pp. 227f.

50. t Sanh 9:7; see also Sifre Deuteronomy, 221 (ed. Finkelstein, p. 254), where the death penalty of being hanged alive "as is done by the [non-Jewish] government" is explicitly mentioned. On the crucifixion in Jewish sources, see

Ernst Bammel, "Crucifixion as a Punishment in Palestine," in idem, *The Trial of Jesus*, pp. 162–165.

51. b Sanh 67a; the Palestinian parallels (t Sanh 10:11; y Sanh 7:16/1, fol. 25c–d; y Yev 16:1/23, fol. 15d) mention only Ben Stada and his execution by stoning, but not that he was hanged on the eve of Passover. On Ben Stada see above, ch. 1.

52. Mt. 26:20ff.; Mk. 14:12ff.; Lk. 22:15 (Jesus tells his disciples that he eagerly awaited eating the Passover meal with them before he suffers).

53. John 13:1ff.

54. John 19:14.

55. The Firenze manuscript emphasizes that the day of execution was on Sabbath eve, i.e., a Friday, which is concordant with all the four Gospels.

56. John 19:31.

57. Josephus gets it right when he says (with reference to the murdered High Priests Ananus and Jesus during the first Jewish war): "They [the murderers] actually went so far in their impiety as to cast out the corpses without burial, although the Jews are so careful about funeral rights that even malefactors who have been sentenced to crucifixion are taken down and buried before sunset" (*Bell.* 4, 317).

58. Mt. 27:17–23; Mk. 15:9–15; Lk. 23:13–25; John 18:38–19:16.

59. According to Matthew, influenced by his wife (Mt. 27:19).

60. John 19:12.

61. This is again the straw man against whom Maier fights (*Jesus von Nazareth*, pp. 231f.).

62. The fact that we are dealing with a Baraita does not necessarily mean that it is an early Palestinian Baraita because not all Baraitot in the Bavli are original; see Günter Stemberger, *Einleitung in Talmud und Midrasch*, Munich: Beck, 8th ed., 1992, pp. 199f. But nothing in this specific case indicates that our Baraita is suspicious.

Chapter 7

Jesus' Disciples

1. Mt. 4:18–20; Mk. 1:16–20; Lk. 5:1–11 (only Simon, James, and John); John 1:35–42 (two disciples of John the Baptist, one anonymous and the other one Andrew, the brother of Simon Peter).

2. Mt. 10:1–4; Mk. 3:14–19; Lk. 6:12–16.

3. Mt. 28:16–20; Mk. 16:14–17 (the longer ending); Lk. 24:36–50; John 20:19–31; 21.

4. b Sanh 43a–b.

5. The full name in Mss. Yad ha-Rav Herzog 1, Firenze II.1.8–9, and Karls-ruhe Reuchlin 2; Ms. Munich has the name and much of the text erased (see the chart below, pp. 140f. and the frontispiece).

6. Or: in secret; in a mysterious way.

7. The list of the names is in Hebrew, whereas the following interpretations are in Aramaic.

8. Maier, *Jesus von Nazareth*, pp. 232f., is very concerned about discrediting the "authenticity" of the text.

9. Indeed, the Gospel of John starts with five disciples that were first chosen (John 1: 37–51: two disciples of John who followed Jesus, one of them Andrew; Simon Peter; Philip; and Nathanael).

10. m Avot 2:8.

11. The historicity of which is even maintained by Klausner, *Jesus of Nazareth*, pp. 29f., who proposes the following identifications: Mattai = Matthew; Naqqai = Luke; Netzer = either a pun on *notzrim* ("Christians") or a corruption of Andrai = Andrew; Buni = Nicodemus or a corruption of Yuhanni/Yuani = John; Todah = Thaddaeus.

12. Mt. 9:9, 10:3.

13. That the verb in the original text is in the first-person singular and in the interpretation in the third-person singular does not bother the author of the passage.

14. The Hebrew word *naqi* can also be read as "Naqqai."

15. Reading *yehareg* instead of *yaharog*.

16. The Hebrew is difficult here; probably also "crushing my bones" (so the JPS translation).

17. Mt. 27:39–44; Mk. 15:29–32; Lk. 23:35–37.

18. A quotation from another Psalm (Ps. 22:1): Mt. 27:46; Mk. 15:34.

19. According to Mt. 27:19, Pilate's wife tells him: "Have nothing to do with that innocent (*tō dikaiō*) man, for today I have suffered a great deal because of a dream about him!" The Greek word used for "innocent" is actually *dikaios*— "righteous," the Greek equivalent of the Hebrew *tzaddiq*, the word used together with *naqi* ("innocent") in Ex. 23:7.

20. John 20:34: "But one of the soldiers pierced his side with a spear, and at once there came out blood and water."

21. "Their fathers" in the Hebrew text, but the singular is much more likely here (see also the ancient translations).

22. Mt. 28:18–20; Mk. 16:15f.

23. Mk. 1:10f.; Mt. 3:16f.; Lk. 3:21f.

24. Mt. 16:5; Mk. 9:7; Lk. 9:35.

25. In Greek: *apo tou xylou*, literally "from the wood."

26. Acts 13:28–30.

27. Hebr. 1:5; cf. also 5:5.

28. Col. 1:15f.; see also Hebr. 1:6.

29. Col. 1:18.

30. 1 Cor. 15:20–22; see also Rom. 8:29.

31. Rom. 9:8.

32. Rom. 9:25.

33. John 1:29; cf. also 1 Cor. 5:7; Rev. 5:6, 9, 12; 13:8.

34. Eph. 5:2.

35. Rom. 3:25; cf. also 1 John 2:12.

36. Hebr. 9:14.

37. Hebr. 9:25f.

Chapter 8

Jesus' Punishment in Hell

1. Lk. 24:51: "While he blessed them, he parted from them" (some manuscripts add "and was carried up into heaven").

2. Could this be the source of the forty days the herald announces Jesus' forthcoming death in the Talmud (see above)?

3. Two angels.

4. Acts 1:9–11.

5. b Git 55b–56a. On this cycle of stories and its anti-Christian implications see Israel J. Yuval, *"Two Nations in Your Womb": Perceptions of Jews and Christians*, Tel Aviv: Am Oved, 2000, pp. 65–71 (in Hebrew).

6. According to Josephus (*Bell.* 2, 409f.), the order issued by the Temple captain Eleazar, the son of the High Priest Ananias, to suspend the daily sacrifice for the emperor was indeed the decisive act of rebellion that made the war with Rome inevitable. The rabbinic literature, in its characteristic way, transfers the events from the level of the priests to the rabbis.

7. Which again is historically correct: they are indeed brought to Rome and depicted on the arch of Titus.

8. The gnat is obviously chosen because it not only is small but also, as the Talmud explains, because it has only an entrance (to take food) but no exit (to excrete).

9. b Git 56b.

10. b Git 56b–57a.

11. *Yeshu ha-notzri* in Ms. Vatican Ebr. 130; *Yeshu* in Mss. Vatican 140 and Munich 95; the Soncino printed edition leaves out either one, and the standard printed editions have "sinners of Israel."

12. Cf. Zech. 2:12: "whoever touches you (pl. = Israel) touches the apple of his [God's] eye."

13. Some printed editions add "the idolaters."

14. So in Ms. Vatican Ebr. 130 and most of the printed editions; Ms. Vatican 140: "R. Shim'on b. Eleazar"; Ms. Munich 95: "R. Eliezer."

15. The Palestinian tradition refers to Aquila as the son of the sister of Hadrian; see Peter Schäfer, *Der Bar Kokhba-Aufstand. Studien zum zweiten jüdischen Krieg gegen Rom*, Tübingen: J.C.B. Mohr (Paul Siebeck), 1981, pp. 242–244.

16. m Sanh 10:1; see above, p. 32.

17. b Ber 17a–b; see above, pp. 30ff.

18. t Sanh 13:4f.

19. t Sanh 13:5.

20. It is God who prevented Balaam from cursing Israel, and Deut. 23:6 says explicitly: "But the Lord, your God, refused to heed Balaam."

21. b Er 21b.

22. "Scribes" (*soferim*) is here understood as referring to the (rabbinic) scholars.

23. b Er 21b.

24. Obviously reading the Hebrew *lahag harbe* ("much study") as *la'ag ha-rabbanim* ("ridiculing the rabbis").

25. How he arrives from *yegi'at basar* ("weariness of the flesh") at *ta'am basar* ("taste of flesh") is his secret. The Soncino translation suggests that he turns the *'at* in *yegi'at* to *ta'* in *ta'am* (not bothered by the fact that the *t* in *yegi'at* is a *taw* and the *t* in *ta'am* a *tet*).

26. In other words, that our narrative in b Gittin refers to b Eruvin, as Maier suggests (*Jesus von Nazareth*, p. 98).

27. See above, ch. 2.

28. Also, the similarity of the punishments for Balaam and Jesus/the sinners of Israel (hot semen and hot excrement) makes it highly probable that the hot-excrement punishment originated in the context of our b Gittin story rather than of b Eruvin.

29. As Maier again takes for granted (*Jesus von Nazareth*, p. 98). Quite the opposite seems to be the case if we follow the logic of the story: Jesus is the climax at the end and as such the "sinner of Israel" par excellence.

30. Mt. 15:1–20; Mk. 7:1–23; Lk. 11:37–41.

31. Mt. 15:17–20; Mk. 7:18–23.

32. The credit—or the blame (depending on the viewpoint)—for this particularly bold interpretation must be given to Israel Yuval: in this case, I still remember vividly that when we were preparing our seminar and were pressing the obvious analogy between Balaam and Jesus, he suddenly came up with this suggestion, which has the advantage of taking seriously the particular punishment of Jesus.

33. Mt. 26:26–28; Mk. 14:22–24; Lk. 22:19–20; cf. 1 Cor. 11:23–26.

34. Ignatius, Letter to the community of Smyrna 7:1 (*Early Christian Fathers*, vol. 1, trans. and ed. by Cyril C. Richardson, Philadelphia: Westminster, 1953, p. 114). And see Justin, *Apol.* I:66.

35. John 6:48–58.

36. Yuval, *Two Nations in Your Womb*, p. 71, comes to a different conclusion. He sees here, put into the mouth of Jesus, an echo of Augustine's theological claim to protect the life of the Jews and to save them for future salvation.

Chapter 9

Jesus in the Talmud

1. Even a scholar like Morton Smith cannot conceal his indignation at the "pure fantasy" and "nonsense" when discussing some of our rabbinic stories; see, e.g., his *Jesus the Magician*, p. 49.

2. On the rabbinic concept of history, see Arnold Goldberg, "Schöpfung und Geschichte. Der Midrasch von den Dingen, die vor der Welt erschaffen wurden," *Judaica* 24, 1968, pp. 27–44 (reprinted in idem, *Mystik und Theologie des rabbinischen Judentums. Gesammelte Studien I*, ed. Margarete Schlüter and Pe-

ter Schäfer, Tübingen: Mohr Siebeck, 1997, pp. 148–161); Peter Schäfer, "Zur Geschichtsauffassung des rabbinischen Judentums," *JSJ* 6, 1975, pp. 167–188 (reprinted in idem, *Studien zur Geschichte und Theologie des Rabbinischen Judentums*, Leiden: Brill, 1978, pp. 23–44; cf. in the introduction, pp. 13–15, my discussion with Herr); Moshe D. Herr, "Tefisat ha-historyah etzel Hazal," in *Proceedings of the Sixth World Congress of Jewish Studies*, vol. 3, Jerusalem: World Union of Jewish Studies, 1977, pp. 129–142; Isaiah Gafni, "Concepts of Periodization and Causality in Talmudic Literature," *Jewish History* 10, 1996, pp. 29–32; idem, "Rabbinic Historiography and Representations of the Past," in *Cambridge Companion to Rabbinic Literature*, ed. Charlotte Fonrobert and Martin Jaffee (forthcoming).

3. Richard Kalmin puts this claim into a much broader context in his new book *Jewish Babylonia: Between Persia and Roman Palestine* (to be published by Oxford University Press): "Chapters Two ['Kings, Priests, and Sages'], Three ['Jewish Sources of the Second Temple Period in Rabbinic Compilations of Late Antiquity'], and Seven ['Josephus in Sasanian Babylonia'] . . . demonstrate that the rabbis' monk-like quality did not serve to seal them off from all contact with the outside world, since . . . we will find abundant evidence that non-rabbinic *literature* reached Babylonian rabbis and found a receptive audience there" (manuscript, p. 12). Professor Kalmin was kind enough to share with me several chapters of this book in manuscript form.

4. For the rabbinic definition of the *mamzer* see m Yev 4:13; Sifre Deuteronomy, 248 (ed. Finkelstein, pp. 276f.); y Yev 4:15/1–5, fol. 6b–6c; b Yev 49a–b.

5. Stoning as the appropriate penalty is explicitly mentioned in the case of adultery between a betrothed virgin and a man (Deut. 22:23). The same is true for the Mishna (Sanh 7:4): "The following are stoned: . . . he who commits adultery with a betrothed virgin."

6. Meticulously listed and discussed by Maier, *Jesus von Nazareth*, pp. 264–267.

7. Ibid., p. 267.

8. F. Nitzsch, "Ueber eine Reihe talmudischer und patristischer Täuschungen, welche sich an den mißverstandenen Spottnamen *Ben-Pandira* geknüpft," *Theologische Studien und Kritiken* 13, 1840, pp. 115–120. Nitzsch explains this allusion to "panther" with the panther's alleged lust and accordingly interprets "Yeshu ben Pandera" as "Jesus son of the whore."

9. Paulus Cassel, *Apologetische Briefe I: Panthera-Stada-onokotes: Caricatur-namen Christi unter Juden und Heiden* (Berlin 1875), reprinted in idem, *Aus Literatur und Geschichte*, Berlin and Leipzig: W. Friedrich, 1885, pp. 323–347 (334f.); Laible, *Jesus Christus im Thalmud*, pp. 24f.; L. Patterson, "Origin of the Name Panthera," *Journal of Theological Studies* 19, 1918, pp. 79–80; Klausner, *Jesus of Nazareth*, p. 24; Karl G. Kuhn, *Achtzehngebet und Vaterunser und der Reim*, Tübingen: J.C.B. Mohr (Paul Siebeck), 1950, p. 2, n. 2. Most recently Boyarin (*Dying for God*, pp. 154f., n. 27) has rediscovered this explanation (wrongly attributing its first discovery to Cassel). All these explanations rely on the (misguided) assumption of a philological metathesis of "r" and "n".

10. Samuel Krauss, "The Jews in the Works of the Church Fathers," *JQR* 5, 1892–1893, pp. 122–157; 6, 1894, pp. 225–261 (pp. 143f.: "*Pandera* is nothing but *pornē*, modified by phonetic influences. *Yeshu bar Pandera* would thus mean Jesus, the son of the prostitute"); idem, *Das Leben Jesu nach jüdischen Quellen*, p. 276 (*pornos*). According to this interpretation, *ek parthenou* ("from a virgin") becomes *ek porneias* ("from fornication").

11. Boyarin, *Dying for God*, p. 154, n. 27.

12. t AZ 6:4.

13. A term that Boyarin ascribes to Shaul Lieberman.

14. *Jesus von Nazareth*, p. 267.

15. See King, *Gospel of Mary of Magdala*, p. 153.

16. Therefore, what happens to the student/Jesus in the inn is far from being a "tragic misunderstanding" (Boyarin, *Dying for God*, p. 24).

17. Justin, *Dialogue*, 10:1 (in *St. Justin Martyr: Dialogue with Trypho*, transl. Thomas B. Falls, rev. and introd. Thomas P. Halton, ed. Michael Slusser, Washington, DC: Catholic University of America Press, 2003, p. 18); see also *Apol.* I:26: "And whether they perpetrate those fabulous and shameful deeds—the upsetting of the lamp, and promiscuous intercourse, and eating human flesh—we do not know."

18. Justin, *Dialogue*, 108:2 (*St. Justin Martyr: Dialogue with Trypho*, trans. Falls, p. 162).

19. Ibid.; see also *Dialogue*, 17:1: "but at that time you selected and sent out from Jerusalem chosen men through all the land to tell that the godless heresy of the Christians had sprung up, and to publish those things which all they who knew us not speak against us." In the third century, Origen compares his opponent Celsus (the pagan philosopher, who in 178 C.E. wrote his attack on Chris-

tianity) with "those Jews who, when Christianity began to be first preached, scattered abroad false reports of the Gospel, such as that 'Christians offered up an infant in sacrifice, and partook of its flesh'; and again, 'that the professors of Christianity, wishing to do the works of darkness, used to extinguish the lights (in their meetings), and each one to have sexual intercourse with any woman whom he chanced to meet'" (Origen, *Contra Celsum*, 6:27; transl. in *The Ante-Nicene Fathers: Translations of the Fathers down to A.D. 325*, ed. Alexander Roberts and James Donaldson, vol. 4, Grand Rapids, MI: Eerdmans, 1989, p. 585).

20. Tertullian, *Apology*, 7:1 (*Tertullian Apology—De spectaculis*, transl. T. R. Glover, London: William Heinemann; Cambridge, MA: Harvard University Press, 1953, pp. 36f.). Tertullian most likely reflects pagan charges against Christianity.

21. Ibid., 8:2–7. A very similar story is reported by the Latin apologist Minucius Felix in his *Octavius*, a dialogue between a pagan and a Christian (*Octavius*, 9:1–7, in *The Octavius of Marcus Minucius Felix*, trans. Gerald H. Rendall, London: William Heinemann; Cambridge, MA: Harvard University Press, 1953, pp. 336–339; and cf. also *Octavius*, 31): "They recognize one another by secret signs and marks; they fall in love almost before they are acquainted; everywhere they introduce a kind of religion of lust (*quaedam libidinum religio*), a promiscuous 'brotherhood' and 'sisterhood' by which ordinary fornication, under cover of a hallowed name, is converted to incest. . . . Details of the initiation of neophytes are as revolting as they are notorious. An infant, cased in dough to deceive the unsuspecting, is placed beside the person to be initiated. The novice is thereupon induced to inflict what seem to be harmless blows upon the dough, and unintentionally the infant is killed by his unsuspecting blows; the blood—oh, horrible—they lap up greedily; the limbs they tear to pieces eagerly; and over the victim they make league and covenant, and by complicity in guilt pledge themselves to mutual silence. . . . On the day appointed they gather at a banquet with all their children, sisters, and mothers, people of either sex and every age. There, after full feasting, when the blood is heated and drink has inflamed the passions of incestuous lust, a dog which has been tied to a lamp is tempted by a morsel thrown beyond the range of his tether to bound forward with a rush. The taletelling light is upset and extinguished, and in the shameless dark lustful embraces are indiscriminately exchanged; and all alike, if not in act, yet by complicity, are involved in incest, as anything that occurs by the act of individuals results

from the common intention." On the custom of extinguishing the light, the scholars are undecided as to whether Tertullian precedes Minucius Felix (in this case *Octavius* would have been written in the early third century C.E.) or whether vice versa Minucius Felix predates Tertullian (in this case *Octavius* must have been penned before 197 C.E.). See on this Hans Gärtner, "Minucius Felix," in *Der Kleine Pauly. Lexikon der Antike*, Munich: Deutscher Taschenbuchverlag, 1979, col. 1342. In any case, Minucius' source seems to be Fronto (cf. *Octavius*, 9:6 and 31:2), the highly influential teacher of the emperor Marcus Aurelius (d. after 175 C.E.).

22. Elias Bickerman, "Ritualmord und Eselskult. Ein Beitrag zur Geschichte antiker Publizistik," in idem, *Studies in Jewish and Christian History*, vol. 2, Leiden: Brill, 1980, pp. 225–255 (original publication in *MGWJ* 71, 1927). See also Burton L. Visotzky, "Overturning the Lamp," *JJS* 38, 1987, pp. 72–80; idem, *Fathers of the World*, pp. 75–84.

23. Josephus, *Contra Apionem*, 2:91–96.

24. In the late fourth century C.E., Epiphanius, the bishop of Salamis at Cyprus, accuses the Christian sect of the Nicolaitans of fornicating with each other and of eating their semen and their blood of menstruation (*Panarion* 26:4f. in *The Panarion of Epiphanius of Salamis*, book 1, sects 1–46, trans. Frank Williams, Leiden: Brill, 1987, pp. 85–87.). This sect is already mentioned by Irenaeus in the second half of the second century C.E. as practicing adultery and eating things sacrificed to idols (*Adversus Haereses* 1, 26:3, in *St. Irenaeus of Lyons against the Heresies*, trans. and annot. Dominic J. Unger, rev. John J. Dillon, New York and Mahwah, NJ: Paulist, 1992, pp. 90f.).

25. The Christian philosopher Clement of Alexandria (ca. 150–215 C.E.) accuses the sect of the Carpocratians of gathering together for sexual orgies, and ironically adds: "I would not call their meeting an Agape" (*Stromata* 3, 2:10–16).

26. Justin, *Dialogue*, 108:2 (*St. Justin Martyr: Dialogue with Trypho*, trans. Falls, p. 162). See also Tertullian, *De spectaculis*, 30 (below, p. 112).

27. Jer. 2:13.

28. Justin, *Dialogue*, 69:6f. (*St. Justin Martyr: Dialogue with Trypho*, trans. Falls, pp. 108f.). For the view of Jesus as magician and seducer see Martin Hengel, *The Charismatic Leader and His Followers*, New York: Crossroad, 1981, p. 41, n. 14.

29. Mt. 28:13–15.

30. Justin, *Apol.* I:30 (*Saint Justin: Apologies*, ed. André Wartelle, Paris: Études Augustiniennes, 1987, pp. 136f.); English translation: *Early Christian Fathers*, transl. and ed. Cyril C. Richardson, Philadelphia: Westminster, 1953, p. 260.

31. Pace Maier (*Jesus von Nazareth*, p. 250), who tries to distinguish between "deception" and "temptation into idolatry"—again in order to separate the pagan from the rabbinic sources.

32. See, e.g., Deut. 18:9–14.

33. Prominent examples are stories of the ten plagues (Ex. 7–12), the "brazen serpent" (Num. 21:6–9), or the so-called ordeal of jealousy (Num. 5:11–31).

34. The rabbis practically distinguished between mere delusion (*'ahizat 'enayyim*), which was allowed, and "real" magic, which was forbidden; see Peter Schäfer, "Magic and Religion in Ancient Judaism," in *Envisioning Magic. A Princeton Seminar & Symposium*, ed. Peter Schäfer and Hans Kippenberg, Leiden—New York—Köln: Brill 1997, pp. 19–43; Veltri, *Magie und Halakha*, pp. 27ff., 54f.; Philip Alexander, "The Talmudic Concept of Conjuring (*'Ahizat 'Einayim*) and the Problem of the Definition of Magic (*Kishuf*)," in *Creation and Re-Creation in Jewish Thought: Festschrift in Honor of Joseph Dan on the Occasion of His Seventieth Birthday*, ed. Rachel Elior and Peter Schäfer, Tübingen: Mohr Siebeck, 2005, pp. 7–26.

35. See above, ch. 3 (p. 35).

36. Acts 8:9–13. On Simon Magus see Karlmann Beyschlag, *Simon Magus und die christliche Gnosis*, Tübingen: Mohr (Siebeck), 1974.

37. One of the seven; see Acts 6:5.

38. Which is also the authority of the individual against the authority of the majority.

39. True, he remains a magician until the bitter end, but he is accepted back into the rabbinic fold after he has satisfactorily answered some questions about purity(!): he dies uttering the word *tahor* ("pure"), and the ban is lifted (b Sanh 68a).

40. Although there are, in reality, strict hierarchical divisions among the rabbis. But this is not the point here: R. Eliezer b. Hyrkanos does not lose the power struggle because he is hierarchically inferior.

41. The Bavli (Sanh 61a–b) distinguishes between the act of demanding to be worshipped and the actual worship: as to the former, two tannaitic rabbis disagree about whether or not such a person deserves death, whereas with regard to

the latter all agree that such a person must be executed. Hence, it is not just the declaration but the successful seduction into idolatry that matters.

42. m Sanh 7:5.

43. Mk. 14:61–64; Lk. 22:67–71; John 19:7.

44. y Taan 2:1/24, fol. 65b. A late and much more developed version of this midrash can be found in the Saloniki 1521–1527 edition of the collection called Yalqut Shimoni, § 765 (end); see Maier, *Jesus von Nazareth*, pp. 87f. (who again explains Jesus away).

45. This latter part is an abbreviated version of Num. 23:19.

46. This last link of the chain is rather loose; in particular, the promise to ascend to heaven has no equivalent in the Bible verse.

47. Maier, *Jesus von Nazareth*, pp. 76–82.

48. Maier (ibid., p. 79) refers to the parallel with the biblical Adam: like Adam, who ultimately was driven out of Paradise (and regretted his hubris), Hiram was ousted from his power (and regretted his hubris). This does not make much sense in our context.

49. In the first part of the interpretation, the emphasis is placed, not on God not being a man/Son of Man, but on God not being a man who lies/a Son of Man who repents.

50. More precisely: it appears, except for Acts 7:56 (in the mouth of Stephen), only in the Gospels and only in the mouth of Jesus. On the "historicity" of the title see Geza Vermes, *Jesus the Jew: A Historian's Reading of the Gospels*, Philadelphia: Fortress, 1981, pp. 177–186.

51. See Ephraim E. Urbach, "Homilies of the Rabbis on the Prophets of the Nations and the Balaam Stories," *Tarbiz* 25, 1955/56, pp. 286f.

52. Maier, *Jesus von Nazareth*, p. 80.

53. PesR 21, ed. Friedmann, fol. 100b–101a. The attribution to R. Hiyya bar Abba is the reason why I include this midrash in my discussion, despite the (relatively) late date of the Pesiqta Rabbati compilation.

54. In the plural.

55. In the singular.

56. The standard prooftext for this is Mekhilta, Yitro 5, ed. Horovitz-Rabin, pp. 219f. (with many parallels).

57. The classical prooftext is BerR 1:7, ed. Theodor-Albeck, I, p. 4 (again with many parallels).

58. As has been argued, quite stereotypically, again by Maier (*Jesus von Nazareth*, pp. 244–247).

59. Ibid., p. 246.

60. Ibid., p. 245.

61. Lucian, *Death of Peregrinus*, 13 (*Selected Satires of Lucian*, ed. and trans. Lionel Casson, New York and London: Norton, 1962, p. 369).

62. See *The Dead Comes to Life*, 19 (*Lucian*, vol. 3, trans. A. M. Harmon, Cambridge, MA, and London: Harvard University Press, 1921; reprint, 2004, pp. 30f.); *The Double Indictment*, 25 (ibid., pp. 134f.), 27 (pp. 136f.).

63. Tertullian, *De spectaculis*, 30 (*Tertullian Apology—De spectaculis*, transl. Glover, pp. 298f.). On this passage, see Horbury, *Jews and Christians*, pp. 176–179.

64. Son of a carpenter: Mt. 13:55; Mk. 6:3; son of a prostitute: see above, ch. 1; Sabbath breaker: Mt. 12:1–14; Mk. 2:23–3:6; Lk. 6:1–11; demon-possessed: Mt. 9:34, 10:25, 12:24; Mk. 3:22; Lk. 11:14–23; John 8:48 (demon-possessed Samaritan), 10:20; purchased from Judas: Mt. 26:14f.; Mk. 14:10f.; Lk. 22:3–6; struck with reed and fist: Mt. 27:30; Mk. 15:19; John 19:3; spat upon: Mt. 27:30; Mk. 15:19; given gall and vinegar to drink: Mt. 27:34; Mk. 15:23; John 19:29 (vinegar only in John); secretly stolen away by his disciples: Mt. 27:64; 28:12–15; the gardener: John 20:15 (only in John).

65. Acts 8:9–13 (see above, p. 105); see also John 8:48.

66. This motif comes back forcefully in *Toledot Yeshu*, as does the motif of Jesus' birth from a whore.

67. Boyarin, *Dying for God*, p. 27.

68. Richard Kalmin ("Christians and Heretics," pp. 160ff.) also emphasizes the difference between the earlier (Palestinian) and later (mainly Babylonian, but also some Palestinian) sources. In addition to the possibility of different *historical* attitudes (earlier sources are receptive to Christianity's attractiveness, later sources are much more critical) he brings into play changing rabbinic *rhetorical* attitudes (p. 163) and, in particular, a "tendency of the Babylonian Talmud to include material excluded from Palestinian compilations" (p. 167). This thought is developed much further in his new book, *Jewish Babylonia: Between Persia and Roman Palestine* (in press).

69. The major proponent is Michael Avi-Yonah, *The Jews of Palestine: A Political History from the Bar Kokhba War to the Arab Conquest*, New York: Schocken, 1976, pp. 158ff., 208ff.

70. Geo Widengren, *Die Religionen Irans*, Stuttgart: Kohlhammer, 1965, pp. 274ff.; Jes Asmussen, "Christians in Iran," *The Cambridge History of Iran*, vol. 3 (2): *The Seleucid, Parthian and Sasanian Periods*, ed. Ehsan Yarshater, Cambridge: Cambridge University Press, 1983, p. 933; Richard N. Frye, *The History of Ancient Iran*, Munich: Beck, 1984, p. 301.

71. See in particular the careful analysis by Josef Wiesehöfer, *Ancient Persia from 550 BC to 650 AD*, London and New York: I. B. Tauris, 1996, pp. 199ff.

72. Ahura Mazda, the "good god."

73. The "evil god," Ahura Mazda's opponent.

74. English translation by Wiesehöfer, *Ancient Persia*, p. 199.

75. On the distinction between the "Nazarenes" (presumably native Persian Christians) and the "Christians" (presumably deported Christians of western origin) see Sebastian P. Brock, "Some Aspects of Greek Words in Syriac," in idem, *Syriac Perspectives on Late Antiquity*, London: Variorum, 1984, pp. 91–95; Asmussen, "Christians in Iran," pp. 929f.

76. On the status of the Jews under the Sasanians see in particular the classical article by Geo Widengren, "The Status of the Jews in the Sassanian Empire," in *Irania Antiqua*, vol. 1, ed. R. Ghirshman and L. Vanden Berghe, Leiden: Brill, 1961, pp. 117–162; and Jacob Neusner, *A History of the Jews in Babylonia*, vols. 1–5, Leiden: Brill, 1967–1970. More recent and more specific are Isaiah M. Gafni, *The Jews of Babylonia in the Talmudic Era: A Social and Cultural History*, Jerusalem: Zalman Shazar Center for Jewish History, 1990 (in Hebrew); Robert Brody, "Judaism in the Sasanian Empire: A Case Study in Religious Coexistence," in *Irano-Judaica II: Studies Relating to Jewish Contacts with Persian Culture throughout the Ages*, ed. Shaul Shaked and Amnon Netzer, Jerusalem: Yad Itzhak Ben-Zvi, 1990, pp. 52–62; Shaul Shaked, "Zoroastrian Polemics against Jews in the Sasanian and Early Islamic Period," in *Irano-Judaica II*, ed. Shaked and Netzer, pp. 85–104.

77. See Asmussen, "Christians in Iran," pp. 933ff.; Sebastian P. Brock, "Christians in the Sasanian Empire: A Case of Divided Loyalties," in *Religion and National Identity: Papers Read at the Nineteenth Summer Meeting and the Twentieth Winter Meeting of the Ecclesiastical History Society*, ed. Stuart Mews, Oxford: Blackwell, 1982, pp. 5ff.

78. Spring or early summer of 337: Timothy D. Barnes, "Constantine and the Christians of Persia," *JRS* 75, 1985, p. 130.

79. Aphrahat, *Demonstration* V:1, 24, in *Patrologia Syriaca* I:1, ed. J. Parisot, Paris: Firmin-Didot, 1894, cols. 183–184 and 233–234.

80. Barnes, in his concluding statement ("Constantine and the Christians of Persia," p. 136), puts the thrust of the blame on Constantine: "It was Constantine who injected a religious dimension into the normal frontier dispute, by seeking to appeal to Shapur's Christian subjects in the same sort of way in which he had appealed to the Christian subjects of Maxentius in 312 and of Licinius in 324. Aphrahat's fifth *Demonstration* illustrates what response he found."

81. *Acta Martyrum et Sanctorum*, vol. 1–7, ed. Paul Bedjan, Paris and Leipzig: Harrassowitz, 1890–1897; selected pieces in German translation by Oskar Braun, *Ausgewählte Akten Persischer Märtyrer. Mit einem Anhang: Ostsyrisches Mönchsleben*, aus dem Syrischen übersetzt, Kempten and Munich: Kösel, 1915.

82. See Gernot Wiessner, *Untersuchungen zur syrischen Literaturgeschichte I: Zur Märtyrerüberlieferung aus der Christenverfolgung Schapurs II*, Göttingen: Vandenhoek & Ruprecht, 1967; and the learned review by Sebastian Brock in *Journal of Theological Studies*, n.s., 19, 1968, pp. 300–309. Regardless of the historicity of the Acts, there can be no doubt that the Acts reflects a cultural climate to which the Jews respond.

83. AMS II, p. 142; Braun, *Ausgewählte Akten*, p. 13; English translation in Brock, "Christians in the Sasanian Empire," p. 8.

84. AMS II, p. 143; Braun, *Ausgewählte Akten*, p. 14.

85. See also *The Chronicle of Arbela*, 54:2–3 (Kawerau), quoted in Wiesehöfer, *Ancient Persia*, p. 202: "And they [the Jews and the Manichaeans] explained to them [the magi] that the Christians were all of them spies of the Romans. And that nothing happens in the kingdom that they do not write to their brothers who live there." Naomi Koltun-Fromm ("A Jewish-Christian Conversation in Fourth-Century Persian Mesopotamia," *JJS* 47, 1996, pp. 45–63) suggests distinguishing between the Jewish involvement in the *physical* persecution of the Christians (which is unlikely) and some kind of *spiritual* "persecution" by seeking converts from the Christian community or undermining their beliefs (p. 50).

86. See Asmussen, "Christians in Iran," pp. 937f.; idem, "Das Christentum in Iran und sein Verhältnis zum Zoroastrismus," *Studia Theologica* 16, 1962, pp. 11ff.

87. Dated 339 C.E., i.e., before the official begin of the persecution (Braun, *Ausgewählte Akten*, p. xvii).

88. *AMS* II, p. 52; Braun, *Ausgewählte Akten*, p. 1.

89. See the apt summary in the martyrdom of the bishop Akebshema: *AMS* II, p. 361; Braun, *Ausgewählte Akten*, p. 116.

90. A good example is Martha, the daughter of Pusai (who was martyred before her), whom the judge strongly urges: "You are a young girl, and a very pretty one at that. Go and find a husband, get married and have children; do not hold on to the disgusting pretext of the covenant [the vow of virginity]!" (*AMS* II, pp. 236f.; Braun, *Ausgewählte Akten*, p. 78f.).

91. Quotation in Asmussen, "Christians in Iran," p. 939 with n. 4; see also Asmussen, "Das Christentum in Iran," pp. 15f. Furthermore the quotation in Ian Gillman and Hans-Joachim Klimkeit, *Christians in Asia before 1500*, Ann Arbor: University of Michigan Press, 1999, p. 115: "The Christians also profess another error. They say that God, who created heaven and earth, was born of a virgin named Mary, whose husband was called Joseph."

92. Asmussen, Christians in Iran, p. 937.

93. *AMS* II, p. 191; Braun, *Ausgewählte Akten*, p. 45; *AMS* II, p. 206; Braun, *Ausgewählte Akten*, p. 56 (the former refers to the sentence on the sixth hour of Friday, the latter to the execution on the ninth hour).

94. *AMS* II, p. 177; Braun, *Ausgewählte Akten*, p. 36.

95. *AMS* II, p. 557; Braun, *Ausgewählte Akten*, pp. 162 (a Friday in November), 184 (a Friday in August), 219.

96. Mt. 27:62–66. John has the interesting detail that Mary believes that the gardener might secretly have taken away Jesus' body (John 20:15).

97. *AMS* II, p. 56; Braun, *Ausgewählte Akten*, p. 4.

98. *AMS* II, p. 374; Braun, *Ausgewählte Akten*, p. 125.

99. *AMS* II, pp. 390f.; Braun, *Ausgewählte Akten*, p. 136. I thank Adam Becker for helping me clarify this passage.

100. Paul Bedjan, *Histoire de Mar-Jabalaha, de trois autres patriarches, d'un prêtre et de deux laiques nestoriens*, Leipzig: Otto Harrassowitz, 1895, pp. 551f.; Braun, *Ausgewählte Akten*, p. 271.

101. See also *AMS* II, p. 206; Braun, *Ausgewählte Akten*, p. 56; *AMS* II, p. 557; Braun, *Ausgewählte Akten*, p. 162; and *AMS* IV, p. 198; Braun, *Ausgewählte Akten*, pp. 176f.

102. This is not to say that the relationship between Jews and Christians in the Persian Empire was exclusively antagonistic; on the contrary. On the

shared cultural space, in particular with regard to the "scholastic culture," see Adam H. Becker, "Bringing the Heavenly Academy Down to Earth: Approaches to the Imagery of Divine Pedagogy in the East Syrian Tradition," in *Heavenly Realms and Earthly Realities in Late Antique Religions*, ed. Ra 'anan S. Boustan and Annette Yoshiko Reed, Cambridge: Cambridge University Press, 2004, pp. 185ff., and in more detail Becker's Princeton dissertation, *"The Cause of the Foundations of the Schools": The Development of Scholastic Culture in Late Antique Mesopotamia* (published now as *The Fear of God and the Beginning of Wisdom: The School of Nisibis and Christian Scholastic Culture in Late Antique Mesopotamia*, Philadelphia: University of Pennsylvania Press, 2006); Jeffrey L. Rubenstein, *The Culture of the Babylonian Talmud*, Baltimore and London: Johns Hopkins University Press, 2003, pp. 35–38.

Another no doubt promising avenue to explore further points of contact between Jews and Christians are the Syrian fathers (Ephrem and Aphrahat). Yet my point is not to review all potential sources for Babylonian Jewish familiarity with Christian traditions but rather (much more limited) to find out why the Jews found it feasible and opportune to speak out against the Christians. Naomi Koltun-Fromm concludes from Aphrahat's *Demonstrationes* and rabbinic sources that rabbinic Jews were indeed engaged in a polemic against the Christians: "Although the Jews did not leave for us an *adversus Christianos* treatise resembling Aphrahat's *adversus Judaeos*, echoes of their complaints against Christianity and proselytizing tactics can be heard in these [rabbinic] passages" ("A Jewish-Christian Conversation," p. 63). I would like to add that the most graphic echoes of such anti-Christian sentiments are the Jesus passages in the Talmud and that it is these passages that come closest to a Jewish *adversus Christianos* treatise.

103. This observation (on a more general basis, i.e., with regard to anti-Christian polemic as such) has also been made by Yuval, *Two Nations in Your Womb*, pp. 39f., 66.

104. Although this does not exclude the possibility that separate versions of the four Gospels were circulating as well (see the article by Barbara Aland below, p. 190). On Tatian and the Diatessaron, see Bruce M. Metzger, *The Early Versions of the New Testament: Their Origin, Transmission, and Limitations*, Oxford: Clarendon, 1977, pp. 10ff., and these useful articles in the *Theologische Realenzyklopädie*: Dietrich Wünsch, "Evangelienharmonie," in *TRE* 10, 1982, pp. 626–629; Barbara Aland, "Bibelübersetzungen I:4.2: Neues Testament," in *TRE*

6, 1980, pp. 189–196; William L. Petersen, "Tatian," in *TRE* 32, 2001, pp. 655–659.

105. See Ernst Bammel, *"Ex illa itaque die consilium fecerunt . . . ,"* in idem, *The Trial of Jesus,* p. 17. On Tatian's harmonizing strategy in general, see Helmut Merkel, *Die Widersprüche zwischen den Evangelien. Ihre polemische und apologetische Behandlung in der Alten Kirche bis zu Augustin,* Tübingen: J.C.B. Mohr (Paul Siebeck), 1971, pp. 71–91; William L. Petersen, *Tatian's Diatessaron: Its Creation, Dissemination, Significance, and History in Scholarship,* Leiden and New York: Brill, 1994.

106. See the list in Wünsch, "Evangelienharmonie," p. 628. A translation of the Arabic version by Hope W. Hogg can be found in *The Ante-Nicene Fathers: Translations of the Fathers down to A.D. 325,* 5th ed., vol. 10, ed. Allan Menzies; reprint, Edinburgh: T&T Clark; Grand Rapids, MI: Eerdmans, 1990, pp. 43–129.

107. The references listed here refer only to allusions to the New Testament directly relating to Jesus; it goes without saying that they do not exhaust allusions to the New Testament in the rabbinic literature in general and in the Bavli in particular. It is striking, however, that they too seem to be more prominent in the Bavli (the most conspicuous example is the reference to Mt. 5:14–17 in the story of Imma Shalom, Rabban Gamliel, and the pagan philosopher in b Shabb 116a–b; see on this Visotzky, *Fathers of the World,* pp. 81–83).

108. However, Martin Hengel reminds me that we should not forget the possibility of a Hebrew or Aramaic Jewish-Christian Gospel, "akin to the later Greek Matthew": see his *The Four Gospels and the One Gospel of Jesus Christ: An Investigation of the Collection and Origin of the Canonical Gospels,* London: SCM, 2000, pp. 73–76.

109. See the broad discussion in Martin Hengel, *Die Johanneische Frage. Ein Lösungsversuch,* Tübingen: J.C.B. Mohr (Paul Siebeck), 1993, pp. 219ff.; Charles E. Hill, *The Johannine Corpus in the Early Church,* Oxford: Oxford University Press, 2004. An extremely early date (68/69 C.E.) has been advocated, not convincingly, by Klaus Berger, *Im Anfang war Johannes. Datierung und Theologie des vierten Evangeliums,* Stuttgart: Quell, 1997.

110. See also 3:35f.

111. See also 6:27.

112. Rev. 2:9; 3:9.

113. John 9:22, 34; 12:42; 16:2.

114. John 10:30: "the Father and I are one." This, no doubt, was the bone of contention for the Jews. Only John mentions the attempt of the Jews to stone Jesus (8:59).

115. It goes without saying that the Diatessaron, as far as it can be reconstructed from the quotations and translations, contains all the major elements so characteristic for John. On a possible affinity of the *Toledot Yeshu* to the Gospel of John see Bammel, *The Trial of Jesus*, pp. 36f. (with relevant literature).

Appendix
Bavli Manuscripts and Censorship

1. Available by subscription only. On the transmission history of talmudic manuscripts, see the recent summarizing article by Shamma Friedman, "From Sinai to Cyberspace: the Transmission of the Talmud in Every Age," in *Printing the Talmud: From Bomberg to Schottenstein*, ed. Sharon Liberman Mintz and Gabriel M. Goldstein, [New York:] Yeshiva University Museum, 2005, pp. 143–154.

2. The Online Treasury of Talmudic Manuscripts site is found at http://jnul.huji.ac.il/dl/talmud.

3. Without attempting completeness, the manuscripts listed below give a fair picture of the textual evidence. In addition, I have used Raphael Rabbinovicz, *Diqduqe Soferim: Variae Lectiones in Mischnam et in Talmud Babylonicum*, vols. 1–15, Munich: A. Huber, 1868–1897; vol. 16, Przemysl: Zupnik, Knoller and Wolf, 1897 (reprint in 12 vols., Jerusalem, 2001/02).

4. The only complete manuscript of the Bavli (only a few pages are missing).

5. The rest of the passage is not legible.

6. Added.

7. A scribe corrects *ba'al* into *bo'el*.

8. Added.

9. A scribe deletes the *waw* in *bo'el* and corrects into *ba'al*.

10. Added.

11. The references according to Maier, *Jesus von Nazareth*, p. 296, n. 305.

12. Editio princeps Venice; the name is deleted in Ms. Leiden, and the second glossator added "Jesus son of Pandera."

13. Editio princeps Venice; the name is deleted in Ms. Leiden, and the second glossator added "Jesus Pantera."

14. The references according to Maier, *Jesus von Nazareth*, p. 299, n. 358.

15. No name.

16. Same.

17. Same.

18. Same.

19. Editio princeps Venice; the name is deleted in Ms. Leiden, and the second glossator added "in the name of Jesus son of Pandera."

20. Editio princeps Venice; the name is deleted in Ms. Leiden, and the second glossator added "of Jesus Pantera."

21. According to Maier, *Jesus von Nazareth*, p. 301, n. 372, this is identical in all manuscripts and printed editions of QohR (with the exception of the Vilna edition which again leaves an empty space for the name).

22. Later addition that is not legible.

23. Same.

24. Same.

25. Same.

26. Same.

27. No name mentioned.

28. With the exception of QohR 10:5: just "son of Pandera."

29. With the exception of New York 15.

30. In Ms. Firenze, just "Jesus."

31. Maier makes this claim over and over again; see his *Jesus von Nazareth*, pp. 13, 16, 63, 98, 110, 127, 165, 173.

32. Particularly revealing is Maier's discussion of R. Yehoshua b. Perahya's attempt to push Jesus away (chapter 3). He quotes here a very similar story from Avraham b. Azriel's *Arugat ha-Bosem*, written around 1234 (i.e., before the implementation of Christian censorship in 1263), according to which R. Aqiva pushes Jesus away with both his hands. Avraham b. Azriel's version is obviously a conflation of the two Bavli stories in Berakhot 17b (my chapter 2) and in Sanhedrin 107b/Sot 47a (my chapter 3), but crucial is the fact that Jesus is clearly mentioned. Instead of concluding that pre-censorship references to our Bavli story do contain Jesus, and that Jesus therefore seems to be an integral part of this story, Maier resorts to the convoluted sentence: "this quotation demonstrates how little we have actually gained by the 'uncensored' text because the earlier

history of the text is crucial" (*Jesus von Nazareth*, p. 110). This is a breathtaking
somersault: he does have even an extra-talmudic proof for a talmudic Jesus story
but conjures up the chimera of the "earlier history of the text" (which he does
not have but claims to be void of any reliable Jesus evidence). Not to mention
the fact that the available Bavli manuscripts all mention "Jesus the Nazarene" (or
have the name erased), including the pre-1263 Firenze manuscript.

Bibliography

Aland, Barbara, "Bibelübersetzungen I:4.2: Neues Testament," *TRE* 6, 1980, pp. 189–196.

Alexander, Philip S., "The Historical Setting of the Hebrew Book of Enoch," *JJS* 28, 1977, pp. 156–180.

——, "3 (Hebrew Apocalypse of) Enoch," in *OTP*, vol. 1: *Apocalyptic Literature and Testaments*, London: Darton, Longman & Todd, 1983, pp. 223–315.

——, "The Talmudic Concept of Conjuring ('Ahizat 'Einayim) and the Problem of the Definition of Magic (*Kishuf*)," in *Creation and Re-Creation in Jewish Thought: Festschrift in Honor of Joseph Dan on the Occasion of his Seventieth Birthday*, ed. Rachel Elior and Peter Schäfer, Tübingen: Mohr Siebeck, 2005, pp. 7–26.

Asmussen, Jes Peter, "Das Christentum in Iran und sein Verhältnis zum Zoroastrismus," *Studia Theologica* 16, 1962, pp. 1–24.

——, "Christians in Iran," in *The Cambridge History of Iran*, vol. 3 (2): *The Seleucid, Parthian and Sasanian Periods*, ed. Ehsan Yarshater, Cambridge: Cambridge University Press, 1983, pp. 924–948.

Assmann, Jan, "Magic and Theology in Ancient Egypt," in *Envisioning Magic: A Princeton Seminar and Symposium*, ed. Peter Schäfer and Hans G. Kippenberg, Leiden–New York–Köln: Brill, 1997, pp. 1–18.

Audollent, Auguste, *Defixionum tabellae*, Luteciae Parisiorum: A. Fontemoing, 1904.

Avi-Yonah, Michael, The *Jews of Palestine: A Political History from the Bar Kokhba War to the Arab Conquest*, New York: Schocken, 1976.

Bammel, Ernst, "*Ex illa itaque die consilium fecerunt . . .,*" in idem, *The Trial of Jesus: Cambridge Studies in Honour of C.F.D. Moule*, London: SCM, 1970, pp. 11–40.

Barnes, Timothy David, "Constantine and the Christians of Persia," *JRS* 75, 1985, pp. 126–136.

Becker, Adam H., "Bringing the Heavenly Academy Down to Earth: Approaches to the Imagery of Divine Pedagogy in the East Syrian Tradition," in *Heavenly*

Realms and Earthly Realities in Late Antique Religions, ed. Ra'anan S. Boustan and Anette Yoshiko Reed, Cambridge: Cambridge University Press, 2004, pp. 174–191.

——, *The Fear of God and the Beginning of Wisdom: The School of Nisibis and Christian Scholastic Culture in Late Antique Mesopotamia*, Philadelphia: University of Pennsylvania Press, 2006.

Becker, Adam H., and Annette Yoshiko Reed, "Introduction," in *The Ways that Never Parted: Jews and Christians in Late Antiquity and the Early Middle Ages*, ed. A.H. Becker and A. Yoshiko Reed, Tübingen: J.C.B. Mohr (Paul Siebeck), 2003, pp. 1–33.

Becker, Hans-Jürgen, *Auf der Kathedra des Mose. Rabbinisch-theologisches Denken und antirabbinische Polemik in Matthäus 23,1–12*, Berlin: Institut Kirche und Judentum, 1990.

Bedjan, Paul, ed., *Acta Martyrum et Sanctorum*, vols. 1–7, Paris and Leipzig: Harrassowitz, 1890–1897.

——, *Histoire de Mar-Jabalaha, de trois autres patriarches, d'un prêtre et de deux laiques nestoriens*, Leipzig: Harrassowitz, 1895.

Berger, Klaus, *Im Anfang war Johannes. Datierung und Theologie des vierten Evangeliums*, Stuttgart: Quell, 1997.

Berkowitz, Beth A., *Execution and Invention: Death Penalty Discourse in Early Rabbinic and Christian Cultures*, Oxford: Oxford University Press, 2006.

Betz, Hans Dieter, ed., *The Greek Magical Papyri in Translation: Including the Demotic Spells*, Chicago and London: University of Chicago Press, 1986.

Beyschlag, Karlmann, *Simon Magus und die christliche Gnosis*, Tübingen: Mohr (Siebeck), 1974.

Bickerman, Elias, "Ritualmord und Eselskult. Ein Beitrag zur Geschichte antiker Publizistik," in idem, *Studies in Jewish and Christian History*, vol. 2, Leiden: Brill, 1980, pp. 225–255 (original publication in *MGWJ* 71, 1927).

Billerbeck, Paul, "Altjüdische Religionsgespräche," *Nathanael* 25, 1909, pp. 13–30, 33–50, 66–80.

Boyarin, Daniel, "Qeriah metuqqenet shel ha-qeta' he-hadash shel 'Toledot Yeshu,'" *Tarbiz* 47, 1978, pp. 249–252.

——, *Dying for God: Martyrdom and the Making of Christianity and Judaism*, Stanford, CA: Stanford University Press, 1999.

Braun, Oskar, *Ausgewählte Akten Persischer Märtyrer. Mit einem Anhang: Ostsyrisches Mönchsleben* (aus dem Syrischen übersetzt), Kempten and Munich: Kösel, 1915.

Brock, Sebastian P., review of Gernot Wiessner, *Untersuchungen zur syrischen Literaturgeschichte I, Journal of Theological Studies*, n.s., 19, 1968, pp. 300–309.

——, "Christians in the Sasanian Empire: A Case of Divided Loyalties," in *Religion and National Identity: Papers Read at the Nineteenth Summer Meeting and the Twentieth Winter Meeting of the Ecclesiastical History Society*, ed. Stuart Mews, Oxford: Blackwell, 1982, pp. 1–19.

——, "Some Aspects of Greek Words in Syriac," in idem, *Syriac Perspectives on Late Antiquity*, London: Variorum, 1984, pp. 80–108.

Brody, Robert, "Judaism in the Sasanian Empire: A Case Study in Religious Coexistence," in *Irano-Judaica II: Studies Relating to Jewish Contacts with Persian Culture throughout the Ages*, ed. Shaul Shaked and Amnon Netzer, Jerusalem: Yad Itzhak Ben-Zvi, 1990, pp. 52–62.

Brown, Dan, *The Da Vinci Code*, New York: Doubleday, 2003.

Brown, Raymond E., *The Death of the Messiah: From Gethsemane to the Grave; A Commentary on the Passion Narratives in the Four Gospels*, New York: Doubleday, 1994.

Cassel, Paulus, *Apologetische Briefe I: Panthera-Stada-onokotes: Caricaturnamen Christi unter Juden und Heiden*, Berlin, 1875 (reprinted in idem, *Aus Literatur und Geschichte*, Berlin and W. Friedrich, Leipzig: 1885).

Casson, Lionel, ed. and trans., *Selected Satires of Lucian*, New York and London: Norton, 1962.

Chadwick, Henry, trans., Origen, *Contra Celsum*, Cambridge: Cambridge University Press, 1953.

Cohn, Haim, *The Trial and Death of Jesus*, New York: Harper and Row, 1971.

Cohn, Haim Hermann, and Louis Isaac Rabinowitz, "Capital Punishment," in *EJ*, vol. 5, Jerusalem: Keter, 1971, cols. 142–147.

Cook, John Granger, *The Interpretation of the Old Testament in Greco-Roman Paganism*, Tübingen: Mohr Siebeck, 2004.

Deissmann, Adolf, "Der Name Panthera," *Orientalische Studien Th. Nöldeke zum Siebzigsten Geburtstag*, vol. 2, Gießen: A. Töpelmann, 1906, pp. 871–875.

——, *Licht vom Osten*, Tübingen: J.C.B. Mohr (P. Siebeck), 1923.

Eisenmenger, Johann Andreas, *Entdecktes Judenthum, oder Gründlicher und Wahrhaffter Bericht, welchergestalt die verstockte Juden die Hochheilige Drey-Einigkeit, Gott Vater, Sohn und Heil. Geist, erschrecklicher Weise lästern und verunehren, die Heil. Mutter Christi verschmähen, das Neue Testament, die*

Evangelisten und Aposteln, die christliche Religion spöttisch durchziehen, und die ganze Christenheit auff das äusserste verachten und verfluchen [. . .], Frankfurt am Main, 1700.

Falk, Ze'ev, "Qeta' hadash mi-'Toledot Yeshu,'" *Tarbiz* 46, 1978, pp. 319–322.

Flusser, David, *Jesus in Selbstzeugnissen und Bilddokumenten*, Hamburg: Rowohlt, 1968.

———, "Jesus," in: *EJ*, vol. 10, Jerusalem: Keter, 1971, cols. 10–14.

Freudenberger, Rudolf, "Die *delatio nominis causa* gegen Rabbi Elieser ben Hyrkanos," *Revue internationale des droits de l'antiquité*, 3rd ser., 15, 1968, pp. 11–19.

Friedman, Shamma, "From Sinai to Cyberspace: The Transmission of the Talmud in Every Age," in *Printing the Talmud: From Bomberg to Schottenstein*, ed. Sharon Liberman Mintz and Gabriel M. Goldstein, [New York:] Yeshiva University Museum, 2005, pp. 143–154.

Frye, Richard N., *The History of Ancient Iran*, Munich: Beck, 1984.

Gafni, Isaiah M., *The Jews of Babylonia in the Talmudic Era: A Social and Cultural History*, Jerusalem: Zalman Shazar Center for Jewish History, 1990 (in Hebrew).

———, "Concepts of Periodization and Causality in Talmudic Literature," *Jewish History* 10, 1996, pp. 21–38.

———, "Rabbinic Historiography and Representations of the Past," in *Cambridge Companion to Rabbinic Literature*, ed. C. Fonrobert and M. Jaffee (forthcoming).

Gaisford, Thomas, ed., *Eusebii Pamphili Episcopi Caesariensis Eclogae Propheticae*, Oxford, 1842.

Ganschinietz, R., "Iao," in *Paulys Real-Encyclopädie der Classischen Altertumswissenschaft*, Neue Bearbeitung, begonnen von Georg Wissowa, . . . hrsg. v. Wilhelm Kroll, Siebzehnter Halbband, Stuttgart: Metzler, 1914, cols. 698–721.

Gärtner, Hans, "Minucius Felix," in *Der Kleine Pauly. Lexikon der Antike*, Munich: Deutscher Taschenbuchverlag, 1979, cols. 1341–1343.

Gero, Stephen, "The Stern Master and His Wayward Disciple: A 'Jesus' Story in the Talmud and in Christian Hagiography," *JSJ* 25, 1994, pp. 287–311.

Gillman, Ian, and Hans-Joachim Klimkeit, *Christians in Asia before 1500*, Ann Arbor: University of Michigan Press, 1999.

Ginzberg, Louis, *Ginze Schechter: Genizah Studies in Memory of Doctor Solomon Schechter*, vol. 1: *Midrash and Haggadah*, New York: Jewish Theological Seminary of America, 1928 (reprint, New York: Hermon, 1969).

Glover, T. R., ed. and trans., *Tertullian Apology—De spectaculis*, London: William Heinemann: Cambridge, MA: Harvard University Press, 1953.

Goldberg, Arnold, "Schöpfung und Geschichte. Der Midrasch von den Dingen, die vor der Welt erschaffen wurden," *Judaica* 24, 1968, pp. 27–44 (reprinted in idem, *Mystik und Theologie des rabbinischen Judentums. Gesammelte Studien I*, ed. Margarete Schlüter and Peter Schäfer, Tübingen: Mohr Siebeck 1997, pp. 148–161).

Goldstein, Morris, *Jesus in the Jewish Tradition*, New York: Macmillan, 1950.

Güdemann, Moritz, *Religionsgeschichtliche Studien*, Leipzig: Oskar Leiner, 1876.

Guttmann, Alexander, "The Significance of Miracles for Talmudic Judaism," *HUCA* 20, 1947, pp. 363–406.

——, *Studies in Rabbinic Judaism*, New York: Ktav, 1976.

Haeckel, Ernst, *Die Welträthsel. Gemeinverständliche Studien über Monistische Philosophie*, Bonn: Emil Strauß, 9th ed., 1899.

Haenle, S., *Geschichte der Juden im ehemaligen Fürstentum Ansbach.* Vollständiger Nachdruck der Ausgabe von 1867 bearbeitet und mit einem Schlagwortregister versehen von Hermann Süß, Hainsfarther Buchhandlung, 1990 (Bayerische Jüdische Schriften, 1).

Harmon, A. M., ed. and trans., *Lucian*, vol. 3, Cambridge, MA, and London: Harvard University Press, 1921 (reprint 2004).

Hartmann, Anton Theodor, *Johann Andreas Eisenmenger und seine jüdischen Gegner, in geschichtlich literarischen Erörterungen kritisch beleuchtet*, Parchim: Verlag der D. E. Hinstorffschen Buchhandlung, 1834.

Hengel, Martin, *Crucifixion in the Ancient World and the Folly of the Message of the Cross*, London: SCM; Philadelphia: Fortress, 1977.

——, *The Charismatic Leader and His Followers*, New York: Crossroad, 1981.

——, *Die Johanneische Frage. Ein Lösungsversuch*, Tübingen: J.C.B. Mohr (Paul Siebeck), 1993.

——, *Studies in Early Christology*, Edinburgh: T&T Clark, 1995.

——, *The Four Gospels and the One Gospel of Jesus Christ: An Investigation of the Collection and Origin of the Canonical Gospels*, London: SCM, 2000.

Herford, Travers, *Christianity in Talmud and Midrash*, London: Williams & Norgate, 1903 (reprint, New York: Ktav, 1975).

Herr, Moshe David, "The Historical Significance of the Dialogues between Jewish Sages and Roman Dignitaries," *Scripta Hierosolymitana* 22, 1971, pp. 123–150.

———, "Tefisat ha-historyah etzel Hazal," in *Proceedings of the Sixth World Congress of Jewish Studies*, vol. 3, Jerusalem: World Union of Jewish Studies, 1977, pp. 129–142.

Hill, Charles E., *The Johannine Corpus in the Early Church*, Oxford: Oxford University Press, 2004.

Horbury, William, "The Trial of Jesus in Jewish Tradition," in *The Trial of Jesus: Cambridge Studies in Honour of C.F.D. Moule*, ed. Ernst Bammel, London: SCM, 1970, pp. 103–121.

———, *Jews and Christians in Contact and Controversy*, Edinburgh: T&T Clark, 1998.

Hruby, Kurt, *Die Stellung der jüdischen Gesetzeslehrer zur werdenden Kirche*, Zürich: Theologischer Verlag, 1971.

Isenberg, Wesley W., "The Gospel of Philip (II, 3)," in *The Nag Hammadi Library in English*, ed. James M. Robinson, San Francisco: Harper, 1990, pp. 139–160.

Jastrow, Marcus, *A Dictionary of the Targumim, the Talmud Babli and Yerushalmi, and the Midrashic Literature*, New York: Pardes, 1950.

Kalmin, Richard, "Christians and Heretics in Rabbinic Literature of Late Antiquity," *HTR* 87, 1994, pp. 155–169.

———, *Jewish Babylonia: Between Persia and Roman Palestine*, Oxford: Oxford University Press (in press).

King, Karen, *The Gospel of Mary of Magdala: Jesus and the First Woman Apostle*, Santa Rosa, CA.: Polebridge, 2003.

Klausner, Joseph, *Yeshu ha-Notzri*, Jerusalem: Shtibl, 1922.

———, *Jesus of Nazareth: His Life, Times, and Teaching*, trans. Herbert Danby, New York: Macmillan, 1925.

Koltun-Fromm, Naomi, "A Jewish-Christian Conversation in Fourth-Century Persian Mesopotamia," *JJS* 47, 1996, pp. 45–63.

Krauss, Samuel, "The Jews in the Works of the Church Fathers," *JQR* 5, 1892–1893, pp. 122–157; 6, 1894, pp. 225–261.

———, *Das Leben Jesu nach jüdischen Quellen*, Berlin: S. Calvary, 1902.

Kuhn, Karl Georg, *Achtzehngebet und Vaterunser und der Reim*, Tübingen: J.C.B. Mohr (Paul Siebeck), 1950.

Laible, Heinrich, *Jesus Christus im Thalmud*, Berlin: H. Reuther's Verlagsbuch-handlung, 1891.

Lauterbach, Jacob Z., *Rabbinic Essays*, Cincinnati: Hebrew Union College Press, 1951 (reprint, New York: Ktav, 1951).

Levene, Dan, "'. . . and by the name of Jesus . . .': An Unpublished Magic Bowl in Jewish Aramaic," *JSQ* 6, 1999, pp. 283–308.

———, *A Corpus of Magic Bowls: Incantation Texts in Jewish Aramaic from Late Antiquity*, London: Kegan Paul, 2003.

Lieberman, Saul, "Roman Legal Institutions in Early Rabbinics and in the Acta Martyrum," *JQR*, n.s., 35, 1944/45, pp. 1–57.

Maier, Johann, *Jesus von Nazareth in der talmudischen Überlieferung*, Darmstadt: Wissenschaftliche Buchgesellschaft, 1978.

———, *Jüdische Auseinandersetzung mit dem Christentum in der Antike*, Darm-stadt: Wissenschaftliche Buchgesellschaft, 1982.

Meelführer, Rudolf Martin, *Jesus in Talmude, Sive Dissertatio Philologica Prior/Posterior, De iis locis, in quibus per Talmudicas Pandectas Jesu cujusdam mentio injicitur*, Altdorf, 1699.

Menzies, Allan, ed., *The Ante-Nicene Fathers: Translations of the Fathers down to A.D. 325*, 5th edition, vol. 10, reprint, Edinburgh: T&T Clark; Grand Rapids, MI: Eerdmans, 1990.

Merkel, Helmut, *Die Widersprüche zwischen den Evangelien. Ihre polemische und apologetische Behandlung in der Alten Kirche bis zu Augustin*, Tübingen: J.C.B. Mohr (Paul Siebeck), 1971.

Merkelbach, Reinold, and Maria Totti, eds., *Abrasax. Ausgewählte Papyri religiösen und magischen Inhalts*, vol. 2, Opladen: Westdeutscher Verlag, 1991.

Metzger, Bruce M., *The Early Versions of the New Testament: Their Origin, Trans-mission, and Limitations*, Oxford: Clarendon, 1977.

Michl, Johann, "Engel II (jüdisch)", in *RAC*, vol. 5, Stuttgart: Hiersemann, 1962, cols. 60–97.

Montgomery, James A., *Aramaic Incantation Texts from Nippur*, Philadelphia: University Museum, 1913.

Morony, Michael G., "Magic and Society in Late Sasanian Iraq," in *Prayer, Magic, and the Stars in the Ancient and Late Antique World*, ed. Scott Noegel, Joel Walker, and Brannon Wheeler, University Park: Pennsylvania State Uni-versity Press, 2003, pp. 83–107.

Naveh, Joseph, and Shaul Shaked, *Amulets and Magic Bowls: Aramaic Incanta-tions of Late Antiquity*, Jerusalem: Magnes; and Leiden: Brill, 1985.

Neusner, Jacob, *A History of the Jews in Babylonia*, vols. 1–5, Leiden: Brill, 1967–1970.

——, *Eliezer Ben Hyrkanus: The Tradition and the Man*, 2 vols., Leiden: Brill, 1973.

——, *The Tosefta Translated from the Hebrew, Fifth Division: Qodoshim (The Order of Holy Things)*, New York: Ktav, 1979.

——, *The Talmud of the Land of Israel: An Academic Commentary to the Second, Third, and Fourth Divisions*, vol. 26: *Yerushalmi Tractate Abodah Zarah*, Atlanta, GA: Scholars Press, 1999.

Nitzsch, F., "Ueber eine Reihe talmudischer und patristischer Täuschungen, welche sich an den mißverstandenen Spottnamen *Ben-Pandira* geknüpft," *Theologische Studien und Kritiken* 13, 1840, pp. 115–120.

Odeberg, Hugo, *3 Enoch; or, The Hebrew Book of Enoch*, Cambridge: Cambridge University Press, 1928 (reprint, New York: Ktav, 1973).

Parisot, J., *Patrologia Syriaca* I:1, Paris: Firmin-Didot, 1894.

Parrott, Douglas M., ed., "The Gospel of Mary (BG 8502,1)," in *The Nag Hammadi Library in English*, ed. James M. Robinson, San Francisco: Harper, 1990, pp. 523–527.

Patterson, L., "Origin of the Name Panthera," *Journal of Theological Studies* 19, 1918, pp. 79–80.

Petersen, William L., *Tatian's Diatessaron: Its Creation, Dissemination, Signifi-cance, and History in Scholarship*, Leiden and New York: Brill, 1994.

——, "Tatian," in *TRE* 32, 2001, pp. 655–659.

Rabbinovicz, Raphael N., *Diqduqe Soferim: Variae Lectiones in Mischnam et in Talmud Babylonicum*, vols.1–15, Munich: A. Huber, 1868–1886; vol. 16, Przemysl: Zupnik, Knoller and Wolf, 1897 (reprint in 12 vols., Jerusalem, 2001/02).

Reiner, Elchanan, "From Joshua to Jesus: The Transformation of a Biblical Story to a Local Myth; A Chapter in the Religious Life of the Galilean Jew," *Sharing the Sacred: Religious Contacts and Conflicts in the Holy Land, First–Fifteenth Centuries CE*, ed. Arieh Kofsky and Guy G. Stroumsa, Jerusalem: Yad Izhak Ben Zvi, 1998, pp. 223–271.

Rendall, Gerald H., ed. and trans., *The Octavius of Marcus Minucius Felix*, London: William Heinemann; Cambridge, MA: Harvard University Press, 1953.

Richardson, Cyril C., ed. and trans., *Early Christian Fathers*, vol. 1, Philadelphia: Westminster, 1953.

Roberts, Alexander and James Donaldson, eds., *The Ante-Nicene Fathers: Translations of the Fathers down to A.D. 325*, American reprint of the Edinburgh edition, vol. 4, Grand Rapids, MI: Eerdmans, 1989.

Rubenstein, Jeffrey L., *The Culture of the Babylonian Talmud*, Baltimore and London: Johns Hopkins University Press, 2003.

Rubinkiewicz, Ryszard, "Apocalypse of Abraham," in *OTP*, vol. 1: *Apocalyptic Literature and Testaments*, London: Darton, Longman & Todd, 1983, pp. 681–705.

Schäfer, Peter, "Zur Geschichtsauffassung des rabbinischen Judentums," *JSJ* 6, 1975, pp. 167–188 (reprinted in idem, *Studien zur Geschichte und Theologie des Rabbinischen Judentums*, Leiden: Brill, 1978, pp. 23–44).

——, "Bileam II. Judentum," *TRE* 6, 1980, pp. 639–640.

——, *Synopse zur Hekhalot-Literatur*, Tübingen: J.C.B. Mohr (Paul Siebeck), 1981.

——, *Der Bar Kokhba-Aufstand. Studien zum zweiten jüdischen Krieg gegen Rom*, Tübingen: J.C.B. Mohr (Paul Siebeck), 1981.

——, "Magic and Religion in Ancient Judaism," in *Envisioning Magic: A Princeton Seminar & Symposium*, ed. Peter Schäfer and Hans G. Kippenberg, Leiden–New York–Köln: Brill, 1997, pp. 19–43.

——, " 'From Jerusalem the Great to Alexandria the Small': The Relationship between Palestine and Egypt in the Graeco-Roman Period," in *The Talmud Yerushalmi and Graeco-Roman Culture*, vol. 1, ed. Peter Schäfer, Tübingen: Mohr Siebeck, 1998, pp. 129–140.

——, *The History of the Jews in the Greco-Roman World*, London and New York: Routledge, 2003.

Schmid, Johann, *Feuriger Drachen-Gifft und wütiger Ottern-Gall*, Augsburg, 1683.

Scholem, Gershom, *Major Trends in Jewish Mysticism*, New York: Schocken, 1961 (reprint, 1995).

Shaked, Shaul, "Zoroastrian Polemics against Jews in the Sasanian and Early Islamic Period," in *Irano-Judaica II: Studies Relating to Jewish Contacts with Persian Culture throughout the Ages*, ed. Shaul Shaked and Amnon Netzer, Jerusalem: Yad Itzhak Ben-Zvi, 1990, pp. 85–104.

——, "The Poetics of Spells: Language and Structure in Aramaic Incantations of Late Antiquity 1; The Divorce Formula and Its Ramifications," in

Mesopotamian Magic: Textual, Historical, and Interpretive Perspectives, ed. Tzvi Abusch and Karel van der Toorn, Groningen: Styx, 1999, pp. 173–195.

———, "Jesus in the Magic Bowls: Apropos Dan Levene's '. . . and by the name of Jesus . . .'," *JSQ* 6, 1999, pp. 309–319.

Slusser, Michael, ed., *St. Justin Martyr: Dialogue with Trypho*, trans. Thomas B. Falls, rev. and introd. Thomas P. Halton, Washington, DC: Catholic University of America Press, 2003.

Smith, Morton, *Jesus the Magician*, San Francisco: Harper & Row, 1978.

Sokoloff, Michael, *A Dictionary of Jewish Palestinian Aramaic of the Byzantine Period*, Ramat-Gan: Bar Ilan University Press, 1990.

———, *A Dictionary of Jewish Babylonian Aramaic of the Talmudic and Gaonic Periods*, Ramat-Gan: Bar Ilan University Press, 2002.

Stemberger, Günter, *Einleitung in Talmud und Midrasch*, Munich: Beck, 1992.

Strack, Hermann L., *Jesus, die Häretiker und die Christen nach den ältesten jüdischen Angaben*, Leipzig: J. C. Hinrichs'sche Buchhandlung, 1910.

Strack, Hermann L., and Paul Billerbeck, *Kommentar zum Neuen Testament aus Talmud und Midrasch*, vol. 1: *Das Evangelium nach Matthäus*, Munich: Beck, 1922.

Unger, Dominic J., trans., *St. Irenaeus of Lyons against the Heresies*, rev. John J. Dillon, vol. 1, book 1, New York and Mahwah, NJ: Paulist, 1992.

Urbach, Ephraim E., "Homilies of the Rabbis on the Prophets of the Nations and the Balaam Stories," *Tarbiz* 25, 1955/56, pp. 272–289 (in Hebrew).

———, *The Sages: Their Concepts and Beliefs*, vol. 1, Jerusalem: Magnes, 1979.

Veltri, Giuseppe, *Magie und Halakha. Ansätze zu einem empirischen Wissenschaftsbegriff im spätantiken und frühmittelalterlichen Judentum*, Tübingen: J.C.B. Mohr (Paul Siebeck), 1997.

Vermes, Geza, *Jesus the Jew: A Historian's Reading of the Gospels*, Philadelphia: Fortress, 1981.

Visotzky, Burton L., "Overturning the Lamp," *JJS* 38, 1987, pp. 72–80.

———, "Mary Maudlin among the Rabbis," in *Fathers of the World: Essays in Rabbinic and Patristic Literatures*, Tübingen: J.C.B. Mohr (Paul Siebeck), 1995, pp. 85–92.

Wartelle, André, ed., *Saint Justin: Apologies*, Paris: Études Augustiniennes, 1987.

Wewers, Gerd A., *Avoda Zara. Götzendienst*, Tübingen: J.C.B. Mohr (Paul Siebeck), 1980.

Widengren, Geo, "The Status of the Jews in the Sassanian Empire," in *Irania Antiqua*, vol. 1, ed. R. Ghirshman and L. Vanden Berghe, Leiden: Brill, 1961, pp. 117–162.

——, *Die Religionen Irans*, Stuttgart: Kohlhammer, 1965.

Wiesehöfer, Josef, *Ancient Persia from 550 BC to 650 AD*, London and New York: I. B. Tauris, 1966.

Wiessner, Gernot, *Untersuchungen zur syrischen Literaturgeschichte I: Zur Märtyrerüberlieferung aus der Christenverfolgung Schapurs II*, Göttingen: Vandenhoek & Ruprecht, 1967.

Williams, Frank, trans., *The Panarion of Epiphanius of Salamis*, book 1, sects 1–46, Leiden: Brill, 1987.

Winter, Paul, *On the Trial of Jesus*, Berlin: de Gruyter, 1961.

Wünsch, Dietrich, "Evangelienharmonie," *TRE* 10, 1982, pp. 626–629.

Yuval, Israel J., *"Two Nations in Your Womb": Perceptions of Jews and Christians*, Tel Aviv: Am Oved, 2000 (in Hebrew).

Zeitlin, Solomon, "Jesus in the Early Tannaitic Literature," in *Abhandlungen zur Erinnerung an Hirsch Perez Chajes*, Wien: Alexander Kohut Memorial Foundation, 1933, pp. 295–308.

Index

Printed in the USA
CPSIA information can be obtained
at www.ICGtesting.com
JSHW020820231223
54242JS00006B/285